Healing Religious Hurts

Stories and Tips to Find Love and Peace

Joanie
Lindenmeyer

Elizabeth Ann
Atkins

Dedication

To you, the beloved,

as you seek love, peace,

and spiritual connection.

God is love!

Acknowledgements

From Elizabeth Ann Atkins

Thank you, God and my Spirit team, for providing the ideas, mental and physical stamina, resources, harmony, and skills that enabled us to create this beautiful book.

Immeasurable gratitude to **Joanie Lindenmeyer** for proposing that we collaborate to write this spirit-inspired book that can bless countless people everywhere. How fun and fascinating to work together to focus our topic, create the outline, and embellish our chapters with the help of our 17 phenomenal contributors from across America.

Teamwork makes the dream work, and it's an absolute honor and privilege to co-captain this literary team with you, Joanie. You are truly an earth angel, and it's been a divine gift to co-create this literary extravaganza that will, as a result, be a gift to people who need it most. May billions of blessings sparkle back on you for being such a blessing to me. Cheers to you, Joanie!

Here's a giant burst of immeasurable gratitude to the other superstars on our team:

Catherine M. Greenspan, co-founder and CFO of Two Sisters Writing & Publishing®. Expressing infinite gratitude and love for your brilliant guidance and editorial expertise throughout the creation, publication, and promotion of this book. You're the best!

Deborah Perdue, founder of Illumination Graphics. Expressing profuse thankfulness and adoration to you for creating the beautiful cover and interior design and formatting. We love how you work your Merlin Magic!

Our 17 contributors from across America. Showering you with billions of thank yous for courageously sharing your stories that can touch lives everywhere. Cheers to YOU!

Jessica Bonosoro, editor and project manager on the Two Sisters Writing & Publishing® team. Thanking you with ebullient joy and relief that you so concisely helped edit this book with great attention to details and deadlines, and helped manage the many facets of this collaboration quickly and efficiently. You are a much-valued member on the Two Sisters team! We appreciate you!

Cat Wilkes, executive assistant on the Two Sisters Writing & Publishing® team. Thanking you for so skillfully tracking and organizing the many moving parts of this project. You make the most beautiful spreadsheets ever, and your help has been a Godsend. Thank you!

Sean Smith, SEO expert and founder of Ikusa. Giant gratitude for your continued support with TwoSistersWriting.com as well as your creative input. You rock!

Meredith Gertz, thank you for your marketing genius to help get this book and others into the hands and hearts of those who need it most. You are awesome!

Natalie Luterman, we treasure your extraordinary skills for editing and proofing. We immensely appreciate you!

And to you, **our readers**, a big burst of gratitude for picking up this book that we hope can help you shine your light from the inside out and cast sunshine into the shadows to illuminate the world with peace and love for all. Stay strong and celebrate!

From Joanie Lindenmeyer

Big, Big, Big thank yous from the top of my heart to each of you . . .
I couldn't have done it without you!
THANK YOU. I LOVE YOU!

Computer helpers: Diane Weir, Sally Roy, Jill Prioreschi, Kennette Babb, Kameron McLean, and Terri Stewart.

Media helpers: Daniel Perry, Cynthia Paulsen, Rebeckah Bustamante, and Andrew Walkup.

Attorneys and legal advisors: Peter Spratt and Leah Halpert.

Organization/office: Carolyn House.

The Two Sisters Writing & Publishing® team: Cat and Jessica.

Book Cover font designs: Scott and Joyce Eason, and Steve Childs.

Book Cover Artists: Gail Baker and Deborah Perdue.

Spiritual team: my unwavering prayer angels: Doris Westoby, Joyce Eason, Ruthie Murray, Maggie Kish, Dan Fowler, Janell Monk, Chloe McCrae, Daniel Perry Walkup, Father Ron Hoye, C.M. and the God Minute Team, and all of St. Tim's Episcopal Church, especially Bernie Lindley and Linda Lee.

Supporters and encouragers: the hundreds of new friends, lifelong friends, and dear family members via texts, calls, and emails, The Brookings Harbor Community Bazaar Ladies, my Brookings Pickleball friends, and my "Lezzi" Tuesday Breakfast LGBTQ+ friends.

Big gratitude for the many people who have shared praise, including: Adalberto Ramirez, Mag Kish, Cherry Kittredge of Qspirit.net Christian books, Daniel Perry, Pastor Dan Fowler of First Presbyterian Church of Ashland, Jenny Leffler, Episcopal Deacon Linda Lee and Mary (Linda's Mother), Marcy Bradbury, Hank Gaus, Wendy Larsen, Rev. Sister Cora Lea Rose of St. Timothy Episcopal Church, Ellen Coffin, and Amber Hintz.

Oh golly, here's a drum roll, please . . . to thank, really thank and I mean really thank the stars of this book!

Our Contributing Writers

To each of you, let me look into your eyes so that you can see and feel the honor and the privilege it is for us to have YOU as a published author, alongside me and Elizabeth in this powerful, life-changing book. Your confidence, courage, and collaboration overwhelm me. Thank you for sharing your personal spiritual journey and truth with us, all in the name of helping and healing others! This is a huge, momentous occasion for you and your beloved that is a legacy all its own. Your unique story will lead to zillions of positive and influential ripple effects. THANK YOU SOOOOOO MUCH. I bless you with a life full of peaceful and loving moments. **I LOVE YOU!**

My Spiritual Co-Authors:

Carol Tierheimer, my beloved angel who is leaping the mountains and singing her heart out in the heavenly choir. My best friend, confidant and my lifetime lover who I "lived every day to the max" with for 40 years!

You will always and forever be inside of me! I celebrate and live *Joyously Free* along with *Healing Religious Hurts: Stories and Tips to Find Love and Peace* each new day, week, month, and year since we met and since your passing on January 20, 2022. Your voice and spirit are alive in words and feelings in this book and beyond. Thank you, sweetie, for your profound love then and now! How fun!

Because of you, I have the courage and awe to live truthfully, lovingly, peacefully and *Joyously Free!* WOWIE! WOWZER! **I LOVE YOU, CAROL!**

Jesus, God, and Holy Spirit, thank you for being the guts, the truth, and the way that burst of your love for me and Elizabeth in this book. You are our Higher Power!

YIPPEE, **I LOVE YOU, JESUS!**

Catherine Greenspan

Extra special praise and thanks to you, Catherine, for your loyalty and devotion as my friend, publisher, and editor! You are always truthful and joyful. Thank you! Your expertise, kind guidance, honest and direct insights for improvements in my writing, your guru skills with finances and business details and all the steps along the way were exactly what I needed when I most needed it. You kept me and Elizabeth on track!

You are AMAZING! SHAZAM!

I LOVE YOU, CATHERINE!

Elizabeth Ann Atkins

OMG! How do I even begin to express the thankfulness and gratitude to you, Elizabeth, for co-authoring this profoundly healing book with me?

Bottom line, I wouldn't and couldn't have done it without you, your spiritual connections, and our intense collaboration!

From the beginning, you took a risk. This was an "us" book, not a me or a you book. Thank you immensely for your trust in Spirit, trust in me, and trust that we could collaborate, adventure, and make bursts of colors and golden sparkles to circle the planet. All evident in our fun, bright, and holy book cover!

Elizabeth, you dreamed bigger, pushed longer and harder, discovered more truths, and poured out your brilliance in brain, heart, and expert writing!

You are the Princess Goddess, an earth angel, a visionary, and a dear friend.

Thank you, thank you, and thank you **SOOOOO** much, Elizabeth, for accepting and celebrating the true me while hysterically laughing at my one-liner jokes and my off-the-wall, silly comments in my writing and with my "props" on podcasts.

Thank you for being patient, compassionate and empathetic, and crying with me as we lived our truths, discovered healing, and found love and peace in new spiritual ways.

In my wildest dreams, I never imagined this moment of writing another book, let alone co-authoring one with a famous and well-respected bionic woman named you, Elizabeth Ann Atkins.

You really are the most incredible expert book coach, amazing publisher, and fabulous editor. It is an absolute HONOR

AND DELIGHT to have my name and picture next to yours on this inspirational self-help book we call *Healing Religious Hurts: Stories and Tips to Find Love and Peace.*

YAHOO! Congratulations, Elizabeth!

I bless you and your sister, Catherine, and TwoSistersWriting.com for continued awesomeness!

I LOVE YOU, ELIZABETH!

Hugs and kisses to all, Joanie

Contents

Dedication iii

Acknowledgements. v

Prelude xv

Introduction 1

Chapter 1: What is Religious Hurt?
Healing & Defining Your Unique Spiritual Path
My Hurts
By Joanie. 9

Finding Peace, Love & Healing after My Parents's Marriage
Triggered Religious Hurts
By Elizabeth 12

Contributors
    Escape from a Mental Alcatraz
    By Vivian Ashton. 24

    Love Heals Religious Hurts
    By Kristen Sheridan. 30
Tips 35

Chapter 2: Sexism in Religion
Let's Make It an Equal Playing Field
How Spirit Helped Me Find the Courage to Write & Publish
Books That Defy Sexism
By Elizabeth 37

Maybe the Root of All Evil is Masculine Dominance
By Joanie. 47

Contributors
    Susannah's Return to Universal Love
    By Susannah Stokes 63
Tips 69

Chapter 3: Escaping Oppression
Erase Religious Brainwashing, Shame and Guilt
Speaking Up at the Library
By Joanie 71

Helping You Escape Oppression Rooted in Religious Shaming
By Elizabeth 81

Contributors
 Finding Freedom from Oppression
 By Deborah Kravitz-Randall. 94

 On Faith and Finding One's Truth
 By Eric Williams, Esquire 98
Tips 103

Chapter 4: Religious Leaders & The Business of Religion
Follow the Money, Honey!
Who are religious leaders? Let's think of them as
spiritual, too!
By Joanie. 105

Money and Religion
By Elizabeth 121

Contributor
 The Business of Religion
 By Zamber Knight 127
Tips 129

PHOTO MOSAIC OF CONTRIBUTORS 132

Chapter 5: Marriage and Death
Eternally Yours
Healing Religious Hurts around Marriage and Death, Widows and
Orphans and Quails
By Joanie. 135

Healing Religious Rifts in Marriage
By Elizabeth 149

Contributor
 Catholic Annulment Pain and Healing
 By Ruthie Murray. 154
Tips 157

Chapter 6: Hypocrisy
Please, Practice What You Preach!
Hypocrites: How to Cope and Heal
By Joanie. 161

Religious Hypocrisy is an Outrage
By Elizabeth 173

Contributors
    Letter to my PASSTOR
    By Pam Ross McClain, Ph.D. 179

    Healing Through Love and Acceptance
    By Jill Prioreschi. 181
Tips 190

Chapter 7: Forgiveness
How to Forgive Religious Hurts
A Deathbed Request for Forgiveness
By Joanie. 191

Give Yourself the Gift of Forgiveness through Meditation
By Elizabeth 195

Contributor
    How to Forgive People Who Caused Religious Hurts
    By Rosie Robles. 206
Tips 215

Chapter 8: Prayer—Go Within to Find Your Answers
Let It Be!
Prayer Creates Joy from Within
By Joanie. 217

God is Within Us
By Elizabeth 219

Contributors
    Accepting the Gifts & Communicating with the Divine
    By Aja Walker. 222

    A Heartbroken Atheist
    By Tay Ryan 224

    "Never Get Rid of the Chair"
    By Michael Ray Hensley 227
Tips 234

Chapter 9: LGBTQ+ and Religion
When You Least Expect It... Rainbows Appear
It's Bigger Than Us!
By Joanie. 237

Follow Your Own Rainbow Path to God's
Love & Peace
By Elizabeth 250

Contributors
    A Jesuit Priest Standing Up for LGBTQ+ People in the
    Catholic Church
    By James Martin. 255

    LGBTQ+ Rejection
    By Michael Irby 257

    A Married Male Couple Hiding the Truth for Their Baby
    Godson's Baptism
    By Derek 264
Tips 268

Chapter 10: Trusting God's Timing
Serendipitous, Inexplicable, and Miraculous Moments
Trust God's Timing to Heal Religious Hurts
By Joanie 271

Why I Trust Divine Timing, and You Should, Too
By Elizabeth 274

Contributor
    Just-in-Time God
    By Reverend Janell Monk 277
Tips 279

Chapter 11
Tips, Tools & Rituals for Healing Religious Hurts
"OMG! I've been healed!" 281

A Love Letter to You 283
About the Authors. 284
Endnotes 290

Prelude

Something has brought you to this book.

You are someone who has experienced a rift with religion, and you're seeking the love, comfort, and peace of spiritual connection.

You may feel disconnected from traditional religion and it may have caused a chasm with your family.

Your spiritual quest to find meaning and solace may have taken you on many paths, but none leading to the idyllic place or space that your heart and soul are yearning for.

Welcome to *Healing Religious Hurts*, a safe space for you to explore new ideas and learn how others have healed and released past pains and found the ultimate peace and love with God, Spirit, or their own way of believing.

Welcome to a new dimension where you're free to express your most authentic self, just as you are, and feel the love and joy of the divine without restrictive rules or fear of rejection or devastating labels.

This book is for you as a guide to inspire your spiritual journey and let you know that you have the power and the divine right to define your own religious and spiritual beliefs, and to create a daily practice that resonates with your heart and soul.

This book is for everyone, regardless of whether you're young or older, LGBTQ+ or straight. Race, ethnicity, national origin, culture, and other labels that are used to divide us are irrelevant here.

God is love. We are all human and our hearts yearn for love, peace, and connection to each other and to the magnificent spiritual powers of the universe.

So, no matter where you are on your journey, let this book be a guide to explore, learn, and celebrate the wondrous powers of *Healing Religious Hurts* so you can finally find peace and love.

Introduction

Consider this book an invitation for *Healing Religious Hurts*! We teamed up to present this book as a valuable, heart-warming gift to YOU!

Enjoy our stories and tips, along with those from brave and diverse people from across America.

Let this book inspire you to define what it feels like to find your love and peace.

You have the power to define what that means.

And since we love to share our life experiences and ideas in books, we ask that *you* select a title for your own story that expresses the essence of your spiritual beliefs.

Call it something like, *Happy, Healed Me, Myself and I, Spiritually Free.*

Or *Finally Finding Love & Peace.*

Or *Opening My Heart to Spirit.*

Or *Becoming the Change I Wish to See.*

Or *WOW, I met an Angel.*

Or *No More Church Shopping.*

Have fun with it! Be creative. Because in each moment of your life, you are literally creating your story that can help those whose lives you touch. *You are awesome!*

Allow the abundance of stories and tips in this collection to inspire you to start a brand new, bold and beautiful chapter in your life, where you've healed religious hurts and embarked on a spiritual journey that fills you with joy and happiness.

For Joanie, that includes her sacred relationship with Jesus and God that is not limited to a religious setting or denomination. Please read her stories and tips with an open mind to see that Joanie's life mission is to show that you *can* be LGBTQ+, religious, healed, and filled with love and peace on *your terms,* the way *you* define your relationship with a Higher Power.

Likewise, Elizabeth's guidance for helping you define your spiritual identity, as well as how to heal from any traumas, involves spiritually-inspired meditation and journaling exercises that are life-changing.

This collaboration aims to be **inclusive of all people**, no matter what your spiritual or religious beliefs and practices are, even if you are agnostic or atheist. We invite you to replace references to Jesus and God with Higher Self, which is the infinite power of the Universe that is within you.

We also decided that the best way to present this message would be to highlight and give voice to people who are on a spiritual quest or have healed their religious hurts, so we asked people we know to contribute their stories. What follows are deeply personal essays that can empower your journey. May their stories inspire you to keep searching for those moments when the truth bubbles up and the world responds.

So many people are still hurting from religious programming and traumas. We are here with this book to help you heal, to understand that you are not alone, and to find love and peace!

Everything happens in divine timing, and it's up to YOU to decide how you want to embark on your spiritual journey. That's why we encourage you to really know your *why.* In knowing your why, you will figure out *how* to find love and peace with God, Spirit, and/or your Higher Self.

So why does the world need this book?

Because hundreds of years ago, men wrote the religious doctrine that today dictates how most of the eight billion people in the world think, behave, make laws, work, love, and control others. These rules are so deeply ingrained in people that society's rules—written and unwritten—affect how we view ourselves and how we operate in the world. When these rules lead to traumas, they can have dire and even deadly consequences. Our book is bold and eye-opening, one of hope, showing that GOD IS LOVE.

That's why more people than ever are embarking on spiritual journeys to find their own path to God/Spirit/Higher Self. We are here to offer tender, compassionate, non-judgemental ways to guide you on that quest, so that you can heal your religious hurts and find love and peace.

Unfortunately, a chilling conservative Christian movement is afoot to impose Biblical beliefs on our modern society, especially as they pertain to oppressing women and robbing people of reproductive rights. Unbelievably, the state of Louisiana has passed a law requiring that the Ten Commandments be hung in every public school classroom. This is a terrible violation of a major tenet of our American democracy: separation of church and state. The Bible does not belong in any public school classroom unless it's being taught in a religion or literature class. Imagine a Jewish or Muslim student being forced to read and recite Christian doctrine as part of their education. This should not be allowed.

Hopefully this 2024 law in Louisiana will make its way to the U.S. Supreme Court and be struck down as unconstitutional. Meanwhile, it's the law in that state, and it is just plain wrong!

This book is a powerful antidote to that unjust reality. Yet, this book is not an angry rant against all of the above.

Our book is a symphony of stories that will make you want to embark on your own healing journey that will empower you to be the change you wish to see in the world, as peacemaker Mahatma Ghandi said. As you read and reflect, feel free to pause and add your feelings, thoughts, insights, and stories, and complete the writing exercises throughout the book as a mini-personal prayer journal or diary. Let your heart and brain be touched as if you are seeing life differently, maybe even by walking in someone else's moccasins.

It's fuel for your heart and soul to dissolve the ominous thunderclouds of opposition with brilliant rays of sunshine. As my friend, book coach, author and publisher Elizabeth has taught and personally shared with me, "The only way to get rid of a shadow is to shine light on it!" I sooo agree with you, dear friend! We are kindred souls. Yahoo!

So we—you!—are each a light. Shine bright into the shadows. Glow up into the person you truly want to become. And together our light will flood the world with positive change on a more progressive trajectory pertaining to religion that exemplifies equality, justice, and love.

So, who are we—Joanie and Elizabeth—to present this information? How are we called, honored, and qualified to help lead this worldwide march?

First, Joanie is changing lives around the world through her 2023 memoir, *Nun Better: An Amazing Love Story* by Joanie Lindenmeyer with Carol Tierheimer. This unique book showcases the beautiful story of how love blossomed between two Catholic nuns and led to a 40-year romantic adventure for Joanie and Carol. Carol went to heaven in 2022, yet her magnificent spirit, wisdom and truths live on as her angel wings soar and swirl, while her soul dwells amongst us.

Both Joanie and Carol ultimately left religious-vowed life

and the church, courageously creating their own LGBTQ+ community during the 1980s when LGBTQ+ singles and couples were enduring hate and deadly violence triggered by the HIV/AIDS epidemic. Also back then, today's freedoms, including legalized same-sex marriage, seemed like a distant, if not impossible, dream.

Now, the popularity and success of Joanie's best-selling book enables her to touch lives everywhere. At frequent in-person events, in churches, libraries, schools, halls, pickleball courts, restaurants, bars, community centers, Prides, pulpits, and events across America, Joanie shines her loving light to create a safe sanctuary for people to reveal their authentic selves with her; this empowers them to speak—and *live*—their truths as LGBTQ+ people, parents, allies, and advocates. Joanie believes that God is Love and is way bigger than a particular Church, that Jesus is her best friend, and that the Holy Spirits of kindness, thankfulness, and joy create our spiritual connection with each other. She has personally been healed in many ways over six decades while on her life's mission to be the best person that her creator-Lord made her to be. For Joanie, it's an ongoing internal and external expression where divinity and humanity combine for the purpose that I do what Jesus tells me to do, so as to abundantly love, help, and serve others. It's so amazing, awesome and BEAUTIFUL! Shazam!

And what qualifies Elizabeth to help guide this transformational journey for you?

As the best-selling author of dozens of books and co-founder of Two Sisters Writing & Publishing®, Elizabeth follows a life mission that's all about cultivating human harmony, with the belief that peace and love begin within oneself. Those who cultivate peace and love within can then embark on their own missions to make the world a better place.

To do this, Elizabeth launched a podcast called The Goddess Power Show with Elizabeth Ann Atkins® to encourage people to create personalized "lovestyles" that free you to experience your greatest joy.

She's also the author of a six-part series of books that help women empower themselves, personally and professionally, by using tools that are deeply spiritual. *The Biss Tribe: Where You Activate Your GoddessPower* is book #1 and was released on August 8, 2024. Elizabeth shares how verbal abuse during a terrible divorce awakened her GoddessPower and inspired her to create a joyous lifestyle and multimedia platform that shows people how to live and love bigger, better, and bolder to manifest their heart's wildest desires.

Elizabeth believes that every human being has the ability to communicate directly with God. We do not need humans to tell us how to communicate with the divine. Nor do we need doctrine written long ago by men to dictate our beliefs and behaviors.

People should be embraced and lavished with self-love, love from others, and love from God/Spirit—exactly as our Creator made us. She believes that when our spirituality is suppressed by trauma, an internal maelstrom brews in ways that can stop a person from experiencing their best life.

When we cultivate a society where people are safe to pray and connect with God/Spirit/Higher Self with healed minds and hearts, then the world becomes a better place.

In addition, Elizabeth long ago became disillusioned by the template that families, religion, and society instill in girls and women the need to conform to the oppressive standards of being a "good girl." Now in *Healing Religious Hurts*, she explains how religious programming perpetuates this dynamic, and how people can break free from it and heal.

Similarly, Elizabeth co-authored *Joyously Free: Stories & Tips to Live Your Truth as LGBTQ+ People, Parents and Allies* with Joanie Lindenmeyer. The June 2024 release that includes 32 contributors from across America shares how to create happiness within the reality of pain, rejection, and grief. This journey can take you on a path that sparkles with stardust, blooms with fragrant flowers, flutters with butterflies and magical hummingbirds, radiates bright beams of colors, and glows under glorious rainbows.

Religion, which is supposed to be a source of comfort, is often a source of conflict and pain. That's why *Healing Religious Hurts* is our gift to you, to help you find the love and peace that you deserve to enjoy life and connect with God/Spirit/Higher Self in ways that bring you joy and fulfillment.

GOD IS LOVE!

Sending you big hugs and lots of love,

Elizabeth Ann Atkins
Joanie Lindenmeyer

P.S.—Dear reader: Please use the blank spaces in this book to write and/or draw your unique vision of YOU, healing your religious hurts, as inspired by each chapter.

Chapter 1

What is Religious Hurt?
Healing & Defining Your Unique Spiritual Path

My Hurts
By Joanie

It hurts so deeply that my gut and every cell inside me bubbles with rage like water boiling over the lid of a pot. My face feels hot and red. But all I can do is silently scream to Jesus as I sit in my church pew, at a staff council meeting or at an adult religion education class.

It hurts so deeply that I seek solace in Mother Nature, taking forceful steps on the thick, sandy beach, yelling at the crashing ocean waves and fighting the ferocious winds that push me backwards before I lunge forward. All the while praying and crying my eyes out for Jesus to take away hate, bigotry, homophobia, division, and **HURT.** My hurt, my family's and friends's hurts, all inflicted for decades by religious leaders's words, actions, and written doctrines. Lord help us. Lord heal us.

Let me share a list, a minute example, of some of my many experiences of religious hurts. Each is a story in itself!

- When my teenage sister was told by a priest in an arrogant tone that missing Sunday mass was NOT ALLOWED.
- When I was not permitted to be an "altar server" because I am female.
- When I sat next to a woman who had an abortion, and the pulpit priest chastised such women.
- When Carol and I were denied a sacramental marriage in the Catholic Church because we were a same-sex couple.
- When we could not be OUT for fear of the repercussions from our church community. We were asked to have individual portraits, not a together-couple portrait, for our church directory.
- When my older sister was not permitted to receive communion after her divorce from her husband.
- When I was denied having the Holy Eucharist put in my pyx (a small round container used to carry the Eucharist) to deliver to an ill family member.
- When my youth friends did not have the courage to go into a confessional to say they had sex before marriage.
- When at John's funeral, his family could not give the Eulogy at mass. John was gay.
- When the priest would not change his ways with the overpowering incense that was causing elderly people to cough and have to walk out of the church building.
- When TV evangelists and news reporters rant about LGBTQ+ people, saying they will go to hell.
- When Christian radio talk shows boldly preach salvation for you, calling you a sinner.
- When my Planned Parenthood educator friends' lives are threatened.
- When I had tomatoes thrown at me in the name of religious beliefs.
  And the list goes on and on!

Was the hostile person who grabbed the *Nun Better* banner and wanted to tear it down a religious person?

Why do I know and feel that these experiences are often a result of religions and church people who are the most arrogant, judgemental, and self-righteous discriminatory ones?

I thank God that I understand that Jesus' life was also filled with such pains. I believe that He feels those pains of mine and thousands of others. Jesus continues to wipe away tears and bring us peace and joy!

Maybe it's time for me to list all the good church leaders, the fabulous works done as holy peoples. I can only be in the downer world for so long.

May healing and peace envelope my being to be better, not bitter. May I stand up stronger because of these pains.

Maybe that's what is meant by carrying the cross.

Finding Peace, Love & Healing after My Parents' Marriage Triggered Religious Hurts
By Elizabeth

My family's story exemplifies the power of finding peace, love, and healing with God and Spirit, to unite families and instill joy and family harmony. I first shared this story in my memoir, *God's Answer Is Know: Lessons From a Spiritual Life* by Elizabeth Ann Atkins, published by Two Sisters Writing & Publishing®, the company that I co-founded with my sister, Catherine M. Greenspan.

It's important to share this story now, to lay a foundation for why I'm here on a mission to help **you** heal religious hurts and find peace and love with yourself, Spirit and/or God. I humbly come to you in this book as the "Princess of Peace" that my father anointed me to become, when he baptized me the day after my birthday.

This story begins before I was born into the bold and brave union of a 19-year-old Black woman and a 44-year-old White man who was a former priest. Back in racially turbulent 1966, Marylin Elnora Bowman and Thomas Lee Atkins sparked a scandal of race and religion by defying the restrictive conventions of the day to marry across the color line. All while breaking a centuries-old rule that Roman Catholic priests were forbidden to marry. The Bishop excommunicated my parents, which meant they were banished from receiving soul-cleansing communion during Mass.

It also meant they were damned to hell.

And my parents believed that.

Yet their love was heavenly, as was the gift of their first child. Back before technology could reveal a baby's gender, they thought I would be a boy.

"David," my father wrote with a magic marker across my mother's pregnant belly. As you probably know, young David in the Bible slayed the giant Goliath with only a slingshot and a rock and went on to become the King of Israel and a forefather of Jesus.

Well, I wasn't a boy.

Shortly after I was born on July 11, 1967, my father named me Elizabeth Ann, after Queen Elizabeth II of England. He nicknamed me "Eli," which means "my God" and "ascended" in Hebrew.

The next day, Daddy—who still had his priestly powers—baptized me in the hospital room. He chronicled it in a hand-written passage in his journal. Here is an excerpt:

It has been a full day. Most significant event was the baptism and confirmation of the baby.

At 8:30 p.m., I asked permission of the nurse in the nursery to Baptize the baby. She in turn asked her supervisor. She in turn asked the floor supervisor. Finally, I persuaded them to say okay. I scrubbed and put on a gown and mask and cap. The nurse got a few "cc's" of distilled water in a small beaker. I had Chrism (baptismal oil) ready and so—muffled by the mask—I said aloud as I poured water across Elizabeth's forehead . . . "I confirm you Ann, in the name of, etc."

Meanwhile my big hand covered her entire head even down to the scapula. And it was my intention not only to give my daughter these sacraments but also to give her membership in the family of David that she might become an instrument of—a literal Princess of Peace and into the royal priesthood of God so far as my power to convey this in these sacraments.

She was born on the 365th day of the year in which I gave Marylin my typed and signed formal engagement. And I admitted Elizabeth into the Church on the exact anniversary of giving this paper to her mother. I have been mindful all day, yesterday and today, of my very strong and oft repeated prayer to God for this child . . .

At the time, the world definitely needed a Princess of Peace. As Daddy was speaking those words, a deadly rebellion was exploding in Newark, New Jersey, killing 26 people, injuring hundreds more, and deepening America's racial divide. Then, 12 days after I was born, the Detroit insurrection claimed 43 lives amidst looting, fires, and the National Guard.

Thankfully, we returned to the safety of our home, where we lived with an elderly family friend. My mother worked the night shift at a bank and my father worked in a flower shop.

While my parents were extremely happy, and my sister Catherine Marie was due to arrive just a year and six days after my birthday, my devoutly Catholic grandmother wanted nothing to do with her defiant son, his pregnant Black wife, or their biracial baby.

But my parents wanted Alphonsine Marie LaLonde Atkins to know her granddaughter. So they drove from the mid-Michigan factory town where they lived, up Interstate 75, for the 90-minute trip to Daddy's forest-shrouded hometown. They went to the house where he grew up with brother George and sister Mary. My grandmother now lived there with Mary, her husband, and their eight children.

My father had traveled such a long and arduous road to arrive at this happy point of his life. If only his family could embrace and celebrate his joy.

But my grandmother, who attended daily Mass, had set her heart on having a son as a Roman Catholic Priest. That seemed imminent when her first son, George, was attending seminary. But he was drafted into the Marines during World War II, and her dream crashed into a nightmare when George disappeared at the bloody Battle of Tarawa. "George Joseph Atkins" is inscribed on the wall of 28,808 missing soldiers in Honolulu, Hawaii.

At the time, my father was a US Navy ensign in the South Pacific. He had graduated with a Bachelor's degree in English Literature from Notre Dame University, and earned a Master's degree in Philosophy from American University. Whatever his career ambitions were, they died with his brother's disappearance, which transferred the family's aspiration for a priest onto the next son.

My father was sent to Sacred Heart Seminary in Detroit. He was ordained in June of 1951 at St. Mary's Cathedral in Saginaw. He served as a Navy Chaplain on ships around the world, then led Mass in English and in Latin at several parishes, finally arriving at Sacred Heart, whose parishioners were a mix of Mexican and Black people.

During that time, his yearning for a wife and children intensified. He was also becoming increasingly disillusioned by the scurrilous and sometimes criminal activity occurring behind church doors: alcoholism, pedophilia, sexual perversion, and the Church's secretive tactics of hiding priests' crimes. He was deeply disturbed that priests who confessed crimes were relocated to other parishes, rather than prosecuted. And he was not allowed, by church law, to report the crimes to authorities.

In 1965, he became one of 100,000 priests who have since left the Catholic Church. At the same time, he was falling in love with church organist Marylin Elnora Bowman, whom he described as "The Queen" in his journal entries.

He was 44 and White. She was 19 and "Negro." On December 19, 1966, they demonstrated radical courage by defying the bishop's damnation. All the while, my father's mother was working with church leaders to have him committed to a mental institution. At the same time, my mother's mother accused my father of unscrupulous intentions.

15

Despite this opposition, my father wanted to make peace with his mother. Little did they know, that his baptismal prayer over me would manifest in a magic moment that shocked them both, as my mother describes in her book, *The Triumph of Rosemary: A Memoir* by Judge Marylin E. Atkins, published by Two Sisters Writing & Publishing®. The book has been developed into a screenplay that will soon be shopped to Hollywood as a feature film. My mother granted permission to share the following excerpt, in which she refers to my father by his middle name, "Lee."

MEETING ALPHONSINE

Sometime during my eighth month of pregnancy, my dear husband decided that it was time for his family to meet us, so we planned to make a trip on the upcoming Sunday. Not a shred of communication had come from his mother, Alphonsine Marie Atkins, since his October 6, 1966, note to her telling her that he had found peace within himself. He had not heard from his sister, Mary, either. Lee always believed that his sister should not have raised her eight children in the same house under the ever-watchful eye of their grandmother.

Lee hoped Mary did not allow the sexually and psychologically repressive atmosphere that permeated his house while growing up to engulf his nieces and nephews. His brother-in-law, Sterling, had always been friendly toward him. He brought balance to the house in Lee's eye. He loved his nieces and nephews, and wondered what his mother and sister were telling them about their Uncle Tom.

West Branch, Michigan, with a population of about 2,200, was situated 88 miles north of Saginaw. Before the drive, I dressed Elizabeth in a pretty pink dress. Her big blonde curls bounced all around her head. Once again, I was as big as a house, and I dressed in my nicest maternity suit.

When I told my parents about our trip, my mother assured me that after all this time, it would be fine. They would be accepting and loving.

Lee responded, "Billie does not know my family like I do."

We started out at noon, arriving in West Branch in the early afternoon. Lee pulled up in front of his childhood home. By this time, we both got cold feet.

"Do you want to go in?" he asked.

"No," I responded.

We pulled away, drove to Bay City which was on the way, picked up some fresh peanuts at the peanut store, ate lunch at a nice restaurant, and drove back to Saginaw. When we arrived home, I called my mother and told her that we chickened out.

"Next Sunday," she directed, "you drive to that woman's house. Put her granddaughter in her lap! If she drops her, call me, and I'll come and take care of her! This is ridiculous!"

Wow! I was not expecting that response.

I told Lee what she said, and he responded, "For once, I agree with your mother. We will go back next Sunday."

The following Sunday, we arrived at Mary's house. This time, we parked the car out front and walked up to the door. We were both very nervous. Lee held Elizabeth. He knocked on the door.

A woman a little older than Lee opened the door, and I immediately saw the family resemblance. This was Mary. For what felt like an eternity, but was probably just a few agonizing seconds, she just stood there staring at us with no smile or other emotion on her face.

"Hello, Mary," Lee said.

"Well," Mary said in a flat tone, "since you drove all this way, you may as well come in."

This is going to be a cold afternoon on a sunshiny day, I thought. I was doing this for my husband. For me personally, I never had to *meet his sister, or his mother, even though this 86-year-old woman was our daughter's grandmother.*

We stepped inside. The living room was neat and tidy with furniture that had obviously been in the family a long time. Mary directed us to sit on a couch directly across from the chair where their mother was sitting.

You mean this tiny, frail-looking lady was the boss of everybody? Alphonsine could not have weighed more than 90 pounds, and though she was sitting, I doubted she stood more than five-foot-two. The resemblance between Lee and his mother was striking. (But later when I saw a photo of his father, Samuel Merritt Atkins, who died in 1945, I was awed that Lee so strongly resembled his dad).

Once on the couch, Elizabeth became fidgety on Lee's lap, looking around at these strange surroundings. Two children, a boy and a girl, appeared in the door to the kitchen.

"Hi, Uncle Tom," they said in unison, then disappeared.

No one introduced them to me. Was I the first black person they had ever seen? I was sure I was the first ever in this house. Okay, Marylin, you can get through this, I thought.

Lee's mother just stared, her eyes moving from Lee to Elizabeth and then to me, again and again without saying a word. She was sitting about six feet away from us.

Finally, a friendly voice said, "Hi, Tom!" as a man I guessed was Sterling, Mary's husband, came into the living room. His tone cut through the tension with its joyful, glad-to-see-you sincerity. Sterling bent down and gave Lee a hug, and introduced himself to me.

He touched Elizabeth on the chin, and asked affectionately, "And who is this little one?"

"This is our daughter, Elizabeth Ann," Lee said proudly, "and we have another on the way."

"I see!" Sterling replied as he glanced at me, careful not to look directly at my protruding stomach.

This man is a saint! I thought.

He sat down and asked, *"Tom, how are you getting along, workwise?"*

He and Lee talked for a bit. Although Sterling had broken the ice, the tension in the room was still very thick and icy stares continued in my direction from his mother and sister.

They must be thinking, "So, this is the girl who corrupted our priest!" I thought. I wonder if Mary is afraid to talk to her brother in front of her mother?

About 20 minutes had passed. We were not offered a glass of water, or asked if we needed to use the bathroom. Sterling was great. I always loved him for making us feel at home. (He died in April of 1986 after a recurrence of leukemia. A good man.)

Just as I was about to say, *"Lee, let's leave,"* Elizabeth began to squirm on her father's lap. Lee put her down on the floor. To my utter amazement, she crawled straight toward Alphonsine. When she reached her grandmother, Elizabeth pulled herself up to her feet by using Alphonsine's long dress for assistance.

Lee and I looked at each other. *Was he thinking what I was thinking? My mother had said to put Elizabeth on her grandmother's lap . . .*

Alphonsine reached down and put her hands under Elizabeth's armpits to steady her. Elizabeth, whose back was to us, must have grinned at her grandmother. To my surprise, a smile came over Alphonsine's face as she looked at her granddaughter.

We could tell that Elizabeth wanted to sit on her lap, but the old lady could not lift her. Lee stood, crossed the room, and lifted our daughter onto his mother's lap. Alphonsine's smile grew bigger, and she even kissed Elizabeth on the cheek.

Is this really happening?

Elizabeth touched her grandmother's long, pointed nose as she reached for her silver glasses.

Mary, my dear sister-in-law, whether she liked it or not in that moment, spoke for the first time since letting us in the house. "She has such beautiful blonde curls! And look at those big green eyes!"

Elizabeth now wanted to get down, so Lee stood, took her in his arms, and returned to his chair.

"We need to get back to Saginaw," he said.

On the drive home, we talked about what transpired. Lee was happy with his mother's interaction with Elizabeth. If either of us thought that the visit would open the lines of communication between Lee and his mother and sister, however, we were wrong.

Lee wrote a nice note to his mother and sister thanking them for the visit. He received no response, nor did we receive an invitation to return. I had expected as much, and understood. They were both still angry over his departure from the priesthood, and that was not about to change. I was not mad . . .

◉

I consider this experience my first act as a Princess of Peace. That afternoon set the stage for slow but dramatic change toward love and harmony in our family. Now we are close-knit and enjoy several large family gatherings and celebrations throughout each year; each gathering is joyous and loving. This family love is a strong foundation for my life mission to share tips and stories that can inspire healing and harmony.

Specifically, as co-author of this book, my family's story establishes my lifetime mission that includes helping you find peace and love with yourself, Spirit and/or God.

Throughout this book, I will encourage you to use the powerful tool of writing for self-exploration. This enables you to identify areas that you want to heal, issues you want to release, and new ideas and practices that you can implement to cultivate love and peace with yourself and the world.

What It Looks Like and Feels Like to Heal Religious Hurts

I am there. I have experienced my family's story as a child, as an adult, and as a writer. And I have—thankfully—had the freedom to explore spirituality on my own terms and craft a lifestyle that is God-centered and focused on using my gifts of clarity to help people like you find your place of peace and love with Spirit. My daily spiritual practice and crystal-clear connection with Spirit directs my every step, fills me with peace, love, and comfort.

I want this for you! Believe that it's possible. We hope that this book will take you a big step closer to being there.

First, what is religious hurt? It's anything that has caused you confusion, pain, trauma, anxiety, rejection, or negativity around religion. That can come in the form of family members, religious leaders, the media, classmates, teachers, books, religious doctrine, and other sources.

This book aims to help you heal from all of the above and find your own unique path to the love and peace that is infinitely available from God, Spirit, and your Higher Self. Your Higher Self is the purest form of *you* that speaks your truth and is unhindered by the fears, doubts, and external noise that cloud our thinking minds.

Now I'm sharing my stories to show you an example of how you can empower yourself to find your way out of the shadows of religious hurts and into the light of love and peace.

As I embarked on my spiritual journey, God sent many amazing people into my life to teach me and help me evolve. I needed help! I desperately wanted to learn to meditate, but the books that I read back in the 1990s—before the Internet put answers, videos, websites, audiobooks, and social media experts in the palms of our hands—I was super confused. The books by spiritual gurus were confusing and the meditation techniques I tried didn't work.

Then my mother serendipitously met a man who became my meditation teacher. He exemplifies the saying that, "When the student is ready, the teacher will appear." Dr. Rama, who is Hindu, taught me a simple meditation technique. Then my spiritual journey connected me with Lori Lipten, a shaman and medium who founded Sacred Balance Academy in Bloomfield Hills, Michigan. From her I learned many meditation techniques that have healed me and my family in miraculous ways. She also taught me how to clear my energy and use intuitive writing to communicate with Spirit to receive powerful guidance that is protective, creative, and life changing. In 2021, I became a certified Intuitive Practitioner after taking Lori's nine-month course, and have led weekly meditations for people across America over Zoom, as well as in person.

These practices are the fast-track to love and peace with yourself first. The act of writing headlines my spiritual practice as I journal in the morning, throughout the day, and before sleep. That's why we're including writing exercises in this book to help you delve deep into your heart and soul to mine the golden nuggets of your greatest desires and help you manifest them in 3D reality. So let's get started.

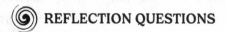 **REFLECTION QUESTIONS**

What are your religious hurts, if any? How do they block you from experiencing love and peace?

_____

_____

What about your family and friends? Do they talk, complain, or express discomfort with religious issues?

_____

_____

Were your religious hurts inflicted by family members, religious leaders, schoolmates, the media, or some other person/entity?

_____

_____

Describe your ideal spiritual life. How does it feel in your mind and body?

_____

_____

What is your vision for finding love and peace with God/Spirit/ Higher Self? Do you want to have a daily spiritual practice in the privacy and comfort of your own home? Do you want to find a faith community that embraces and celebrates you just as you are? Do you want to create your own prayer group or spiritual organization to express and teach your views on spirituality? Your vision can be as simple or as grandiose as you desire. Write about it.

_____

_____

What do you need to do to bring the above vision to life? If you're not sure, please keep reading, because this book may inspire ideas.

_____

_____

Escape from a Mental Alcatraz
By Vivian Ashton

I *was* a good boy. I was born into a conservative family that taught me the many laws of righteousness. Especially ingrained in my head was the great guilt of man—that we are carriers of sin, like rats with the plague. In every action I took, there were critiques that sometimes became long, incessant homilies about failure. My failure, someone's failure, the failure of being human. Everywhere I went, I was reminded of failure.

I remember helping set up a Christmas tree once. The job was to take out the stand and fill it with water. A simple task. It seemed as though everything I was doing was wrong, from the stand's positioning to the amount of water that I was supposed to give. I followed things as exactly as I could, and yet it was still not to code.

The sharp vetoes that would follow my actions pushed me to a boiling point, and the glass dome of my patience cracked. Through that crack, my ability to care gushed out of me as I left the room for my bedroom to cry. Then, my father came in and asked why I wasn't doing anything to help. In tears of self-loathing, I cried that nothing I was doing was helping, so I figured I'd just not be present and stay out of the way for everyone else. As a mere human, a disgusting displeasure to God and my parents by His command that I was told I should honor, there was nothing that I could do that would be perfect. So in search of Heaven, I did nothing.

To recount things more specifically, I was born into an American Baptist family in the mid-2000s. We were headstrong Bible-thumpers and patriots, the horror of the conflicts in the Middle East stealing our zeal. We culturally felt the ripplings of the Cold War, with great disdain for socialism, communism, and the Devil, who was apparently behind both. To me, communism felt more like an alright idea that was bastardized by dictators, but I kept that opinion mostly to myself to avoid being "the enemy." There were many opinions I kept to myself for these reasons, such as my opinion that one's relationship to God should be more informal.

I was in a car ride with my dad once, talking about God. I cannot quite remember the quote, but the meaning of my dad's words were clear: God was the heavenly father, yes, but first and foremost the Triune God is the *Lord*. He was not someone who was going to reassure you that everything was okay, he is a God that demands something from his *servants*. My heart sank upon truly internalizing this. I was a servant, a failure of one at that.

After that, my middle school years involved my family frequently changing denominations until we found something that suited our legality far more: Catholicism.

I kept to myself in general, really only talking at great length to my family until the very late 2010s when I grew to have more friends. Whenever I socialized, I would commit too many *faux pas* and usually got a long "talking at" (because it was not even a conversation) afterwards. I was usually doing something "wrong" anyway unless I was just standing there, holding something for someone, or just going to grab something when asked for help.

Even on the corrections that were genuinely fair, everything was still adding up as misstep after misstep. Any desire I had to interact with people was greatly waning. It seemed better to just stay mentally shackled to my desk, either playing video games or doing schoolwork. I was schooled online, which was not an inherent problem (it was beneficial to learning) but this experience provides context.

I spent all day in my room, with some exceptions such as helping with errands or visits, and eating meals. Anything else would invite folly. I had been offered a few escapes by my father, but I never took them. It all looked like nothing but an emotional drain, which would be better spent on schoolwork.

As mentioned, I did indeed have friends. My parents questioned me on whether or not they seemed conservative or Christian. (How was I supposed to know? Was I supposed to interrogate them for their beliefs?) I had better questions to ask, like which Pokémon was their favorite, or if they liked Minecraft.

Even as a kid, this amount of questioning thy neighbor was not something I was keen toward. Many of them were good friends to me, people I still consider friends to this day. My friends both in online school, some of whom I actually saw on rare occasions at school events, and my friends from church, were the people who helped heal my hurts the most. They taught me to open up and form connections, even when those connections were painful. Some connections stayed during times where I failed. It taught me a kind of love and life that no denomination of Christianity I experienced had taught me.

This is the story of my escape from a mental Alcatraz.

It wasn't until mid-high school that I truly started to break free from the beliefs tethering me, thanks to my friends. I met a friend of a friend over a casual call one day. I found out very quickly that this friend of a friend was a trans man named Will. At the time, I was still rather transphobic, although I was admittedly better than my parents in that I did not develop social indigestion in his presence. Will and I began to bond immediately over a mutual fascination with jester characters. But the combination of a Catholic would-be priest and a transgender man was not the most novel thing about our relationship.

I strived to use his preferred pronouns, correcting myself when I misgendered him. I gave his gender respect, and what he called himself didn't matter to me. Before I knew it, I had developed a crush on him. He was such an interesting, friendly, strong, intelligent human, essentially the opposite of what I was told that people of the 2SLGBTQIA+ community were. I wanted to be there for him in his struggles, and I wanted to spend as much time as I could with him, but it was not safe to do so, as my parents, too, found out he was trans. *She*, they insisted, *she* was "batting for the wrong team." I didn't agree with them, but rhetoric and ideology kept me bound. I found myself pleading to God for forgiveness, because I couldn't stop loving him just because he was trans.

I felt greatly betrayed by my faith and at the same time like its betrayer. The God of infinite love extends His promise to only the "saved," yet I broke the laws of God by loving someone who is not "saved." There was a contradiction, but would I be a heretic to say so? I began to feel lost, as this identity-consuming belief about the world began to crumble around me.

Worse yet, I had a potent nightmare of a daydream that I now understand as gender dysphoria. (To put this in perspective, I used to visually hallucinate.) I was lying on the bed, taking a rest from school for the day. Kneeling on my chest was a woman in a black dress and a glowing mask. I could feel life and energy behind her mask, and an immediate sameness with this woman that paralyzed me. This was yet another seed sown whose growing roots would one day break the concrete sidewalk of religious hurt. By being a good person who didn't believe in God, one man mangled the neck of my beliefs before leaving it to die with a sickening crack. I was left alone with a shattered image of a plastic Christ.

About a year after we met, that man and I established a romantic partnership, which was interfered with by a cruelly convenient move that my family made to Ohio. Will and I still kept in contact, and we grew closer than before, facing the challenge of a long-distance relationship that I had to hide from my parents.

Over the two years I spent in Ohio, I began to look to augment my quickly disintegrating faith. I studied philosophy and alchemy, but nothing made sense until I discovered Daoism. I'd heard references to it in media, so I thought to give it a shot. I listened to an audiobook of the Dao de Jing. It opened my eyes to a new perspective of how the world works, and things began to make sense for me. It answered questions that Christianity did not answer for me, and it answered questions in a manner that felt more natural and realistic. It taught me that God is not a corporate overlord breaking His servants' backs, but a loving, gentle guide. Later, about half-way through my stay in Ohio, I came to realize I was not a man, and with some experimenting, I found myself as a woman.

I find that I can comfortably call myself a Daoist now. I found a new appreciation for Christianity after leaving it and being free to declare so. I remember kindly two priests, one who did my first confession and boldly proclaimed in a homily that the Muslims were our brothers and sisters, too (for context, it was late 2000s and early 2010s, so the shock of 9/11 and the War on Terror were painfully fresh), and another priest from my time in the Midwest who acted like a member of the parish just as much as a leader of it.

I have met several Christians (including the lovely Joanie) who have made me remember that being Christian is about loving people and showing love. Even though I no longer follow the faith, I was able to find the God I've been praying to—a loving God, like a gentle parent, guiding Their children through life, not ordering them around like a CEO demanding more hours from their overworked employees.

I spent 16 years stuck in a ritualistic remnant of faith and three years questioning it, leading me to where I am now. All it took for the process of healing to start for me was to find the love I shared with one man, whom I can call my husband now. (We ditched the paperwork and kept it to feelings. Besides, tax season is already over at the time of writing, so we wouldn't get any benefits from a legal marriage until next year.)

Today, I am outside the prison, despite still shaking off the cuffs. For anyone still going through the hurts of a mentally shackled upbringing: You're not a burden for being flawed. It is something I still grapple with to this day, but being flawed is what makes us beautiful. We can find beauty in times of struggle because of our strength.

If you so choose to stick with your faith, please remember its principles beyond just what your parents or community tell you. Especially in a time when Christian love is so far distanced from the love that Christ taught His people, remember that love does not judge like an executioner. This applies to any religion, not just the Christian faith. You are free to explore your religion. Take some time to beseech the help of bodhisattvas if you are inclined, try out a protective Wiccan spell (if it is safe to do so), or even just take some time to wonder if the god you've been praying to this whole time may come to you by another name.

Thank you for listening.

Vivian Ashton is a trans game developer and writer.

Love Heals Religious Hurts
By Kristen Sheridan

My biological mother was 15 years old when she gave birth to me. By the time she was 21, she was raising two children and was addicted to meth and alcohol. Life with her was understandably chaotic, and I experienced many abuses.

However, I had the freedom to watch or listen to anything I wanted to. I was essentially the adult in the house, making sure we had food, that the rent was paid, and that my brother was safe. I was a mini-adult in a lot of ways. When I was 12 years old and my brother was six, a family friend stepped in and gave my mother two options: let me and my brother go live with them or have Social Services called and put us into foster care.

My mother chose to send us to live with the family friend. At the time, I was excited. Regular meals, clean clothes, and a home with heat were the most ideal things for me. I was excited to live without fear.

The family that took us in was a married couple in their late thirties or early forties. They were conservative and regular church attenders. They expected me and my brother to participate in church activities as well. In the beginning, I had no problem with this because I was just so grateful to be out of the situation with our mother. However, many things quickly became apparent.

I was not allowed to listen to the music I enjoyed or watch the movies and TV shows that interested me. I was expected to attend and participate in church services and youth group. I was discouraged from having friends who did not attend church, even though I went to a public school and none of my friends from youth group attended my school.

In short, I went from being a mini-adult to being expected

to be the perfect Christian kid, all in the span of a month or so. I did love youth group. I got to go to summer camp and travel to Mexico to work at an orphanage that helped adults with developmental disabilities. We went on trips to amusement parks and Christian music festivals. My youth leaders were great and didn't make me feel less than because I wasn't fully raised in the church.

My adopted parents even took me on the annual church trip to Israel as a sort of pilgrimage. That trip was so much fun. It is there that I learned that those of the Jewish faith do not write the name of G-d, but write it as I have. Since then, I have tried to follow this out of respect for people of the Jewish faith or any other faith that follows this.

The main issues I had with the church were the emphasis on purity culture, the impending rapture, and the negative attitude towards getting professional help for mental health.

Meanwhile, my biological mother had frank, and honestly inappropriate, conversations about sex with me. I was taught that sex can be for procreation, but also pleasure. In church, I was taught that sex was for procreation only, and you may go to hell if you had sex before marriage.

Getting married right out of high school was the norm for most of my church peers. The idea was to date to marry. If you couldn't see yourself married to a person, there was no need to date them. I was given a promise ring and encouraged to make a vow before G-d that I would save myself for my husband. I was taught that the more sexual partners I had, the less value I had to anyone.

The head pastor was obsessed with the end times. Every major news event out of the Middle East was a signal that the rapture was coming, and you better make sure you are right with G-d so you don't get left behind. We were even encouraged to read *Left Behind: The Kids* by Jerry B. Jenkins and Tim LaHaye. This series of 40 books is about teenagers who were "left behind" after the apocalypse and find faith in Jesus. Our pastor wanted us to know how terrible things would be if we were left behind. He preached the rapture almost every Sunday. There were many altar calls made after services so people could be saved to avoid being left behind when Jesus came back.

At the age of 15, I finally opened up to my adopted parents about the many abuses I had experienced as a child. Instead of finding me professional help, I was introduced to a woman from church who had a "similar testimony" as mine. I was encouraged to pray that the negative feelings would stop and that G-d would show me how to forgive my abusers.

I wasn't taken to get professional mental health help until my adopted parents discovered I was self-harming. I think their motivation for getting me professional help was to avoid any "scandal" at church. I was only in therapy a short while because my adopted parents didn't like that my therapist encouraged me to set boundaries.

During my senior year in high school, I met a girl and I was attracted to her. We dated in secret, but eventually my adopted parents found out and told me I was going to hell for the things I was doing and that no man would ever want me if they knew I was a lesbian (actually they didn't say lesbian, but I don't like the word they used).

Once I turned 18 and moved out, I went a little crazy. Lots of drinking, drugs, and men. And even though I was making those choices for myself, I felt a huge amount of guilt that I was letting Jesus down and that I would be burning in hell for sure when I died. But I also remembered the teachings of Jesus and how He spent most of His time with the sinners. How He commanded people to love their neighbor. In my heart, I know that G-d gave us free will for a reason and that Christ loved me no matter what. That thought helped ease the guilt a bit.

I think I stopped feeling guilty right around the time that I got pregnant with my first child. I was terrified to tell my adopted parents I was pregnant because I was unmarried. This is ridiculous to think about because I was 24 years old, lived on my own with my boyfriend, had worked since the age of 16, and had gotten my act together regarding substances. But I just knew none of that would matter without a ring. Turns out, my adopted parents were willing to overlook that for a grandchild.

I'm definitely not completely healed from my religious hurts, but I no longer feel overwhelming guilt and anxiety when I make choices that go against what I was taught. I do still have moments where I feel like I have failed or that I fear death because I'm going to hell. Then I remind myself that G-d is love and Christ preached love. I have attempted to build a faith on that alone.

I also make sure I have frank and honest conversations with my children about religion and explain they can believe what they want to believe. While my children attend church with my adopted parents, I keep a close eye on how they are feeling and understanding what is taught, so I can get ahead of any anxiety or guilt they may have.

At the end of the day, love and acceptance are the most important lessons I learned in church. All humans desire love and acceptance and that is what Christ teaches in the New Testament.

I really believe in people finding their own ways to believe and worship whatever G-d or creator they want. Unfortunately, Christian leaders have done a disservice to their congregations by focusing on the wrong things in the Bible. They cherry-pick what they want to believe and usually what they pick are the things that oppress women, the LGBTQ+ community, and other religions. What they should be focusing on is the teachings of Christ. The gospels tell us that Jesus preached love and spent his time with the "sinners."

For anyone struggling to reconcile the life they live with their Christian upbringing, I encourage you to remember this: Jesus said there were only two great commandments: love your G-d with all your heart and love your neighbor as yourself (Matthew 22:37-39). In those verses, there are no commands to judge, to live or be a certain way, or to do great works.

He calls on all of us to just love. That's it. **Just love.** I think that is what this world desperately needs right now. I hope that everyone on their healing journey can find that love.

Kristen Sheridan is a wife, mother, and avid reader.

Tips

- Identify, be honest, and name the hurt to yourself first.
- Realize you are not alone.
- Write it down. Clarify and start healing.
- Break off a relationship if it is unhealthy, demeaning, and devastating to you. Stick up for YOU!
- Share the hurt with a trusted person. Get it off your chest.
- Confront the source of the hurt in person with an ally for backup.
- Write a letter or many letters.
- Take legal action if necessary.
- Get professional help not related to the organization or person(s) that caused your pain.
- Decide to go public or not.
- Pray for yourself and pray for those who hurt you.
- Grow from it and turn it into something beautiful and thankful.
- Get closer to your Higher Power/maker because of it.
- Sit, be quiet, and find peace.

Chapter 2

Sexism in Religion
Let's Make It an Equal Playing Field

How Spirit Helped Me Find the Courage to Write & Publish Books That Defy Sexism By Elizabeth

I believe women can be deeply spiritual and highly sexual at the same time.

I totally reject the virgin-whore complex that society has inflicted from the beginning of time. This phenomenon—that a woman is either a pure virgin **or** a dirty whore—is presented in the Christian Bible and the majority of religious teachings, whether written or spoken. This is also called the Madonna-whore complex, which categorizes women on the two extremes of being either virginal and pure like Mother Mary, or sexually promiscuous.

Humans are programmed with this information starting at birth, which prompts men to enforce it and women to comply with it. Defiance of this deeply-rooted system of control can result in horrific consequences, including death to girls and women in some religious cultures.

In general in society, women are punished for expressing our natural desire for physical pleasure. A long list of names awaits any women who are sexually liberated and break the "rules." They are "slut-shamed," which means degrading a woman who independently expresses her sexuality, especially if she has multiple romantic partners. The instant and worldwide reach of social media and AI makes it easier than ever for people to use this centuries-old tactic to hurt girls and women, sometimes so traumatically that they choose suicide.

In contrast, men are praised and celebrated for their sexual conquests. They're called "a stud" and "Romeo" and "a lady's man." Amazingly, even those who are proven adulterers can still bask in the superstar glory of their industry as athletes, politicians, executives, and musicians. All while this belief is emphasized and perpetuated in music, movies, popular culture, on social media, amongst friends, and in families. This is especially promulgated by societal norms rooted in religion.

Sadly, it guilts and shames people, especially women, so profoundly that they feel and fear they can never enjoy our God-given right to enjoy the pleasures of the flesh, even in a committed and loving relationship. As a result, many women, including Catholics, are too emotionally, physically, and spiritually shut-down to orgasm. They feel so shamed and guilted by religious brainwashing that they are disconnected from this beautiful gift. They're told that they have to "stay pure" in order to attract a husband who does not want "used goods."

Sexism in religion outrages me!

I have not ascribed to my family's Catholic roots for multiple reasons.

First, the Church damned my parents to hell for being in love, and they believed it. They were excommunicated, which means, according to the Oxford Languages Dictionary on Google: "to officially exclude (someone) from participation in the sacraments and services of the Christian Church."[1]

Catholics take Communion, which is a small wafer and a sip of wine that symbolize the body and blood of Jesus. When someone is excommunicated, they are allegedly banned from this sacred ritual that happens during every Mass. Thankfully, my parents were still given Communion when they attended church, and I say thankfully because it was important to them. I don't know why they were still given Communion after they were excommunicated.

Let me say thankfully again to this: our parents never forced me or my younger sister Catherine to go to Sunday School or catechism, a series of classes that indoctrinate children with Catholic teachings. Our parents taught us that as girls we can be and do anything we want in life. And they did not impose the sexual oppression that many Catholic families inflict on girls.

My second reason for rejecting Catholicism is that it is unbelievable and unacceptable that the Catholic Church's leadership is entirely male, yet they are dictating to millions of people around the world how women should live, love, and have no power over our reproductive rights—while millions of women actually follow what these men command!

Unfortunately, many of the world's major religions do the same thing, often with even more strict rules for women.

My third reason for opting out of Catholicism is that it's a man-made tool for control. Humans—men in particular—wrote the Bible and most religious texts that influence how billions of people think and behave. In the Bible, women are wives, concubines, and whores. In reality, we are so much more, with infinite potential to be and do any and everything! So I refuse to allow rules that men wrote centuries ago to control me just because I was born with a vagina and not a penis. It makes no sense!

Here's where I flex the power of my pen to defy this. A quick play on words. Look at the word pen. It's the first three letters of penis. Not a coincidence, considering again that men wrote and enforce the world's religious doctrine.

So my mission is to use my pen-power to write and publish books that inspire new ways of thinking about these dynamics, especially spirituality and women's empowerment. Please read *God's Answer Is Know: Lessons From a Spiritual Life*, and my new book, *The Biss Tribe: Where You Activate Your GoddessPower*, published on August 8, 2024. This six-part series of self-help books is all about helping women activate the infinite power within ourselves to lay a foundation of Power, Pleasure, Prosperity, Protection, and Peace to build a personal and professional empire that we rule from a throne of power wearing a crown of confidence.

I've done this for myself and now I'm teaching these tools to women everywhere to help them live bigger, better, and bolder and manifest their heart's wildest desires.

As co-founder of Two Sisters Writing & Publishing®, I created a global platform to share information on the pages of books like *Healing Religious Hurts* that can help people find their own empowered journey to love, peace, and spiritual connection.

Having a publishing company and writing books is how I aim to be the change I wish to see in the world, and Spirit encourages me every step of the way.

On this topic of sexism in religion and breaking the chains that restrict women from living and loving as we truly desire, I write erotic fiction. Ironically, I composed an erotic trilogy with graphic love scenes and language during my spiritual retreat in 2013. During that time, as guided by Spirit, I withdrew from the world and spent every day meditating, doing yoga, eating a strict vegan whole-foods diet, praying, journaling, and writing books. I ate no meat or dairy, had no sex and very little social life, only listened to gospel or spiritual music, and blocked out the noisy world. My spiritual connection was so strong, it was psychic and psychedelic, and this launched me into my creative genius zone. As a result, I wrote several books, including my erotic trilogy called *Husbands, Incorporated.*

The women in this story played by society's rules, but ended up disillusioned and divorced, feeling discarded and dissatisfied. Now they're seeking the power and pleasure in romantic relationships, on their terms. So I created a world where that is possible. I believe very strongly in many of the themes that I worked so hard to illustrate through four couples in the book.

However, writing erotica seemed totally incongruous with my extraordinary spiritual experiences. How could I simultaneously be a spiritual teacher talking about Jesus and the power of God within us, and be an erotica writer with radical viewpoints about marriage and monogamy?

This question made my heart pound with anxiety. I feared I would not publish *Husbands, Incorporated.*

"Yes, you will," Jesus told me in meditation.

(Please know that the Jesus who appeared to me in meditation during my spiritual awakening is an all-inclusive, non-denominational Jesus who loves everyone of every culture, religion, ethnicity, and national origin. Prior to this moment on August 20, 2011, I had had zero relationship with Jesus, for some of the reasons stated in this chapter. And when He appeared, I was filled with the most tremendous sense of peace and love, a feeling that I want **you** to experience by reading this book and embarking on your own journey of healing and spiritual awakening. Jesus spoke to me during meditations with clarity, and you can read more about this in *God's Answer Is Know.*)

"Jesus," I asked in meditation, "how can I talk about you and testify about my spiritual awakening—and publish and promote erotica?"

"It will be part of your mission," Jesus said, "to show the world that one person can integrate the erotic and the spiritual and the teaching and everything that you offer."

41

I expressed my trepidation.

"Publish it anyway!" He exclaimed. "You will force the world to see a woman as many-faceted, the merging of the virgin and whore, my love."

Receiving guidance directly from Spirit—whether it's Jesus, an angel, your ancestors, God, the Universe, Creator, Source, your Higher Self, or whatever name you use to describe your beliefs—is the ultimate affirmation! Please know that this is possible for you and anyone, and when you use the tools in the final chapter, you can begin to attune to this energy and create a clear channel for two-way communication that will help you heal, find your purpose, tap into your creative genius, and experience life in exhilarating ways that you may never have imagined. You can do it!

So let's get back to the virgin-whore complex. Since time began, this dynamic has ranked women at either one end or the other. When I became aware of this damning social construct during Women's Studies classes at the University of Michigan, I was infuriated. I felt that the "Virgin Mary" concept only perpetuated this. After that, I gained a new understanding of Mary Magdalene—who was wrongly portrayed as a prostitute in the Bible—and was relegated to unscrupulous end of the Madonna-Whore scale. In my meditations, I learned that Mary Magdalene was actually the wife of Jesus.

This revelation prompted me to spend hours online, reading and watching videos about Mary Magdalene. She was with Jesus during the crucifixion, and she was the first person to see Him upon his resurrection. After He went to heaven, she fled on a boat across the Mediterranean, landing in the south of France, where she retreated for 30 years in a cave in a mountain called La Sainte Baume. People pilgrimage to the cave every summer to celebrate the Feast Day of Mary Magdalene on July 22. Many believers consider this trip third in line after visiting the holy sites in Jerusalem and Rome.

Mary Magdalene was one of many wealthy women who provided financial support for Jesus's ministry. She was not a prostitute. She was a wealthy woman from Magdala, a fishing town on the Sea of Galilee. And she was Jesus' wife. He sought her counsel on many topics, much to the jealousy of Saint Peter.

It's very suspect and not surprising that the *Gospel of Mary* is missing significant portions of her story and is not widely known or included in the Bible along with the gospels of Jesus's all-male disciples.

The ancient manuscript that is the *Gospel of Mary* was discovered near Akhmim in upper Egypt during the late-nineteenth century, according to gnosis.org. In 1896, German scholar Dr. Carl Reinhardt bought the well-preserved manuscript and took it to Berlin, where it's now kept in the *Berlin Gnostic Codex* (codex means ancient manuscript).[2]

We'll never know portions of her story in her own words, because the *Gospel of Mary* is missing 10 pages: six from the beginning and four from the middle.[3]

Mary Magdalene exemplifies sexism in religion. The men who wrote the Bible portrayed her as a prostitute, and if you mention her name today, that's what most people will say, because the Bible-writers didn't want us to know her financial power, influence with Jesus, or position as the wife of Jesus. Then somebody long ago absconded with 10 pages from her manuscript. If this topic interests you, please explore online and watch the many documentaries about this amazing woman and her important place in religious history.

So, back to my point about sexism in religion and specifically, the virgin-whore phenomenon. I believe that this idea should be abolished altogether. It's all about shaming women and attempting to make us conform to society's rules to control us. This deeply ingrained and insidious rating scale keeps many women living under the radar, playing by its rules, because the consequences of defying it can still be extremely detrimental to a woman's reputation and life.

That's why *Husbands, Inc.* became my literary response to a global society where men typically make the rules about women's sexuality. In my books, women make the rules and have the power. I loved Jesus's extremely progressive support and prophecy, but I was afraid of criticism from humans.

Determined to proceed, I considered using a local printing company that had produced copies of my best-selling novel, *Dark Secret*, or Lightning Source, a print-on-demand company that would make my book available on Amazon.com and online retail sites around the world.

"Use Lightning Source," Jesus said on January 17, 2014. "It has greater distribution." In my meditation, He was holding a lightning bolt in each hand. "Use Lightning Source because you will be like bolts of lightning over the world."

Jesus said the book would be successful: "It will make an extremely loud and big splash, Elizabeth. Like a whale slamming on the water, causing great waves and commotion."

I continued to write and publish books that defy the rules and show new ways for people—especially women—to live and love.

In order to clean the window, we need to see the smudges. So let's get a clarity on examples of religious sexism that may have hurt you and are stopping you from living your best life.

Writing is a powerful tool for self-exploration that can help you heal and release old thoughts and behaviors that are disempowering you.

So, describe examples of how religious sexism may be hindering your mind, body, and spirit. Where and how have you witnessed religious sexism?

REFLECTION QUESTIONS

What beliefs do you hold—that you want to release—that are rooted in religious sexism? These beliefs may not at first seem religious, but many of society's beliefs come from religious teachings.

_____

_____

Describe an example of how religious sexism may have affected the way you think, speak, live and love.

_____

_____

What can **you** do to express new ideas that disrupt, halt, and challenge religious doctrine—and as a result, societal norms—to help others find love and peace with themselves and with Spirit/God?

_____

_____

If you believe that sexism from religion has stifled, hindered, shamed, guilted, and/or scared you into thinking and behaving a certain way, describe your mindset, your feelings, and your lifestyle that you'd like to experience after you've freed yourself from these beliefs and behaviors.

_____

_____

Dwell on this vision in your imagination every day. See it, feel it, and take steps to make it your 3D reality. Write what you need to become that version of yourself who is liberated from religious sexism.

_____

_____

Maybe the Root of All Evil is Masculine Dominance
By Joanie

All through my years, I've been faced with sexism in sports, school, church, and society. As I discovered my true self and my sexual identity as a lesbian, I've lived through both homophobic and crude, sexist remarks and assumptions. It's been frustrating, darn it.

As a kid with my baseball hat sitting precariously backwards on my head, my freckles sprouting like popcorn kernels, I was called a boy, a tomboy and queer by people who did not even know me. I shrunk with fear and anger. These stereotypical comments were assaults on my personhood.

So, is there a correlation between sexism and homophobia? Yes!

Are either one contagious? No, but they are learned behaviors.

Thank goodness I had a healthy, happy family that appreciated and loved me for who I was. In the 1960s, I, a little kid, was affectionately called Joanie Baloney, "Bones" by Tom and Gail, my older siblings, and Joan of Arc, my namesake, by my mother. I was gifted with extra athleticism, extra enthusiasm and an extra spirit I called, "love of life."

Sexist and Homophobic

As I grew older, the sexist and homophobic jokes and pokes appeared out of nowhere in judgmental and subtle ways. Most people didn't even realize that actions and words could hurt my sensitive nature. I discovered that sexism was predominantly found in simply belonging to the human race, in institutions that seek to serve others and in belonging to a community of faith believers.

Did you know that now in 2024, Jewish, Christian, Catholic and Islamic religions are considered the top male chauvinistic religions? Yucko! That's sad.

Will we ever learn how to raise children without gender stereotypes and sexism? I think baby colors are not only pink and blue; they are orange and turquoise and red and purple and magenta and okra. Think of the *Joseph and The Technicolor Dreamcoat*. Please listen to the song, "Coat of Many Colors" by Dolly Parton.

Babies are pure joy and filled with abundant possibilities. Toddlers like a zillion things, so please share with them a multitude of activities, music styles, languages, toys, books, adventures, and diverse people, places and eats. Raise them with positive -isms, not sexisms.

Under my Catholic school plaid uniform skirt, I wore my play-sports shorts, my freedom attire. When the school bell rang at 3 PM, I hooped and hollered at the top of my powerful lungs, "Wahooo," as I twirled my arms in a circle and stripped off my skirt. I was pulled aside, verbally criticized, scolded and reprimanded for making such a raucous yell and for running down the side steps of the second floor in the school building at St. John's Elementary School on Normal Street in San Diego, California. By the way, it was the late 1960s and early 1970s, and it was not a religious sister who scolded me, but a female lay teacher.

"Control yourself, Joan," she said, "you are a young lady, not a wild animal."

From then on, I kept my joyful noise contained until I straddled my fat-tire blue Schwinn bicycle, leaving my skirt on and riding happily and vigorously home in my hidden shorts. At home, after hugging my mom, dumping my homework and books on the dining room table, I went to my bedroom, and turned into the real bionic amazing kid wearing shorts and a T-shirt.

A most important life lesson is to value the dignity and uniqueness of every person.

Girls in Church

I remember so vividly the first time at Catholic mass, in the 1980s, seeing a young girl as an altar server! Exhilaration! She and her male friend, dressed in a red cassock or alb, their stoic faces, steps in unison, sharing the altar space, holding the lectionary and ringing the bells. They shared the altar duties with grace and elegance. I was pumped up, seeing this female teen absorbed in an age-old, male-dominated ritual, carrying and holding the water bowl and towel for the priest to cleanse and dry his hands. I had chills of joy as I watched her bow in reverence as her eyes twinkled with angel dust. It was about time! Finally, the church's sexist monopoly was changing to be more all-inclusive. A huge mindset and perspective change!

Society and church had equally progressed to oust a male-dominated norm. Oh, I relived the same excitement I had felt when I attended a professional baseball game, seeing a ball girl dressed in a baseball hat, tennis shoes, a nylon sports jacket and a baseball glove permanently secured on her hand. She was on the same playing field as the bat boys. Similarly, the Catholic Church was moving and grooving forward. Yippee!

Female altar servers were officially allowed in 1994. In 2021, Pope Francis ordered a modification to canon law, from temporary to stable, allowing women and girls to serve on the altar. On a disgusting side note, in 2024, there are still dioceses that don't allow female altar servers.

So much for a universal Catholic Church!

49

For centuries, male priests were the only ones allowed on the church altar, while nuns or sisters were only allowed to clean the altar. The role of women and men serving the church and on the altar has been sexist and still carries residual pains and scars that need to be healed. Lay lectors are another biggie. It's not just a male-female issue; it's for all baptized people, said Pope Francis. Another yippee!

Many joys rang through Carol and I regarding serving and celebrating in Catholic communities and parishes. A highlight was Carol's 25th year of jubilation as a vowed sister. She asked me, "Joanie, would you give a short, five-minute sermon at my jubilee mass?"

"Of course, Carol! I would be honored!"

She chose one of her hundreds of favorite scriptures—Jeremiah 29:11-14: "For I know the plans I have for you," declares the Lord, "plans to prosper you and not to harm you, plans to give you hope and a future . . . "

The kicker was, it was 1986 and our religious order, the Sisters of St. Joseph of Carondelet, and Carol had a fabulous rapport with the male Jesuit priests. She had requested of them that I and a lay woman speak the sermon as lessons. It was AMAZING; she and I stood together sharing the podium and microphone that once was only male-priest territory. Carol and Sister Frances knew this was the time and place to celebrate sisterhood. That this would, and it did, lead to more women roles, more women on the altar, and more lay women religious leaders. It was the best win-win-win-win for the Catholic Church in Lewiston, Idaho.

Can love win without stigmas and sexism? Absolutely yes!

At home growing up, I was raised in a "you can do it" spirit. Be kind, be respectful, be the best you. We were taught a dress code for school and church; there were appropriate ways to behave in public and we practiced how to walk with a book on our head for posture, how to sit like a lady with ankles crossed, (I had a hard time with that one because I felt silly) and don't antagonize or hit your little sister. "Girls don't hit," we were told. However, in high school, I did get into two fights, both while defending myself and my softball teammates.

I, like my sweetie Carol, marched to our own drums! We learned to let sexist issues roll off our backs, and we were able to do that joyfully because we had each other. We loved each other so incredibly deeply, profoundly and proudly. We were each other's "better half." It was a lifetime adventure of making each day the best ever, enjoying every person we met. It might sound cliché or dreamlike, but that was us!

Catholic Sexism

As nuns, and as laity, Carol and I, in our same-sex couple-hood, withstood Catholic sexism. Many times, Carol would say, "Let's do this; we can ask for forgiveness later." We were each other's cheerleader, rock, and bulletproof vest.

We were blessed with progressive priests as our collaborative leaders. We found that the Jesuit order of priests and some diocesan priests who lived in community with other priests/ brothers were much more advanced in working in cooperative relationships with women and lay religious leaders. They actually enjoyed having discussions and collaborations.

Only a handful of priests we encountered were jealous of us and had great difficulty letting go of power. The sexist male mindset friction seemed to surface like oil on water. We females were fun, joyous, relatable and available to listen with our parish friends. They, the ego power-driven men, were not pastoral people and would rather *manage* "their" parish (not "our" parish) versus living amongst them. This was a lonely sexist

51

attitude they held tightly to. Of course, many of them tooted their hierarchical masculinity because they were the chosen men approved to consecrate the bread and wine into the body and blood of Christ. I never understood how testosterone and a down-under body part gave them that honor.

Imagine you are a young child. Who and what is your role model for religious leadership? I loved playing priest, giving the communion host in the form of an Oreo cookie to my little sister, Ter, in our shared bedroom. She "played priest" too, giving me cookie communion. How fun! We were just decades ahead of the times.

The first time I witnessed a female priest consecrate the bread and wine was one of the most profound spiritual experiences in my life. It was in 2023!

My eyes were twinkling with delight, mesmerized by watching her as she spread her arms like a soaring eagle to greet the gifts presented at the altar. Her voice was like a Dolby sound system of thankful prayers. With her gentle hands placed elegantly above the gold chalice and paten (plate), she spoke with a voice quivered with emotion as she recited the consecration words over the miracle of bread and wine becoming the body and blood of Christ. OMG!

A tall female Episcopal priest, Reverend Janell Monk, had executed an ancient memorial meal celebration, once designated for only men. She was the woman, holy, chosen, and called by God. With both hands, her finger ring glistening, and sunlight sending prisms through the stained-glass colors, she held the cream-colored host. She raised her outstretched arms high above her head, looking up to the ceiling of heaven and then looking intently around the church at all of us; the Jesus host was front and center.

"You are all invited to the feast!" she said. Her smile radiated throughout the historic old wooden 1894 Trinity Episcopal Church in Ashland, Oregon. I'm sure all of our vibes also sent joy around the world. Tears streamed down my face, the breeze of the spirits lifted me, and I felt light, so peaceful and extremely joyful. I knew Carol was present with me, as my hands felt warm as I held them gripped together in my lap. It was a connection of heaven and earth, of the dead and the risen. Of a church community that accepts, honors and celebrates women priests. This was my happy place!

Disconnections and Oppositions

Unfortunately for us and many others, there is a huge disconnect between religion and the divine. Churches, temples, synagogues, and other houses of worship have rules and laws that often contradict spirituality during a worship service.

An example is, at mass or service, where it's supposed to be all about God and or Jesus, right? The scriptural Bible word is alive, songs of unity and peace are sung, a feeling of oneness, solidarity, joy and hope occurs. At the conclusion, we all begin a fresh start to go into the world, the streets, the personal relationships and interactions with others to serve the Lord/God/Spirit and each other. How beautiful!

Until service concludes and people race out of the parking lot and everyday life resumes where reality strikes and we are back to the normalcy of life with cold wars, divisions, negative attitudes, and judgments. It's so easy to revert back to old habits, but I challenge you to move forward and wonder, "What if?" What if we desire and commit to stomp out sexism? Why not?

Take a look at religious websites, "rule books," and catechisms; almost all were written and finally approved by males. When I visit these websites, I see a list of oppositions. They say, "We oppose" sex before marriage; we oppose LGBTQ+

ordination of ministerials; we oppose same-sex marriages; we oppose interracial marriages; we oppose marriage between two distinctly different religious denominations, such as a Jewish person loving and marrying a Protestant person; we oppose divorce; we oppose birth control; we oppose abortion; we oppose VSED (voluntarily stop eating and drinking); we oppose salvation coming from Jesus Christ; we oppose eating this and that; we oppose this; we oppose that; we oppose! Yikes! What's your problem? Opposing too many things does the heart bad. It's the opposite of free will.

Oh golly, centuries of male-dominance collided with "love your neighbor as yourself!" Did we not see it? Can we name it for what it is? Sexism.

 A disconnect happens after a lovely prayerful service when we dive back into the reality of family problems and sexist work scenarios. What a mess! What a disconnect that needs healing.

Can we ever learn that church and our faith institutions are meant to love, to share, and to serve? That it's not limited to the time sitting with one's butt planted in a seat inside the safe cocoon space while listening and obeying one preacher-man.

I finally had to make the break. The disconnect for me was the Catholic culture of opposing same-sex marriage, women and laity not having a voice in decision-making, and women not permitted to be ordained ministers. All of this is a combination of sexism and phobias.

My alleluia was finding the Episcopal Church and being received into their faith in August of 2023. After 66 years, I found my freedom, love, and peace in a faith community where I am happy and celebrated.

My recommendation for anyone who feels a disconnect is do what you have to do to make the connection to bring you happiness. For example, the United Church of Christ, UCC, is known for radical love, justice, and welcoming. There are options and you can find a place and people who fit your desires.

Let's stop the sexist root of evil!

Back in time, the holiest of all, the supreme being, the highest of power was named God: Father, Abba, Yahweh, king, majesty, etc. Then came along a man called the **Prince** of Peace! All are sexist archaic male terms that fit right into the society of their times and continued through the dark ages, the light ages, and all ages. Male dominance began this problem, the root of evil.

So, how do we stop the sexist root from spreading and choking out other good men, women, and LGBTQ+ people?

The spirit of love and truth is the answer! It was emphasized by many ancient prophets in visions, apparitions, feelings, and holy spirit maneuvers that blocked earthly sexist realities. Hope and faith are mysterious, mystical and magical. Great people stormed and followed their open hearts through deserts and famines. They learned to be more all-inclusive in families and in communities for survival's sake. We are the same.

Freedom is joy! Free will and forgiveness are about an all-encompassing love of self and others. That's the eternal gift available to everyone in heaven, on earth and in everyone's heart of hearts. That's the power of a Higher Power!

Personally, my God is gender-neutral, my Jesus is among us as human and my spirit messengers are the angels of the deceased and the living. Together in relationship, I and they seek to live life joyfully, every NEW day!

That was Carol's and my expression as individuals and as lovers.

Tell me about your name for your Higher Power. For fun and reflection, draw a picture of your supreme being.

Jesus happened to be the way and the one to open the window, open the door, and buck society and chains of religious sexism. Pope Francis is doing similar things today with his synod process, his inclusion of world women ministers, and his guts to oust high-ranking church members who are sexist and exclusive. YIPPEE!

Is your personal life, religion, parish, or faith community gaining momentum in countering sexism?

Jesus is Male. Why not Female? Or LGBTQ+? Or Demi?

So named, Jesus came in the human form, male (not female), to show that God loves us so much and is willing to risk everything for us. God's goal was and is to share a common human being, to bring us closer in friendship and loveship.

God chose a baby boy who grew to be a young and then an adult man. Thousands of years ago, a "man" was the selected gender, the best way possible for God to make a difference in getting us to "him" in a male-dominated society. Ingenious! RELATABLE! Way to go, God! Not sexist, just in tune with human nature at that point in time. I wonder how and who God selects now to bring about divine love.

Speaking of men, I always wondered about human development amongst the 5-15% of people who are born LGBTQ+. Imagine Jesus being LGBTQ+. Imagine Jesus ministering, healing, recruiting, blessing, and marrying same-sex or trans couples. Imagine that women, LGBTQ+ people, and men have equal religious and societal opportunities and responsibilities, with equal say, equal pay, equal voice, and equal everything! Healthy, with no malice and hate circling or underscoring their beauty. Imagine we are all truly inter-denominational.

How cool! Don't box Jesus or Spirit in!

Keep your hearts, ears, and eyes open as John Michael Talbot sings in "Open My Eyes." Help me to LOVE!

Living an authentic, truthful life and, as the subtitle of our book, "to find love and peace!"

Strong women with strong collaboration! Who were and are outstanding women prophets, saints or disciples? Let's name some. My favorites are: Sarah, Hannah, Esther, Elizabeth, Ruth, Catherine, Mother Rivier, Theresa, Maria Francesca, Margaret of Antioch, Dr. Linda Le Mura, Monica, and Joan of Arc.

I hope you can add many more.

Who are the LGBTQ+ saints, prophets, and disciples?

Sergius and Bacchus are the most famous in the Eastern Orthodox church. Two male saints loved each other as Roman soldiers and Christian martyrs united in "brother-making," a kind of early Christian same-sex marriage called adelphopoiesis. Will the Catholic Church, someday, make LGBTQ+ sainthood visible and relatable? Hope so!

QSpirit.net by Kittredge Cherry presents profiles from the LGBTQ+ saints series. Check it out. By the way, my memoir, *Nun Better: An AMAZING Love Story* by Joanie Lindenmeyer, was one of the top 23 QSpirit Christian books Bestsellers in 2023.

Think about it; Jesus did not personally write the Bible. Males mostly did! Jesus was too busy healing, interacting with men and women, leading others to God, and simply doing life! Leading others to find love and peace! Just like Elizabeth and I are doing. Collaboration and dialogue along with all care, were Jesus's mode. Ours, too!

How many times do you think Jesus snuck away to a mountain top, or stayed awake at night communing and collaborating with "His" spiritual advisor, God? Probably a lot! Maybe we could all learn to listen to our spiritual advisor better.

That's why Elizabeth and I are co-authoring this book! Two heads and two hearts are better than one. Collaboration and dialogue really are the main points and that's why I repeated it. As Elizabeth says, "teamwork makes the dream work."

⟲ REFLECTION QUESTIONS

Do you think we need more collaboration and dialogue about religious sexism? Is this book helping? Why do you think that?

_____

_____

Here's a conversational icebreaker about sexism: Score yourself and your church/religion/spirituality: true or false or both? Write your responses now, then retake the quiz in three months to see if you think or believe differently.

_____

_____

T for true, F for false, B for both.
1. Some men, and definitely not all men, are sexist.   ___
2. Some women, and definitely not all women, are sexist. ___
3. Traditionally in religion, men are martyrs, and women are the blessed virgins. ___
4. Men are the founders of religions and orders; women are the companions or addendums. ___
5. Men are the religious leaders; women are the behind-the-scenes workers. ___
6. Men are popes, bishops and priests; women are sisters, nuns, laity. ___
7. Men have decision-making power; women's voices are stifled in discussions. ___
8. Men are honored; women are tolerated. ___
9. Men preach from the altar pulpit and relish in front-row

seats; women stand on the outside or perimeter, kneel, genuflect, or curtsy. ___

10. Men consecrate the bread and wine; women make the bread, chill and serve the wine. ___

11. Men hear confessions; women heal and forgive with love and empathy. ___

12. Men baptize in massive dunk tanks; women baptize infants in bathtubs of grace. ___

13. Men have a sacrament called ordination, and women make vows but are not ordained. ___

14. Men pray for peace; women strive to live in peace. ___

15. Men are more spiritual; women are healers. ___

16. Men have seminaries; women have universities. ___

What does the future look like? This might surprise you.

One cold, wet December day in 2023, I was attending a book discussion group where I had the rudest shock of the month . . . actually of the year!

Sitting on padded chairs in our close circle, an elderly man launched a verbal attack, furiously voicing his opinion that Jesus condemns homosexuality. That the Bible and Jesus tell us that homosexuals are sinners. That there is no place in our world or in our churches for such grotesque people. That homosexuality is our biggest problem in society and Jesus told us so.

I was absolutely floored by this guest. He was extremely rude, his comments did not match our discussion, he had not read our book, and his hateful mouth repeated, "Homosexuals are sinners!"

With a white beard and glasses perched firmly on his nose, he stared and glared at us women. We were shocked by his words, his demeanor, and his outburst. He was a controlling man who was not going to intimidate me, my female friends, or others.

After what seemed like an hour, when he came up for air, I calmly retorted, "You're talking about me. I am lesbian. You used the word homosexual. I am homosexual. God made me this way. It is not my choice. I feel hurt. You hurt me. You don't even know me and you are calling me names and you are hating me. That's wrong to do that!"

He started in again! He hadn't heard a darn thing I said. He was verbally demanding, abusive, and out of control, ranting and raging, raising his voice louder, saying, "We are all sinners and homosexuals are the worst kind of sinners."

I have heard these ugly statements so many times. I could feel my escape mechanisms of numbness kicking in and I didn't want to put any more energy towards him. Nothing I could say would change his mind. Our poor world!

I silently mouthed: *He does not understand. Lord help him and help me, too.*

Yay, I know the end of the story, the cross, and then the resurrection! Out of death, new life will come. Oh, sweetie Carol, your death and resurrection have once again been laid in my lap. Let me sit here, my palms open, my calmness present.

I said to myself, "This man is full of hurt. What has triggered this for him? Is he always this hateful, judgmental, and vocal? Why here, today? Let love win!"

The Episcopal female deacon jumped in, with a fire in her belly and jaws, and looked him directly in his eyes. She raised her hand like a stop sign and fiercely yelled, "STOP. We, the nationwide Episcopal church, accept and celebrate all people, including gays, lesbians, and homosexuals. I need to ask you right now to stop it or we will ask you to leave!"

He immediately got quiet! Was he taken by the white collar around her neck? Did his ears open up to the severity of conviction in her voice? Did my words settle in his soul? Was it two powerful women chasing and destroying the devil in his actions and words? I think her lightning bolt carried the Spirit of God!

First off, this was the second time, in front of me, that she, an Episcopal deacon, had stood up against homophobic hate! I felt comforted and protected, like a baby blanket wrapped around an infant. She had guts to wear her faith, our church's commitment, and stance on her sleeve! Her amazing female voice had the power to go to battle and combat an elderly male sexist bigot. She faced the "good old boys" of centuries-old male chauvinistic attitude, Goliath, and took him down with a single blow.

He no longer could hold his conditioned and programmed sexist truth.

Deacon Linda was sticking up for me and even bigger, she was showing the other people present that the Episcopal faith is all inclusive, not discriminatory, not sexist, and not homophobic, biphobic, or any phobic!

As our book discussion continued, the elderly gentleman sat in silence and stillness. We talked about the gifts of the spirit. How appropriate was that?

One more time, the troubled man surfaced hate again and WE all jumped in with louder voices, sticking to our topic and at the same time drowning his voice. We channeled the conversation in a positive direction, leading me to enthusiastically invite him to our 10 AM Sunday service. I felt sorry for him and thought that maybe being around more lovable people would be a good thing for him. He declined.

Our time was up. "Can I give you a hug?" I asked him.

"Yes," he said, and we both stood, arms extended, reaching out to exchange a nice hug. *Actions speak louder than words* rang through my blood cells from my head to my toes. *Joanie, you did good*, I heard my self-talk say.

He quietly released our hug and walked out of the room.

"Hope we see you Sunday, all are welcome," members of our group said. And we meant it!

Just maybe our influence and my hug will add to his life experience and he can leave his learned sexist and homophobic behaviors far behind. Maybe in that moment, he let go of an anchor that was pulling him down and keeping him stuck. Maybe he felt love today? I believe that love always wins!

Oh, my emotions burst forth, I looked at Linda, we tightly hugged, tears streaming down my face as I thought, *how wonderful it is to be a part of a NATIONWIDE CHURCH FAITH FAMILY THAT HAS YOUR BACK!* I was feeling weak and strong, most loved and most cared for by our female deacon.

I had just shared two amazing hugs, one with a male sexist homophobe and one with an earth angel saint. OMG!

Jesus hold you; God bless you!

Susannah's Return to Universal Love
By Susannah Stokes

I grew up on an organic blueberry farm in the Georgia countryside, which by all accounts, was like a dream. I spent my days playing with our many rescued dogs and horses, running through the forests and helping my parents with the various chores.

I still remember the smell of freshly mowed grass after a summer rain, and the humid air creating a layer of fog that gently settled over the field that sprawled out in front of our log cabin. I now know that living close to the Earth on Foxbriar Farm taught me most of what I needed to know in this life, but social norms—and my family—had other plans for my education.

Like most American children, I was expected to go through school and attend church to become a "productive member of society." In my family, exploring spirituality was particularly encouraged, since every man in my father's lineage—back at least four generations—was a pastor, minister, missionary, or church leader, primarily in the United Methodist and Quaker traditions. My own grandfather was a well-known Methodist Bishop who held a position as the Assistant Dean of the Emory School of Theology for more than 30 years. Needless to say, organized religion was a powerful force amongst our kind.

On one hand, this meant that I was exposed to spirituality and a connection with God very early in childhood. On the other, the expectations to "be a good Christian," and act in accordance with "Christian values" were drilled into me from many different angles. It was expected that I would study Methodist teachings–especially since my grandfather had quite literally written the book on *Major Methodist Beliefs*, learn the Bible, and eventually marry a "good Christian man." My curiosity was at first strong enough to explore these teachings purely from a place of wonder, asking the questions that I couldn't get answers to from Mother Earth herself.

If people who haven't accepted Jesus into their hearts go to hell, what happens to infants or people in the far-off regions of the planet who never hear about Jesus before they die?

Why would God create us in His image and then punish us for being our human selves?

Why is our religion/belief system better than others? Aren't they all worshiping the same God?

I remember asking these and many other questions of my grandfather, Bishop Mack Stokes, as I worked toward confirmation in the Methodist Church around the age of 11. His answers were always gracious and open-minded, offering me a more academic view of philosophy and spirituality. Although his perspective was still rigid in many ways, I learned through his teachings that no one would be excluded from God's love. This was a powerful, foundational concept for my personal spiritual evolution and a fundamental viewpoint that eventually helped me piece together my own spiritual belief system.

Around this same time, I began to attend church service at the local Baptist Church, which happened to be just down the road from our farm and was a gathering place for many of the children in the area. Ironically, this "safe" space where I found connection with the local kids became one of the primary roots of my personal trauma. The surrounding community was steeped in Georgia's notorious Southern traditions, and although this church was not technically part of the "Southern Baptist" lineage (an important distinction), many of the sermons were full of Southern Baptist "fire and brimstone" concepts.

I was suddenly introduced to the idea that we are naturally sinners, with no hope for forgiveness unless we repented and were "saved by Jesus." Each service would include an altar call, in which individuals who were ready to be saved would come to the altar to accept Jesus Christ into their hearts. I remember always feeling hesitant to participate in this ritual, not under-standing its purpose or how it might help me.

Slowly but surely, I was encouraged to attend more and more services by the elders in the church. I started by going to youth service on Sundays, then began to return for Sunday evening service and after a few months, joined for Wednesday evening services as well. After a year or so, I was attending three to four services per week and even attended daily summer Vacation Bible School courses and many gatherings at the church elders' homes.

The culture was a new kind of evangelical that I had not experienced before. When I didn't attend a service, people would ask where I was and why I could not be there. The pressure to show up, participate, and spread the "Good Word" was incredi-bly strong, especially for a young girl who had not been taught boundaries in my own family system.

During my middle school years, the church began to offer the "True Love Waits" program. This course radically shifted the course of my life. While I currently have a greater perspec-tive on why my soul chose such an experience, it has taken me nearly 20 years to understand and integrate the trauma that this course had on my sexual freedom.

True Love Waits is a program focused on the abstinence of young people, encouraging them to keep their bodies "pure" by completely abstaining from sexual activity, and repenting for past sexual experiences. Although I believe the intention behind this program was to reduce unintentional pregnancy, prevent the spread of STIs/STDs, and help young people be more thoughtful about their sexual endeavors, it ultimately accomplished the opposite for me and many others. The teaching of total "purity" and abstinence—going as far as to have each graduate wear a "purity ring" on their wedding finger—added layers of shame and guilt to my psyche that have taken decades to untangle.

I remember sitting in our small classroom with 10 to 12 other middle- and high school-aged youth group kids, being told things like . . .

No one should ever touch you in any place a bathing suit covers.

Sex before marriage is a sin and you should remain pure for your husband.

If you've had sex before, you can ask for forgiveness from Jesus and He will help purify you, so you can become a virgin again.

Whoever becomes your spouse should replace the purity ring on your finger with a wedding ring.

The narratives around the "sinfulness" of sexual activity, the glorification of virginity, and the shaming of my physical body reached deep down into my womb and remained there for years, until I began to explore why I felt so sexually repressed. As the years went on, I integrated these teachings so fiercely that I actually did "remain pure" for the man who ultimately became my husband, and replaced the True Love Waits ring with an engagement ring, and then a wedding ring.

The Baptist Church system had worked. I was a total believer.

Looking back, I now see how my repressed sexual freedom drove me to seek a monogamous relationship and hold it as closely as possible, if only to have the "permission" from God that it was okay to have sex. I even see how this program influenced my desire to get married to this man at age 22, which then led to a painful divorce at 27, simply because I was certain that I needed to find "the One" as early as possible so I could share my purity with him (and satisfy my unconscious sexual urges).

It was only when I was on my second deployment to Afghanistan as a U.S. Marine Corps Officer that I began to deconstruct everything I knew about what Protestantism had taught me. Seeing the destruction of war first-hand, I began to ask questions and dissolve these constructs, layer by layer. I wondered:

How could a "loving God" allow such tragedies to happen?

Does the God that I learned about growing up even exist?

Is it possible to love more than one person at the same time—and what is so bad about being sexual with more than one person?

This last question came about because I met my current partner, André, while deployed and we began to fall in love—or perhaps lust at first—with one another. Our connection caused me to feel a deep knowing that I could, in fact, love more than one person at a time. And if I could love and be sexual with more than one person at a time, then what else had these institutions taught me that was no longer true for me?

As I explored and deconstructed my understanding of the existence of God, and the "truth" in the philosophies I had grown up learning, I also discovered the trauma that these teachings had left in me. This process of disillusionment and full reconstruction of my belief systems led me on a powerful journey of healing and growth, culminating in a powerful spiritual awakening and the reclaiming of my own version of spirituality. I realized, after much healing with the support of plant medicine, ancient and modern healing modalities, as well as several mentors and coaches, that I was the creator of my own reality and my belief system.

This journey, while challenging and unexpected, was a journey back to love, connection, and my Self. And for that, I am deeply grateful for the grace of trauma that the church gave to me.

After two combat tours as a Marine Corps Officer, Susannah experienced a powerful spiritual awakening facilitated by psychedelics that called her into service as an Energy Priestess and Embodied Consciousness Guide. Susannah is the co-founder of Metamorphosis Ventures and House of Embodied Metamorphosis, dedicated to bridging the gap between the clinical and ceremonial to create human transformation.

You can connect with her on Instagram @susannahroses or @embodiedmetamorphosis.

Tips

to Heal Hurts from Sexism in Religion

- Decide that you refuse to allow man-made religious doctrine to oppress your thoughts and behaviors based on your gender.

- Explore how these ideas have influenced the way you think, live, and love.

- Identify ways you can think, live, and love to disrupt the stifling rules of religious sexism.

- Find a faith community that offers gender equality in its leadership and members.

- Create your own faith community where everyone is equal.

- Get therapy from an excellent counselor or psychologist who can help you resolve any deep-rooted thoughts, beliefs, traumas, and behaviors that were caused by sexism in religion.

- Take an in-depth look at how religion perpetuates sexism in society. Take steps every day to shine light on these topics—in conversations, in social media, on blogs, in videos or whatever way you prefer to express yourself— to get people thinking and talking about these topics and to inspire change.

- Be alert, be aware, open your eyes and ears.

- Name it for all that it is: sexism, homophobia, transphobia, and biphobia (the 2023 highest phobia rise).

- The past is the past . . . forgive, let go, and move forward.
- Find your happy place and/or person(s).
- Educate yourself on the history of sexism, church sexism, and other current hurtful -isms.

Chapter 3

Escaping Oppression
Erase Religious Brainwashing, Shame, and Guilt

Speaking Up at the Library
By Joanie

ere are my mother and my brothers, for whoever does the will of my Father in heaven is my brother and sister and mother."

Matthew 12:48-50

The November night was brisk and dark, the clouds playing hide and seek with the full beaver moon. Here I am grabbing last night's leftover green salad to inhale, quickly changing out of my orange beach-walking shorts, green T-shirt and white tennis shoes with pink laces, and multitasking like a crazy woman.

How fun to sit at the kitchen table to personally address my just-arrived, *Nun Better* thank-you cards with handwritten words: "Thank you, Library Board Members," signing it with my name Joanie, I'm pacing from the living room to the office using both copying machines, producing the January 2024 book event flyers to share. Yes, tonight is the night of our small but mighty rural community monthly library board meeting.

Doris, my dear 89-years-young, hard-of-hearing, spunky progressive mother, grandmother, great- and great-great-grand-mother, wanted to attend with me on the "buggy ride," a 10-minute drive to the Forest conference room at our community library. We are both dressed with our winter sweater warmth, me in the green and white snowmen and snowwomen pullover sweater and her in her red and green Christmas tree-decorated sweatshirt with long, warm pants on this chilly, 40-degree night. Her in her black leather shoes and me in the tennies with pink laces, our smiles shining brighter than our high-beam car lights.

With our anticipation and excitement, being together, we know that our friend and board president, Pat, will open the meeting with a call for audience participation to be kind, controlled, with no threatening rudeness or pointing of fingers at the volunteer board members, as happened at the last month's outburst of hate.

When we arrive, the parking lot is almost filled to the brim, bringing us more excitement in the night air. Two gentlemen, carrying books that look like Bibles, walk in behind us.

Doris and I greet them with smiles as I say, "Hi, what a great night!"

They say, "Hi," and I pull the door open for Doris and remain there holding it for them like an elementary school door monitor; they are only a few steps behind us.

"Doris, please save me a seat; I need to stop and make copies. I'll be right there."

I travel through the foyer and enter the large, beautiful library where I greet and ask Karla, a friend and the library staff helper, to please show me how to make three-dollars' worth of 30 copies of the *Nun Better* book events flier. She pops up from her desk chair and as a tremendous wizard, pushing buttons on the copying machine as if she's done this a zillion times before.

She mentions, "New shoes Joanie? They look great, so white and with your pink laces."

"Thanks." I complimented her with her shiny black boots.

"They're warm and comfy," she says.

I grab my blue backpack and warm just photocopied flyers and dash into the large conference room. The overhead lights are super bright as the packed room of people are all sitting in chairs facing the honored board members. I spot Doris seated on the right side, third row from the front with a saved seat for me.

"Thank you, Doris, great seats," I say.

Behind me is Kelly, mother of Will, and 17-year-old Will. We touch hands as our hello. Will says, "Great to see tonight, Joanie."

I nod and agree, "Same to you, Will." Two rows up, I wave to Jason and Kat.

I searched my backpack, which is more like my traveling office, to find my thank-you cards and book. *Have I signed enough?* I jump up and approach each of the board members. Kathleen instantly stands and we hug. I work my way around, greeting each board member with a hug, asking head librarian, Julie, "How many board members are there?" She says five. I come to the newest board member and stick out my hand to shake hers.

"Hi, I'm Joanie."

"I'm Sue," she says.

"Welcome."

Great, I have enough signed cards to hand out. I return to my seat. I turn around again and comment on how great Will and Kelly look!

"Joanie," Kelly says, "we need to have you over for that Greek meal to celebrate Will's writing." This was a promise we all made when Will was just forming thoughts on what to write for another book we named *Joyously Free!*

"Yes, that sounds wonderful," I said. "Can we do it when I get home? We have a new baby in the family." I show them a photo of baby Onyx and they both respond, "Oh, so cute!"

Will then says, "That makes you a great Auntie, Joanie." I think, *how sweet of Will to say that to me. Always so kind Will is!*

President Pat speaks and sets the verbiage and tone that the board is ready to sit and listen, but she will not tolerate outrage and if you do not follow the protocol, you will be asked to stop and to leave. She mentions her late husband as the model for being a Lutheran minister and a devout Christian. He was an example of being polite.

"So tonight, let's be considerate and respectful," she says. "If you choose to speak, share your voice, state your opinions clearly while sticking to the three-minute allotted public remarks time."

The white timer is positioned on the table of the head librarian, who is seated in the front of the horseshoe-shaped table and chairs. "Please state your name and where you live. We are here to hear from you tonight."

About 30 people fill the room. The sound of the shuffle of more chairs being added breaks the silence of a low murmur. I spot a few people I know, waving hi and saying, "Good to see you." Now we have 40 or more attendees, with no more chairs and people leaning against the back wall.

"Who would like to go first?" asks Pat.

Kat steps up to the podium. She introduces herself as a library staff member and wants to be silly tonight. She reads a beautiful children's Christmas book about Santa and reindeer. Kat is theatrical and throws a few fun gestures as she reads from the book; her closing line is, "Thank you, board members, for having a variety of books on our shelves for a variety of readers."

Point well taken!

I jump up next, with my paperback *Nun Better* book, flyers, and thank-you cards in my hand. I speak my name loud and clearly into the microphone and then proceed to walk around the horseshoe table arrangement, handing each board member a thank you card and flier. A person in the front row remarks, "Those are some bright shoes."

At the wooden podium, with microphone in hand, I responded, "Yes, and they are on the cover of my book, too!" Giggles erupt! Looking into each of their eyes with my big smile, I compliment our board experts for being instrumental in the success of my 2023 book when they hosted me in a launch celebration back in March, just eight months ago. I dish out my gratitude and accolades to their helpful staff and especially to Eric who is the staffer in charge of promoting and organizing the hundreds of events our library involves itself in. I provide an update of me being a top 100 Amazon best-seller in the category of LGBTQ+ Parents and Family. Then I say, "I'm not even a parent. What a hoot!"

My jubilance must be contagious, because they clap and congratulate me. I was very humbled. I turn to the audience, proudly holding the beautiful pink, fun cover of *Nun Better: An AMAZING Love Story.*

"I invite all of you to our next celebration, on January 6, 2024, right here in this room!" I say. "Come meet one of the co-founders of Two Sisters Writing and Publishing, Catherine Greenspan; she will be here in person."

A few sighs erupt throughout the room from a few people.

"Have any of you ever met a publisher?" I ask. Heads shake and they look perplexed. "How about have you ever met an author? That's me!"

People laugh and I smile with them. I give a quick synopsis about the book and how recently an 84-year-old woman came out to me and then in our own county, a 16-year-old came out. "This book has touched so many lives; even a heterosexual couple told me that this is the best love story they have ever read. I hope you can all read it and have your heart be touched, too! Again, thank you Chetco Library for the use of your facilities, and I'll see you in January. By the way, two more books will be written by October 2024. Stay tuned."

Then everything changes. The people who had walked in carrying what looked like Bibles launch into a verbal assault on queer people and LGBTQ+ books.

Then for the next 30 minutes, people zealously state their anti-LGBTQ+ opinions, disgust with trans people, and the fervent judgment of how our library is promoting children to look at queer pictures in books by the unacceptable placement of the books on lower shelves (not true!). Someone even barks at the immoral and inappropriate graphics in queer books. I think in non-queer books you can find the same evidence.

Sprinkled in the public remarks are a few pro-inclusivity values of having many books available on many topics. A library is about you choosing your style of book and/or parents okaying the books their children read.

An older, white-haired woman says, "I love our library because we have a diversity of subjects, styles and genres. I don't like gory or murder books, so I don't check them out." Her point is well taken!

The icing on the cake comes from Will. You can read his story in detail in *Joyously Free: Stories & Tips to Live Your Truth as LGBTQ+ People, Parents and Allies* that Elizabeth Ann Atkins and I co-authored.

Age 17, articulate, courageous, sincere, honest and integrity-filled, Will speaks from his heart in front of the adult naysayers, some who are hardline Christians who rail, oppose, and spread false accusations about LGBTQ+ people. Tonight is no different than the past few months. Will had heard plenty of outrageous remarks directed at the board members, but of course it was a ploy to all of us; it was intimidation without a gun. The board members remain expressionless, silent, listening, and taking notes. I am impressed with their professionalism.

He carries his cell phone to the podium, looking sharp with his black hair, beautiful deep brown eyes, and all-black pants and boots with a tight-fitting multi-colored long-sleeve shirt. He looks so professional and exquisitely finessed, he would have received the award for best dressed tonight. And he has a high energy bounce in his step.

I feel his power, his true self alive and beautiful! I've known Will only since summer, about four months. He is a kind soul with an IQ beyond me. He has been a recent devoted caregiver for his mother while staying on top of his senior high school graduation work and looking forward to advancing his educational goals and making a game plan for his future.

His mom, Kelly, is sitting directly behind me, when she whispers into my ear, "Joanie, please hold my hand!"

I turn my body half-way around, grasp her outreached hand as she leans forward on the edge of her seat. We grip skin to skin, finger and palms holding on for dear life. She wraps her other hand on top. I feel a shimmer, then trembling, shaking. Her thumb's pulse beats faster; she is frightened, she is nervous, she is proud of her son, and who knows what else she is feeling. I can only imagine, is this what Mary felt when Jesus did his outspoken activism ministry?

We do not know how this will go. Would Will be interrupted? Would Will faint, be heckled, be condemned, or God forbid, be physically attacked? What is he going to say to the group and to the board tonight? The suspense is in his mother's heart and mine, too!

I am poised for action, not trusting the naysayers in the crowd. I would do anything to save him from anything negative that might happen. I have seen horrendous things in the past when people suddenly "come out" in public. I silently pray and feel enormous peace: "Please Lord let this beautiful young man be well received!"

All 40 to 50 of us watch and listen to every soft detail of his presence. Oh golly, it's like listening to a modern-day Martin Luther King, Jr. speech. Will is eloquent, positive, and forthright, owning every word and standing taller than the highest mountain in the world, Mount Everest. You could have heard a pin drop. He has everyone's attention! His melancholic voice, added with a few trembles, ripples through the room! I'm sure that the spirit winds took it outside to spread it to the world. Kelly and I relax our hand grip; I could hear her breaths become more natural and normal. I keep beaming my smile, imagining Will has eyes in the back of his head to carry on and know that we are one hundred percent with him!

I'm going to paraphrase, but the gist of his less than three-minute oratory was profound! In summary, he said:

My family and parents are wonderful. They have always loved me, let me be myself, fed me with knowledge, challenged me to read and be a sponge for information. We are an honest family, and they have encouraged me to learn from every experience and from everyone. I believe I have! I am a trans man! This is who I am! I've always been this way! Treat me kindly!

Don't slander or say things about me when you don't know what you are talking about. That hurts me. You are not me. I have been through a lot of discrimination in this town, but I also have great friends and support.

So, respect me! Yes, I am different from you, but you don't have to be afraid of me, either. I am a part of this community, and this library is my friend. I appreciate and need what it offers me. Others also need this library!

Thank you!

He quietly steps away from the podium and turns down the aisle with all eyes glued on him. He had broken a judgmental stereotype of what a trans person is. He holds his head strong and high while a smile appears on his face. He is a man on a mission and he made it happen! The room remains silent, a compliment to his strength, courage and guts.

He enters his row, sits next to his mother, she puts her hand on his leg, and I turn and pat his leg. He looks each of us directly in our eyes. His eyes are deep and I feel like I'm in a spiritual world called heaven on earth. It is pure joy! Yahoo! Wowzer!

Will sits relaxed, peaceful and probably relieved. He had conquered something that many people take years to do or they go to their grave without ever having done:

To discover, celebrate, and tell their personal true self to the world. He had escaped oppression and was a risen Phoenix! He is AMAZING! He is Saint Will tonight. Will, this was your moment! Will, this was all of our moment. THANK YOU! Thank you! Thank you!

What an incredible role model Will was for all of us. Being the youngest person in the assembly, he was the last to speak and the one with the most to say! You touched people in places they had never been!

I hope our community members, on both sides of the aisle, reflect on his composure and his voice of conviction.

Facts alone don't elicit change in people, but emotions do. Will had us all wrapped in a cocoon of humanity's feelings. It was a God Moment, as Catholic author Matt Kelly would say.

Oh readers, I wish you could have been there!

Continue on, LGBTQ+ people and allies, live your life with gusto, continue to help each of us grow! Young people show us how to behave and relate. They, like Will, remind us that some days you can't sit still and take it anymore. Even though you are scared, you have to say something, do something. In the spiritual sense, this is escaping oppression! It is the purpose of prayer turned into action. It is the healing expression of one's inner true self becoming joyously free!

It's the same way Jesus lived, taught, and preached.

Oftentimes, people like the homophobes who ranted at the library express vitriol that they try to back up by citing the Bible.

But the bottom line is that God is love, and only in speaking up and out against hate speech can we escape oppression. So speak up and speak out whenever you witness oppression in the name of religion. Sometimes the religion part is so hidden, it is like a tree in the middle of a forest. Be aware and be an agent of change!

Helping You Escape Oppression Rooted in Religious Shaming
By Elizabeth

I'm on a mission to help people escape the internal and external oppression that society inflicts on us, especially around love, romance, sex, and sexuality.

It has always **enraged me** that double standards exist to dictate how women are "supposed" to think, speak, behave, live, and love, while men enjoy so much freedom that's void of the name-calling, condemnation, and even deadly consequences for their own behavior around these topics.

This double standard is rooted in and reinforced by most of the world's most influential religious doctrine, and it is enforced by believers who brainwash us starting at birth to conform to these rules. Unfortunately, many people never wake up to the fact that this is happening. But when you do, it's infuriating.

No more!

These rules ruin people. They indoctrinate innocent children with guilt, shame, fear, worthlessness, anxiety, and depression that can even lead to suicide.

Religion is supposed to be a conduit to God's love and peace. Instead, it is a man-made construct and a manipulative tool to control people through domination, fear, and the bogus belief that you can only access the infinite love and comfort of God/Spirit/Higher Self through the human conduit of a religious leader and the physical place of worship where they operate.

You have so much power, and now's the time to tap into that love and peace that will heal you and empower you on every level. I have done this, and it feels miraculous. It's free and accessible to you 24/7. You can do it!

During my meditations that you can read about in detail in my memoir, *God's Answer Is Know*, I experienced the inexplicable bliss of the divine where I saw and felt the love and peace of God. Every person is free to believe whatever they want about God and Spirit, and in my book and here, I'm sharing mine.

You can love it or leave it, but I hope my information here emphasizes for you the essence of this book: **that you have the power to connect with God/Spirit/Higher Self all by yourself**, in the privacy and comfort of your mind and your home or wherever you are, and it is the most blissful, comforting, peaceful feeling you can ever imagine.

The problem is that most people follow what the male leaders of churches and other religious institutions tell them about what God is, and how they can or cannot experience God.

The way that you can achieve this is first by escaping the oppression of what you may have been taught about God/Spirit/Higher Self. The powers that be don't want us to know that we have the power to enjoy two-way communication with God/Spirit/Higher Self. They want us to remain dependent on the human leaders of religion for a long list of reasons.

The religious institutions need to keep people hooked on believing and practicing their ideologies, attending weekly (or more) services, and making financial contributions.

The religious leaders are running businesses—as our contributor Zamber Knight so brilliantly expresses—that depend upon followers faithfully tithing 10 percent of their income to fill the coffers and keep the church, synagogue, temple, or other religious building and organization in business.

It is in their best interest to control their flocks so that the business of religion thrives. We have a whole chapter on that in this book.

But first, let me just say that my mission to help people to escape the oppression of religion is not an indictment of all religion or its leaders.

I absolutely love attending nondenominational services—especially Black churches. It is so overwhelmingly joyous when I hear the music, feel the electrifying energy of the people around me—singing, crying, wailing, praising—and listening to the pastor share powerful messages that give me chills and make me cry. I've had some profound revelations in church.

I love religious/spiritual services of all kinds. I have enjoyed joyous prayer and song gatherings amongst 50 people in the home of my meditation teacher, Dr. Rama, who is Hindu and Hare Krishna. And I recently attended two Jewish funerals where the music, messaging, and collective love were overwhelmingly inspiring.

And I have been uplifted and saved so many times by inspiring words and sermons from mega pastors such as Joel Osteen, Joyce Meyer, and Reverend T.D. Jakes via YouTube. I love them! They play a very important role in our world!

So again, anything I say here is not an indictment toward them or their divine missions to share the word of God that is so very healing and empowering. During some of my lowest points, Joel Osteen's engaging, 30-minute sermons on YouTube were a ray of sunshine that lifted me from shadowy mind spaces.

So my mission in this chapter is to share with you, dear reader, my perspective that in general, religion imposes oppressive ideas that set the standard for society's rules on how we should or should not think, speak, behave, live, love, work, and play.

This especially pertains to women, as the world's most-believed religious doctrine was written by men a very long time ago, and for the most part is preached by the religious patriarchy, as all the major religions are ruled by men.

So how am I escaping oppression and helping others do the same?

Through my multimedia Goddess platform that includes books and my podcast, as well as my women's empowerment retreats where I lead guided meditations to show women across America and beyond how to connect with Spirit through their own minds and souls, from the comfort of their homes.

As I've said, my parents taught me and my sister that we have the power to connect with God in our own way. Every night before bed during our childhood, our father led us in reciting aloud *The Lord's Prayer*. I've always been a fervent prayeress, especially as a child if I were scared, and I was always protected. That laid the foundation for my direct connection with God and Spirit.

Then, my spiritual awakening as an adult blessed me with the password to connect to the divine wi-fi of God's communication network that provides knowledge and guidance.

It is my life mission to teach this to any and everyone who is eager to learn how to escape religious and societal oppression to liberate their minds, bodies, and spirits so they can connect with God/Spirit/Higher Self to find love and peace, which lead to self-love and a more fulfilling life.

So here are the major ways that I'm helping people escape oppression that's rooted in religious teachings that set the standard for society's rules.

First, through my new book series that begins with ***The Biss Tribe: Where You Activate Your GoddessPower* by Elizabeth Ann Atkins.**

This six-book series teaches how to access and activate the infinite energy within ourselves that directly connects with God/Spirit/Higher Self. This enables two-way communication that provides the love, peace, and guidance we need to become the greatest versions of ourselves while creating our dream lives.

In the books, I refer to this powerful awakening as your Supernatural Self. God is supernatural. Spirit is supernatural. Your Higher Self is supernatural. Google defines "supernatural" as something caused by a force that defies scientific explanation and the laws of nature.

If you'd like to read about the science behind this phenomenon, please read the 2017 book, *Becoming Supernatural: How Common People are Doing the Uncommon* by Dr. Joe Dispenza, which is the #1 bestseller in the chakras category on Amazon.[4]

I recommend that you try it for yourself, and it will be so fantastical and nourishing to your mind, body, and soul, that you won't need any scientific documentation. Seeing is believing.

So what inspired my Goddess mission? More than two decades ago, during one of the worst periods of my life, I was at the gym, praying for God to please relieve me of the emotional torment of verbal abuse, while the terrible words were reverberating through my mind.

"No, QUEEN! I'm a queen!" I declared this over and over, out loud, to silence the person's voice and erase their face from my thoughts. I didn't care how I looked, talking to myself and praying in the noisy gym.

God, please help me feel better . . .

Suddenly, out of nowhere, my mind filled with the vision of a small silver box. It was positioned inside the middle of my head. And those foul words were flowing—like letters dancing through my mind—into my right ear, through my brain, into the silver box. Then, as if it were a word-processing program, the silver box rewrote the insults, and a new word streamed out from the other side: Goddess!

Euphoria rippled through me. It pushed a reset button on my frazzled emotions, and a geyser of joy exploded inside me.

Something deep within felt like a starburst of energy that sent sparkles through every cell in my body, glowing around me like an aura of light that was creating a forcefield of protection, like a giant bubble. My body felt strong and inexhaustible as I climbed the stairs with a sudden surge of energy.

As the word "Goddess" echoed in my mind, my spirit seemed to dance.

"Goddess!" I announced out loud.

Then a voice within me—a voice that was not mine—declared clearly:

"You are Goddess, Elizabeth. Know that. Be that."

"Goddess!" I declared out loud. "Yes, I am Goddess!"

In that moment, I felt like I had just been given a secret password that connected me to a supernatural network of divine wi-fi—that's just as invisible and powerful as the Internet connections on our devices that enable us to phone anyone, anywhere, or access any information we desire.

By simply saying, "Goddess," I plugged into an infinite and divine Source of power and peace. It was as instantaneous as flipping a light switch that sent an energy surge through my entire being. It jolted my brain and body with confidence that:

Yes, I have the power to make all my dreams come true, including transforming this terrible situation into harmony while my career and family flourish.

I felt limitless, protected, powerful—and thankfully—and peaceful.

All from a single word.

Goddess.

That moment in the gym so many years ago was a spiritual awakening that happened a split-second after I prayed for help. Now I teach this power in my books, at retreats, and in videos, by sharing simple techniques that people can use to activate their superpowers, then transform into the boldest version of themselves while creating their personal and professional dream lives.

I'm proof that it works, because I practice what I teach. These techniques have helped me lose 100 pounds, celebrate that as a guest on *The Oprah Winfrey Show*, and become more fit, peaceful, and confident than ever . . . manifest material abundance and relationships in magical ways . . . write and publish more than 50 books with my sister Catherine Greenspan through our company, Two Sisters Writing & Publishing®, and activate my own power to live and love myself and others as I truly desire.

My mission is to empower people to break free from self-sabotage, negativity, wrong relationships, and unfulfilling work, so they can finally create the self-love and dream lives that until now have been stuck in their imaginations.

This dream life is possible when we escape the oppression of societal rules that are rooted in religion and trigger shame, guilt, and fear. These rules permeate and hinder every area of our lives. That's why The Biss Tribe series covers the five foundations of your best life: Power, Pleasure, Prosperity, Protection and Peace.

I'm not trying to sound like a commercial, but the way I'm combating oppression is through books. That's why my mission continues in Book #2, ***The Biss Tribe: Where You Activate Your GoddessPleasure*** by Elizabeth Ann Atkins, scheduled for release in October 2024 with many events planned. Please visit TwoSistersWriting.com, click on the book cover, and check out the events tab.

Meanwhile, it's infuriating to wake up and realize that life is flying by and—because of religious programming—we've been too scared, stuck, or sad to truly enjoy it. So I'm on a mission to show how to seize the power and pleasure of life's limitless potential and experience our hearts's greatest desires in ways that make a positive contribution to people everywhere.

You can learn how to use these transformation tools in videos that you can access via this QR code:

GoddessPower Tools

The guided meditation videos help you attune to the divine channels where you can communicate directly with God/Spirit/Higher Self. As a certified meditation teacher through Lori Lipten's Sacred Balance Academy in Bloomfield Hills, Michigan, I have for years led guided meditations for people across America every Wednesday night. Every person walks away empowered with this life-changing knowledge.

Another way that I'm helping people escape the oppression of religious programming that sets societal standards is through my podcast.

The Goddess Power Show with Elizabeth Ann Atkins® explores provocative and often taboo topics that inspire people to live bigger, better, and bolder to manifest their deepest desires, both personally and professionally. You can hear it on Spotify, Apple Podcasts, iHeart Radio, and wherever you listen to podcasts, and you can watch it on the YouTube channel for The Goddess Power Show. It presents new ideas, insights, and instructions that liberate a person's mind, body, and spirit from oppressive beliefs and behaviors that have kept us small, stuck, and scared, while conforming to the mold that society imposes on us from birth.

Here's something that totally defies religious brainwashing that tries to shame us around sexuality. I created content that emphasizes that pleasure is the portal that activates the power to create a unique personal and professional empire—however you define that—where you rule wearing a crown of confidence while sitting on a throne of power. I believe that owning, enjoying, and even flaunting our divine right to enjoy life to the max—is the ultimate act of empowerment.

Why? Because for many people, especially women, our pleasure and power have been stolen from us through oppressive cultures, religions, and traditions that have used fear, guilt, shame, and even violence to confine us to patriarchal society's definition of what a person should be.

So when a woman embraces and celebrates her birthright to enjoy her body and all the glory of her six senses, as well as every aspect of her life, she rejects society's conventions on the most intimate level, and that empowers her to create a life that sparkles—explodes!—with passion and purpose.

This message is really important for men, LGBTQ+ people, and all human beings, because the complicated tentacles of religious and societal programming are twisted and intertwined in our psyches and subconscious minds, influencing our thoughts, emotions, behaviors, and ability to live a happy life.

This can make us feel that something is missing. That our daily realities just aren't in synch with our deepest desires to truly enjoy how we feel about ourselves, and how we experience other people and the world. That's why it's imperative to explore how to flip the switch inside to activate the energy to manifest the mind shifts, the lifestyle changes, the people, and the experiences we need to maximize our infinite potential.

Very importantly, this Goddess concept isn't about being a diva or lying around being fanned by palm fronds and eating chocolates. It's about the infinite energy that we can summon during the worst moments to find the peace and power to persevere and ultimately FLY up into our greatest lives.

My podcast guests explain how people are doing that. Episodes feature experts and everyday people who are blazing new trails to think, act, live, and love in ways that buck convention and ignite bliss. Many of my guests (and people I know!) express how religious programming as children and adults stifled their ability to self-actualize and become empowered to live their authentic truths. They broke free of their own volition, reprogrammed their thinking and behavior, and stepped into lives that make them happy. They are amazing role models, and it is my honor to showcase them for you on the podcast.

As I've said earlier, Women's Studies classes at the University of Michigan awakened my understanding of the tremendous inequities in society, which are usually rooted in religious teachings.

That triggered a fascination with how "the personal is political," a feminist phrase from the 1960s that was also important during the Civil Rights Movement and the Black Power Movement. It means what happens in our one-on-one interpersonal relationships is a microcosm for the macrocosm of society at large. This means that the power dynamics between people that are based on race, gender, LGBTQ+ identity, socioeconomic status, and other factors, all reflect the power dynamics of the world in general. If a person or a people lack power in the greater society, they usually lack power in personal relationships.

So, when we make changes on a personal level, we can affect change on a worldwide scale. Change begins with understanding where things are out of balance, and you're reading this book on a quest to heal religious hurts, so we're starting there.

On the podcast, I've found the courage and confidence to escape the oppression of being a "good girl" while exploring questions such as:

How does pleasure boost a woman's power? What's the

connection between pleasure and women's wellness? How can we level the pleasure playing field so women always get ours, our way? What is polyamory, and how do you do it? Is monogamy a myth? What is pansexual? How does a loving, soulmate couple that has an open relationship coach others on how to do the same. Anal sex! Why is there a stigma, and how can that stigma end? How can the powerful energy exchange of intimacy infect you with negative, toxic energy, even if you use protection?

These fascinating and titillating topics open minds and hearts! They give people a new blueprint to build a better mind-set and life. They shatter the fear around talking about topics that—through a religious lens—are usually viewed as scandalous, inappropriate, and even sinful. I find it thrilling!

This exciting purpose and passion are waiting for you on the other side of religious oppression. There you'll discover a starburst inside you that, when you ignite it on your healing journey, you will glow from the inside out to illuminate the shadows within yourself, then light up the world in your own unique way. So let's do this!

I love providing this portal into provocative topics that can help you learn to live and love in ways that transform you from the inside out to live your wildest dreams. I hope that when you heal your religious hurts, you can either level up what you're already doing or discover a new passion and purpose that excites you and helps you make a powerful, positive impact on the world.

Another tool that I use to help people escape oppression is **Writing Erotic Books.** Sex is the ultimate taboo in religion, so writing about it for all the world to see is a powerful act of liberation. My erotic fiction and the "romantic thriller" novels that have become best-selling books all express love, soulmate connections, passion, and pleasure in an intelligent, tasteful, and thought-provoking manner.

I've been doing this for decades, starting with romantic thrillers *White Chocolate*, *Dark Secret*, and *Twilight* (written with the actor Billy Dee Williams), published by the Tor/Forge imprint of St. Martin's Press. When these books were published in 1998, 2000, and 2002, they were groundbreaking explorations of race, specifically about mixed-race people, at a time when those topics were not widely discussed or explored in books.

I invite readers to experience provocative plotlines and luscious love scenes that are much more than a titillating tangle of limbs: they showcase the magic of deep, passionate love and romance, and the bliss of finding your soulmate.

Again, I'm not trying to sound like a commercial for my books. But this is how I communicate to the world with a free and even rebellious spirit to share oppression-shattering ideas. Some people blog, some people go on a public-speaking circuit, some people create podcasts and blow up their social media, and some people stand on a proverbial soapbox and rant to whomever will listen. I write books. Please choose a platform to share your ideas that can liberate the minds and hearts of others!

So, after my fairytale wedding led to a nightmare divorce, I conceived and composed an erotic trilogy called *Husbands, Incorporated*. It was first published under my name, then re-released by Two Sisters Writing & Publishing® under my pen name, Sasha Maxwell. This story showcases two women—both divorced and disillusioned with marriage and monogamy—who start a company that offers fantasy marriages for women who wield the power and receive the pleasure of their wildest dreams.

The sex in these books is not for procreation, as religion often dictates. It is for pleasure, and it is for women to finally get the satisfaction on their own terms that they may have been craving for their whole lives. Writing these stories was fun, and the mission motivating them was to express my philosophies about monogamy and marriage that spun in an unconventional direction after divorce and subsequent dating disappointments.

Please let this creative consequence of my life experiences inspire you to escape the oppression of religious programming by doing something daring and provocative—if that interests you—to help people explore new ideas for how to live and love.

⊚ REFLECTION QUESTIONS

How do you feel that religion has oppressed your thinking, behavior, lifestyle, relationships, and career?

_____

_____

Describe how you would feel and live after you have escaped the oppression of religious programming that sets the standards for societal norms.

_____

_____

What big dream do you have—but you have been too afraid to manifest—because of religious programming? Describe the dream and the thrill of achieving it after you have escaped the oppression.

_____

_____

Finding Freedom from Oppression
Deborah Kravitz-Randall

I would say that the traditional definition of religion or being religious does not apply to me. I have spent a lot of time over the past couple of years mulling this over and questioning myself as to what my beliefs are. Am I an atheist? Am I agnostic?

I am not religious. What I have concluded is that for me now, in this stage of my life, and especially after experiencing life-altering events such as retirement and the break-up of a very long-term relationship, it is about exploring my spiritual path and what role spirituality plays in my everyday life.

My life didn't start this way. I was raised by a loving mother who also happened to be a devoted Catholic. My mother insisted that I was going to follow in her steps and become a devoted Catholic as well. First, I was baptized in the Catholic Rite, then when I was in First Grade it was off to Catechism every Saturday morning and mass on Sundays. On July 2, 1967, I received my First Holy Communion along with my Marian Children's Mass book, and added Saturday Confession to my religious routine. That was my life growing up attending St. Martha Catholic Church in Valinda, California.

As a young girl, I recall sitting in my Catechism classroom thinking about everything else but what I was there for. I was being asked to accept all that was being taught in those classrooms as the irrefutable truth and I was expected to accept it without questioning. I remember actually being scared at times of what would happen to me or my loved ones if we didn't follow the rules or laws of the Catholic Church.

When I went to Confession, I remember struggling to come up with sins to renounce. Maybe I should have confessed that I was really there for the donuts that were served in the Community

Hall after mass or the once-a-year carnival, or that I really didn't understand what was being taught. I struggled to understand and connect with all of this. To make matters worse, my brothers didn't have to attend church. I was on my own.

So why me? I believe the answer has everything to do with my mother. She grew up a devout Catholic. She attended all-girl Catholic schools her whole life. My mom was also a divorcée who ended up remarrying a non-Catholic. A double whammy! Reflecting back on this, I have come to believe that my mom was living her Catholicism vicariously through me.

I continued going to Confession and attending Mass and special events at church up until middle school. I think that my mom was distracted by family dynamics while dealing with alcoholism and my father's illnesses; at some point, I just stopped going to church. I was absolutely okay with that.

School and extracurricular activities—such as being with my friends, playing sports, band, and Girl Scouts—were more important to me. In high school, I became best friends with a girl who was a practicing Catholic. On occasion, I would attend Mass with her—usually on a Friday or Saturday evening before going to some high school friend's party!

At this time, I really started to question things. Religion seemed so routine and impersonal. Yet I didn't feel completely disconnected, as it provided some sense of being comfortable. And it was all I really knew.

Fast forward to being a college graduate and any connection with Catholicism had totally faded away. GONE. I was about to marry a young man who happened to be Jewish. This presented a small problem when it came time for us to decide who would marry us and where we would get married. We found a minister who performed a lovely secular ceremony for us at Disneyland!

Our son was born three years later in Southern California and eight years later we moved to Crescent City, California. I wanted more children and we tried, but I was not able to get pregnant again, so we adopted three children. We raised our children with love, compassion, respect, and kindness, but no religion.

Unfortunately, our marriage ended, but as co-parents, we felt that if our children wanted to explore any religion, then they were free to do so at any time with our unconditional support. Now my children have children and know they have my support in whatever choices, if any, they make in terms of actively pursuing religion for themselves or their children.

As I have lived my adult life, my feelings and beliefs have evolved. I have always loved science and over the past several years I have discovered the cosmos and love reading anything about the origin and structure of our universe. Science makes sense to me. I have questioned whether there is really a God and whether I ever had a connection with God or Jesus or the teachings of the church. Is there really a Heaven or a Hell? I think not... I wonder if when I die, everything will just shut off. Will it be the same as before I was born? I'm thinking so...

I have begun exploring my spirituality more (better late than never, right?) Do we have a soul? Is our soul and consciousness the same thing? I am exploring my personal journey and discovering what is important and meaningful to me versus religion, which felt more like a specific set of rules or practices that needed to be followed and one that I blindly accepted as faith passed down by my mother.

Every day that I wake up, I start right where I am. My church is exploring my spirituality and my religion is love, kindness, joyfulness, compassion, and empathy towards all living things. I have respect for those who believe differently than me. I am at peace with my beliefs.

I HAVE A GREAT LIFE AND AM SO GRATEFUL!

Deborah Kravitz-Randall is a joyous mother and grandmother who prioritizes wellness by having fun with friends, playing pickle-ball, and spreading kindness. She welcomes emails at dkravitz57@ gmail.com.

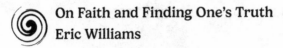

On Faith and Finding One's Truth
Eric Williams

Faith. *The assurance of things hoped for, the conviction of things not seen.* The key to success in this life and salvation in the next. *For by grace, you have been saved through faith.* Faith. Demanded by God, feared by demons. The starting point, the path, and the destination of man's spiritual journey.

I grew up surrounded by people of faith. From Kindergarten to 8th grade, I attended a Lutheran elementary school in Detroit. An hour of religion class every day. Gold stars for memorizing the books of the Bible in order. Two stars if I spelled them all correctly. Genesis, Exodus, Leviticus, Numbers . . . The Apostles' Creed recited after The Pledge of Allegiance.

> I believe in the Holy Spirit,
> the holy Catholic Church,
> the communion of saints,
> the forgiveness of sins,
> the resurrection of the body,
> and life everlasting.

Faith. But it wasn't the same faith they spoke of during my summer vacations with my mother's parents in Hopkinsville, Kentucky, at Freeman Chapel CME Church (established 1866). Less order, more inspiration. Better food after service. It was easy to be inspired. I had a crush on Teresa Franklin, a grown woman, when I was a child, and I went to church just to hear her voice rising above the rest of the choir... *We are not ashamed of the gospel of Jesus Christ . . . to everyone that believes it.* Women in the front, dressed in white, swayed when she sang. I got hard. I was there every Sunday. Except on those Sundays, I went with my great aunt Martha to Virginia Street Baptist (established

1852), which was right next door. My mother never went to either church.

On school breaks too short to go to Kentucky, I went to Chicago to visit my father's family. Their version of faith was less gentle. Scary. Faith. To the Church of God in Christ (COGIC), it was not only the key to happiness in the next life, but protection from demons in this one. Their Faith was in the infallible written word of God. So many rules. No smoking. No drinking. No Teresa Franklin, either. My father never joined us.

Faith in all its varied Christian glory.

Then while walking across campus in Ann Arbor, Michigan, I heard something different. Not the soulful music I associated with worship, but something more real, more relevant:

> "The honorable Elijah Muhammad said, 'You, Black man, are not American citizens or members of the White man's world. The only American citizens are the white people who are originally from Europe. Why fight a losing battle by trying to be recognized as something you are not and never will be. I am not trying to disillusion you, but merely telling you the truth.'"

This was spoken by members of a group on the Diag—the tree-lined gathering place at the center of the University of Michigan's campus—while they were giving out brochures and copies of *The Final Call*, which is the newspaper for the Nation of Islam.

No mention of Faith, just the reality I faced as a Black man in America. I began to think Faith was overrated. After all, I could see Louis Farrakhan on Saviors' Day. I could see the system that empowered a 12-year white kid in Hoptown to call my grandfather, "boy." **The system that prompted my high school counselor to say,**

"You're not college material." My mother, a child of the segregated South, often lamented that integration was the worst thing to happen to Black folks since slavery. My personal experience was that the presence of White people seldom made my life better. I didn't need Faith to understand Black empowerment.

At age 19, I joined the Nation of Islam.

I wore a kufi. Sold *The Final Call.* I drilled with the FOI. I stopped worrying about Faith. For a while.

I don't know which muezzin recited the adhan that day. With all the mosques in Dearborn, I'm not even sure where it was coming from. *Allahu Akbar.* God is Great . . . . *Aayya 'ala-s-Salah.* Hurry to prayer. *Hayya 'ala-l-Falah.* Hurry to salvation. I could feel a tickle in the place I assumed my soul resided. I felt my Faith growing.

At 21, I became Sunni.

The Shahada. The Muslim declaration of Faith. نَّمَّحَمُ هلللا الَّإ هلإ الَ لُوسُرَ هلللا *There is no god but God and Muhammad is his messenger.*

Have Faith and you will be rewarded. And I was. The mosque was like family, particularly during Ramadan. When the fast fell during summer, the long days were simply the price to take Iftar among my brothers. Water washing down the sweet taste of dates. Lamb and hummus passed around. Smiles. Love.

But slowly, even when prostrating towards Mecca, I realized what I felt was love for my fellow Muslims, not Faith. And I suddenly worried Faith was beyond me. *What if I can't believe? Why does my mind reject an omniscient and eternal being equally enthralled by birds, masturbation, and the Boston Red Sox?*

But I wanted to believe I was capable of belief. I told myself I could learn to believe, even if I had to brainwash myself into believing I believed.

She was Jamaican. Her mother and aunts told her, "Do not be unequally yoked with unbelievers . . . "

She married me anyway.

On September 10, 2001, my family spent the first night in our new house in South Orange, New Jersey, after living in Brooklyn while I went to law school. The following day, we caught the 7:15 Midtown Direct to Penn Station. My wife was headed to work at Columbia. I was headed to my firm in the MetLife Building. We'd forgotten my son's vaccination papers, so he couldn't go to school. He rode with us and was going to transfer at Penn Station to head to his grandmother's house in East Flatbush. We'd pick him up after work. As we approached the Hudson River, my son, sitting across from me, facing towards NYC, said, "Dad, look. That building is on fire."

I told him it was just a reflection. It was a beautiful, sunny Tuesday.

Just before the train entered the tunnel beneath the river, the conductor came on the intercom: "Ladies and gentlemen, if you look to our right out of your window, you can see the World Trade Center on fire."

My Faith lies somewhere on the Brooklyn Bridge, covered in dust among broken and burned office furniture. In its place is a gritty morality. There is no god to judge, so it falls to me to do the sorting. The good. The bad. I see people of faith in both groups. It no longer surprises me that none of the good people are good because of their Faith, but many of the bad tread in darkness because their Faith led them there. It's what I expect.

I'm now 56, and the prospect of death, a final end to all I know without hope or fear of a next stage, has become more imaginable. A sudden, unexpected death is far less likely with each passing day. I'm years removed from the crack epidemic in

Detroit, running with the bulls in Pamplona, and travels through the former Yugoslavia during its civil war.

I am statistically more likely to be ushered from this mortal coil by heart disease or cancer than by my bad judgement and sense of adventure. On the day I am no more, I expect to be judged by those I left behind. But that will matter far less than how I judge myself every day before that day. Am I a good father? A good friend? Do I try to make the world a little better than I found it? That is how I judge myself. My Faith, or lack thereof, is not part of the equation.

Eric Williams is a father, a grandfather, and a social justice lawyer in Detroit, Michigan.

Tips

- Identify how you may feel oppressed by religious programming. Journal about it.

- Think about and describe in your journal how you would feel, think, live, and love if you were free of the oppression of religion-induced guilt, shame, and fear.

- Speak with a caring professional therapist to identify your wounding and begin a process of healing.

- As you become empowered, take action every day to affirm your divine right to be free of oppressive rules from religion that hinder your happiness and best health.

Chapter 4

Religious Leaders & The Business of Religion
Follow the Money, Honey!

Who are religious leaders? Let's think of them as spiritual, too!
By Joanie

*W*ho are they? Can you name your favorite religious leader(s)? The ones associated with a specific religion? What did they do or not do that makes them your favorite leader?

When I think of religious leaders, I wonder about their amazing ability to quiet their insides with peacefulness and then invite me or others into that space. I call them spiritual guides or confidants! Spiritual leaders!

I've experienced exuberance and joy with such leaders who are fantastic listeners and hope-filled role models. Have you experienced phenomenal spiritual/religious leaders or faith communities? What religions, if any, were they representing?

I've also experienced religious leaders and the organizations they represent that caused me and others grave pains: mentally, emotionally, spiritually, and physically. Not fun to talk about, but it is reality and everyone needs to get it off their chest to move on. Throughout recent book events while interacting with people, the top hurts that people express to me stemmed from judgemental preaching and teaching, labeling LGBTQ+ people as sinners, and the no-remorse attitude from those who dealt the hurtful actions. Do you harbor resentment towards any spiritual/religious leader(s) or organizations?

Religious leaders are "normal" people, you and me included

Maybe you are a spiritual leader living the dream? Maybe you are discerning your next step in getting closer to your Higher Power and when, where, why, and how you play into that?

Well for starters, I believe each one of us is a spiritual and religious leader! Yes! Yahoo, Amazing!

It's not about a title or even a promise that you make to a church, synagogue or temple, an organization, a community, an individual, and/or a location.

It is about what you believe and how you want to live! It's about being the best YOU that God, Spirit or your Higher Power calls you to be. It's a calling to be selfless every day in every way! It knows no boundaries or limits; it is abundant love at its best, freely given and freely shared, not expecting anything in return!

You'll feel happy from the inside out and nothing can stop that feeling! Even if you are denied, rejected, or invisible to others.

You will sparkle, shine, and smile, your joy will be contagious, and it just happens. You don't think about it, you don't plan it, it is just YOU! You are a spiritual leader!

I am a religious leader, how about you?

Am I a religious leader? Yes, I am. So was my honey, Carol. Individually and together, a lesbian couple in love with life and daring to share love and Jesus with others. We did that within the Catholic Church.

Dead or alive, we continue to lead others deeper into their souls, into who they really are, and who they can become, in being the image of God!

Sharing life in a normal daily way was our key—listening, playing, laughing and being 100 percent present with friends! We would go out to dinner or gather for games and cards and say, "No job talk, no business talk tonight." We want to know you, the real you! So much fun! Yippee! (Some people find conversation and dialogue only exists within work or business mode; I think they are missing out on true treasures.)

I can talk about specific religious spiritual people who are my least favorite leaders, but I won't use their names. Some have been involved in illegal issues and others have been asked or chose to leave their religious institutions on their own accord. They were judgmental, not loving, not accepting, not kind, and did not walk the walk in being a Christlike disciple. They contradicted themselves with complicated talk of dishonesty, disharmony, and disease.

They were frightening zealous people I saw on TV and heard on radio talk shows who delivered sermon fires with hell and damnation and how they enjoyed seeing vulnerable people burned at the stake. Personally, I saw how they were manipulative, strategic in selecting specific councils or circles of friends, which promoted their personal agendas and ideas, and some were high on a pedestal as the king or queen, very egotistically self-centered.

I felt victimized and scared to speak up. Probably the exact place they wanted me. It was power and control for them, unhealthy and disturbing to me, and after months and years of feeling frustrated by trying to collaborate to make our faith community better and more welcoming, I resigned. I quit. In the end, it was all wonderful. I learned so much about myself and how important it is to be an "outspoken activist" as Elizabeth describes me in *Joyously Free.* All of my life, my actions have spoken louder than my words! Today, my words are powerful, gentle, and loving as I am living my truth.

I feel sad for them. I feel badly for the hurt that was incurred. But I chose to move on, to forgive, to let go, to face the facts that a person can only change themself. *All in divine timing, I believe.*

This enabled me to look and find leaders who spread hope, as I imagined a man named Jesus did.

If you've been hurt, let it go! Don't waste any more talk, time, or energy reliving the hurt. Name it and move on. Shake the dust off your feet and move forward! Now. Today! Get professional help if you need it.

At the same time, maybe that ugliness and hurt etched something, stirred you into action that you can control, share, and use to help someone else. Like the old saying goes, make sweet lemonade out of sour lemons. Make a delicious healthy drink; you can do it!

Who are some of my, our, favorite religious leaders?

Many and from all walks of life! From poets to musicians, to dancers to animal lovers, to authors and speakers, to married couples, singles, divorced people, and those living in alternative three- and foursomes. They are LGBTQ+, straight, and unsure. They speak languages that are unfamiliar to me, but their smile and love exude profoundly and joyously. They are poor and rich both in money, assets, and friendships. They are honest, open, and sincere. They are happy, kind, thoughtful, caring earth angels, and they are everywhere! They are a surprise around the next bend! They will be there when you need one! Or two or three!

When *Nun Better: An Amazing Love Story* was published in March 2023, I knew it would circle the globe. My heart said so and so did Elizabeth Ann Atkins and Catherine Greenspan, my

God-sent publishers and experts about book coaching, writing, creating, and publishing. Our book is a universal love story that many people can relate to.

How funny that two ex-nuns, queer as all get-out, could be the universal symbol for love, happiness, forgiveness, tenderness, loyalty, and holiness. The best-selling book is "a trip" of godly spirit humor! Wowie! You can order the book at TwoSistersWriting. com. I have autographed, sold, and given away many copies of *Nun Better* since March 2023. I was even bold and brave, sending them to people with prestigious religious titles, with initials behind their names that looked like alphabet soup. I distributed the book out of my backpack, the trunk of my SUV, and at planned book events to those who didn't have a dime to spare. Fun is my middle name! Hugs are free, too!

I loved finding a fun way to raffle off a book, stage the winners, and make sure that it wasn't based on a lack of finances. I love having *Nun Better* in local libraries for check-out. I love it when someone tells me they are sharing their book with another person. As long as I cover my expenses, I'm a happy camper. I absolutely appreciate all of you who order and purchase the book. It is a book to read and reread with zillions of golden nuggets hidden in our stories. All are welcome to read, be inspired, and be uplifted.

Oh, how the goose pimples rose on my arms as I placed the bright pink signed *Nun Better* books in gray, book-size waterproof envelopes to mail to the whoop-de-do, big-wig well known religious leaders. My heart did flip-flops as I Googled or personally phoned, asking for the direct mailing addresses of a variety of Catholic leaders who are the influential decision-makers for their organizations, parishes, and dioceses.

In my handwriting with a permanent black ink marker on the first of many envelopes, I prayerfully, happily, and excitedly printed the names of Sisters of St. Joseph leadership council members from the Los Angeles Province. That was Carol's and my congregation, and we were thrilled to share with them our life before, during, and after living out our vows—me for five years and Carol's 32 years. Sending them the book in March 2023 revealed our true self and who God had called us to become. I was overjoyed and proud to do so because they, the congregation sisters, were an integral part of our love story! I was so complimentary and thankful for the years and deep friendships that resulted from serving as a nun.

Next was the wild and crazy inspiration and awe that I spontaneously heard and felt to mail the book to Cardinal Robert Walter McElroy in San Diego, California. We had communicated with him in the past, congratulating and thanking him for his compassionate and endearing response to the LGBTQ+ Pulse nightclub in Orlando, Florida, where 49 people were killed in a massive, grotesque shooting attack on June 12, 2016. That began our solidarity in prayer and correspondence with a hand-written note wishing blessings upon us and with *Nun Better*. Thank you, Cardinal McElroy.

Next was Pope Francis. This was a super wild idea that came during my daily prayers. Carol and I had sent him a beautiful letter and card of thanksgiving when he succeeded Pope Benedict in 2013. As a Jesuit and with his band of brothers, we knew he was destined to lead and make great changes, including the acceptance and celebration of LGBTQ+ people, the healing of abuse from priests, and confronting the ministerial leaders who secretly buried issues that caused grave wounds for individuals and families. We hoped Pope Francis would improve and heal worldwide cultural and environmental setbacks and for the Catholic Church to move progressively forward with an open mind and heart to 21st-century living. We were jazzed that he was not going to take us backwards. *That's why Latin is called a dead language.* We were thrilled and vocal as we stood together with the "pope of the people!"

We had mailed both of these Catholic leaders our wedding picture of August 5, 2020, and then I sent them Carol's obituary flier in February 2022. Our thoughts were always to keep the leaders in tune with us, important specks in the common flock. We were excited to be on the same team with them and it was fun to invite them into our lives.

On March 22, three days after the official *Nun Better* book launch, I was led by Spirits to send both Cardinal McElroy and Pope Francis our book. It was the right time to send this spiritual gift to them. Spontaneity is one of my gifts and I rolled with it! My heart was beating faster and faster, knowing, *"This book is bigger than I can imagine; this is bigger than me. This is God's plan. I just need to mail it to them!"* Yahoo, go for it!

It was Tuesday, March 21st, 2023, when the second book launch for *Nun Better* took place at our local Chetco Community Library. I was still on an incredible natural high for having finally met my publisher Elizabeth Ann Atkins in person, after she had flown from Detroit and drove three hours from Medford, Oregon, to be present for the March 19 book birthing. It was a feeling of ecstasy. The Two Sisters Writing and Publishing business ladies had escorted me in a kind, loving way of book coaching and editing. I had written my story in five months, grieved, laughed, and cried, and now it was giving people chills and I patted myself on the back for accomplishing this biggest project ever of my life.

REFLECTION QUESTION

Have you ever thought about writing a book? You can do it! Who would you want to read it?

_____

_____

I was so grateful for them and for the publication of a book. Never in my wildest dreams did I see myself as an author, let alone an author about my love life with Carol and Jesus. And even wilder, an author who was willing to remain vulnerable and gutsy, sharing the book EVERYWHERE!

On Wednesday, March 22, 2023, my sister Gail, my number one family cheerleader and original designer of the *Nun Better* book cover, was busy at my house, sitting at the dining room table while drawing and coloring in beautiful artwork-plaque announcements. She was preparing these for our six-foot tall pink promotional banner, a photo-op billboard of location and date. On the docket was the next 30-day book tour and a thousand-mile road trip adventure. We would embark toward Southern California via stops in Ashland, Oregon, and San Francisco, California.

Enthusiastic vibes circled Gail and me as shooting stars from heaven, Carol's new home. Somehow, I just knew something big was going on. I couldn't define it or explain it, but oh, I could feel it. Carol was running the show and I was the laborer, the feet, the hands, and the mouth. My energy level was phenomenal and it was similar to the hype of a playoff volleyball game. Wowzer!

"Gail, I'm going to the Brookings Harbor Mailroom to mail a

book to the Pope and Cardinal McElroy. I won't be long. Catch you later big, sis!"

Large steps I took out the front magenta-painted door. I carried the purple and white cloth bag with my book that was going to two holy, powerful, top men in the Catholic faith, all the way from San Diego and across the Atlantic Ocean to Rome, Italy.

"Go get 'em, Joanie!" Gail called out.

This 11 AM drive north on Oceanview Drive felt like I was boarding a jet to both locations. I was super jazzed with happy visions of both men in their black and white collars glancing at the return label of *Nun Better*, Joanie Lindenmeyer. Did they wonder, *What is Joanie up to now? What is this? It feels like a book.*

Yes, a book that tells a story of two women in love, having served years in and for the Catholic Church. A book that they could learn from and use to improve the Catholic Church. A story of how God is alive and well in a same- sex marriage—and loved until death did they part.

I arrived at Boardwalk Mail and again, with a fast-paced stride, my smile beaming bright, I said, "Hi Nan, How are you? I have a few packages to mail."

"Of course, Joanie."

"The book envelopes work great," I said, "thanks so much for your suggestion."

She focused, typed contact information into her computer, printed the address label, and off it went to Cardinal McElroy. Shazam!

"One down, one to go!" I said.

"Oh Joanie, you'll need to go to the Brookings Post office to mail this next book to Rome. You'll need to fill out a customs form."

"Oh really, wow. Okay. Thanks so much. See you next time."

"You are welcome, see you next time."

"Have a great day!" I'm thinking, *Wow, I need to go to the main post office, this really is a big thing! Okay God, let's go!* I skedaddle out the door, dance around a water puddle, and hop back into my vehicle.

With the purple and white Hawaiian-print bag draped over my shoulder, the book that could open eyes and hearts and possibly even change the Catholic faith, shifts in the bottom of it.

My foot, with my signature pink-laced tennis shoes, pushes down on the gas pedal. I slide my hand on the floor gear shift to D for drive. I'm thinking, *Let's get Pope Francis his Nun Better book. I hope he reads English. Of course, he's smart and/or even better, someone could read it to him, then two people would have read it. Wow! That would be soooo cool! Or he could look at the pictures and get the idea of our life. Either way, it will be marvelous. How fun!*

The post office parking lot is crowded with 10 or so cars in my small town whose population is 6,000. Grooving and moving like a child on their birthday, I smile and my eyes are big and happy. I might have even had a skip in my step.

I wait in line, only two very quiet people in front of me standing on the COVID keep-your-distance circles on the floor. I don't say anything, a rare one for me. Within a few minutes, I walk forward to the large gray counter.

"Hi! How are you?" I ask. We make small chit-chat. Then I flash and smile and explode, "I finished my book! I was advised to come here to mail my book to Pope Francis at the Vatican in Rome. Will you please help me with this?"

Whipping to her side, she pulls out a thick bunch of paper with varying colors and pulls out one form. "Here is a required USPS Customs Declaration and Dispatch Note form for you to complete. Step to the side and then return here when completed.

Print hard and clear because there are multiple copies that it needs to show on! Be specific!"

"Oh Golly, wow! Okay, great, thanks!"

Standing at the gray counter next to hers, I pull a pen from my blue backpack, also known as my traveling office. The form has microscopic print instructions and lots of short lines for answers. *I can do this! I can fill this out correctly!*

"Joanie, print clear and hard!" I tell myself, out loud in a soft "teacher voice."

Sender information . . . I got this. I proceed to print slowly and accurately with my black ink pen and push hard with my hand, but not too hard to tear the paper. I check the layers of copies to make sure my printing is going through. This is all good, Joanie. I can feel Carol cheering me on. *Keep going. Remember, No Hurry in Curry; that's our local Curry County motto how we move slower than a bustling city slicker.*

Last name, First and Initial. *Yep, that's me.*

Business Name . . . *Nun Better. How fun it is to say that!*

Address: easy peasy, because it's been the same for 31 years.

ADDRESSEE'S INFORMATION:

I start to panic. *Oh God, help me.*

LAST NAME ?????? FIRST INITIAL:

Oh my gosh, my heart skips a beat. What is the Pope's last name? I left my phone in the car, so I couldn't Google it. So I turn around with a *please help me* puppy dog look and I ask with my booming enthusiastic voice to the half-dozen people standing 12 feet behind me in line: "Does anyone know the pope's last name?" I think I shocked people into silence. They all glared at me. It was like a movie scene and felt surreal, like time standing still.

"No, I don't know," comes a response, as others shake their heads sideways. Bummed, I look at the only postal employee and she shakes her head "no." But she is smiling. Yippee! I'd be really happy if someone could help me. You never know. Right? Bold and proud, I was on a mission and it's so much more fun to involve others.

Oh well . . . I print POPE in the space for last name... I giggle aloud. Everyone hears me. Why not? POPE is a good first and last name, I chuckle some more.

First name: I print FRANCIS.

Middle initial: I leave it blank! No clue, I definitely don't want to lie. (Smiles.) I pray to God that I get a positive form reviewer, not an anal pencil-pusher.

BUSINESS NAME: Oh man, I think I'm starting to sweat. My underarms feel moist. I turn around again to the people in line, hoping for a miracle, "What would you call the Pope's business name?" I ask in my booming voice once again to the remaining four in line who are joined by a few newcomers.

People are smiling and their heads are shaking and saying, "Nope, don't know."

"I got it, let's call his business the Catholic Church," I proclaim with a wink. *It fits in the short line. Yahoo!* I hear a few tiny laughs; I feel them with me in spirit.

ADDRESS 1: Apostolic Palace. *Good job Joanie,* I say under my breath, *that you carried your lime-green sticky note with the address written on it. Keep pushing hard.*

ADDRESS 2: 00120 Vatican City

CITY:

PROVINCE:

COUNTRY: *Oh boy, hope this works. Italy two times, why not?* I print hard and clearly: "Vatican City State, Italy, Italy"

Description . . . value, quantity and purpose: *Nun Better* Paperback book $20 and thank-you card, $1.00 total $21.00. A gift.

How exciting, I'm sending a gift to the Pope! This is a first! Way to go, Joanie and Carol!

The declaration is complete. It looks good as I read and review it to make sure I didn't miss anything. I stand tall and proud. My underarms are definitely wetter.

"Come right up," the employee says.

I slide a few feet to my right, hand her the package with the book and the completed document form.

"Looks great," she says with a smile.

"Thanks!" I paid the mailing charge with my *Nun Better* credit card. EXHILARATION! Wowie! By the way, the mailing was more than the cost of the book. I think it was $28.00 to mail this AMAZING gift to the pope.

What a hoot, what a day, what a trip I'm on, and what a trip this book will make! I thought, *I wonder what really is the value of my book?* Probably way more than $28 dollars. Maybe priceless! Big smiles. God only knows!

Carol, it's up to you, sweetie! Please make sure it gets there and in Pope Francis's gentle hands.

My mind switches into a daydream mode. I see Pope Francis sitting comfortably in his white smock, holding our pink-cover book with the two happy healthy, in love, nuns. He was smiling and his eyes were dazzling and sparkling! No, I did not see doves flying around, nor did I hear the angelic choir. Maybe next time.

I asked the postal clerk if I could touch the package one more time before she tossed it into the large parcel bin on rollers. She looked perplexed, but placed it in front of me. I put both my hands on it in a blessing-slash-hug to the pope! I felt lighter than a feather and happier than a clam. Off it went, like the meatball rolling off the table.

I have never heard if Pope Francis received it, touched it, or read it. Oh well, I did my part. My gut feeling as of today is *yes, he did!* I trust that Angel Carol and God took care of that detail! Yahoo and yippee.

On December 21, 2023, Pope Francis declared that same-sex relationships may now be blessed by Catholic priests around the world, just not in a liturgical setting. Wow, wow, wow! My phone and computer went ballistic as friends called and texted saying, "Joanie, we think Pope Francis read your book!" Such a monumental step for the universal Catholic Church! I guess it is.

Is it enough? In my opinion, absolutely Not!

Carol and I waited 39 years, 39 years, 39 years to be married in the Catholic Church. Many people would have died by then. FYI: We got sacramentally married by an Episcopal priest.

My dear friend Maggie said, "The window has been opened, but the door is still closed."

Maybe *Nun Better* had something to do with the pope's proclamation! That would be profound if it had an impact on the pope. Maybe it did?! And maybe the many countries where *Nun Better* has been ordered and read are impacting common people, the hierarchy or the Pope's decision?

Nun Better is bigger than we know!

I can only hope that our love story led him to that spiritual awakening and action, and that it has done that for others. Sure hope so. It would be fun to know that *Nun Better* was inspiring and uplifting to Pope Francis! What a hoot! God only knows! I did my part.

It's amazing; we lived our life and we wrote our storybook. Now it's circling the globe and changing lives and churches. It's absolutely AMAZING and mind-boggling to think of the possibilities for where it and I go from here.

Maybe when I send this *Healing Religious Hurts* book to Pope Francis, he will read it and Angel Carol will do the rest again. A double hoot! Shazam!

Since then, I've mailed, hand-delivered and discussed *Nun Better* to females and males, young and elderly, straight and LGBTQ+ religious leaders. Some with titles and positions such as bishops, priests, deacons, vicars, ministers, chaplains, clergy, pastors, reverends, rabbis, and sisters. More exciting to me are the faiths, denominations, and organizations they represent: Catholic, Episcopal, Presbyterian, Methodist, Lutheran, Jewish, Baptists, Latter-day Saints, Protestants, Scientologists, Nazarenes and Unitarian. Some are authors, speakers, theologians, spiritual directors, healers, counselors, professors, chaplains, retreat directors, musicians, youth ministers, teachers, fishermen, wardens, and attorneys. Hats off to those who are former, retired, or active with earned and vowed religious titles: Chip, Bernie, Linda, Cynthia, Amashia, Janell, Alyssa, Paul and Evelyn, Dan, Karolyn, M, F, R, S, E, M, S, I, R, Judy, Diana, Michael, Patty, C, Silky, Rosie, John, Jim, Dana, Skip, Mary, Penny, Diana, Suzanne, Colleen, Sally, Karolyn, Ron, and the Fairfield University Alumni Library.

And the countless people who are spiritual leaders in their own ways.

May all religious leaders foster a deeper relationship with their maker. I admire your gusto, tenacity, and fortitude. Religious leaders will serve, come, and go in a dynamic, changing world. I pray for them to keep their minds and attitudes open like a parachute and celebrate life joyously with God and Company.

Anyone, anything, and anytime makes it possible for mountains to be moved! Are you the next spiritual guru? Sure hope so! Answer your call and all will be well!

I pray for you and our world to be healed! For solitude and peace for those who are hurting! If I were there in your presence, I would offer my broad shoulders to cry on, my big hugs to console you, and my tears will flow in empathy and sympathy with you.

Remember, you can let go, forgive, and live anew.

Be the best you! Be healed! Be outrageously bold and loving! That's the best description of a religious leader, don't you think?

Money and Religion
By Elizabeth

The church had a purple-carpeted altar with several steps leading up to where the pastor and his wife sat in gold throne chairs. As the gospel music blasted, it roused goosebumps on my skin and made my heart soar. I felt intoxicated by the energy of hundreds of people all around me, praising, singing, moaning, crying, and responding out loud to the pastor's extremely charismatic preaching.

Then, upon his command, the people began to rise, row by row, in an almost hypnotic state, walking up the two aisles to the purple steps, where they dropped cash and checks.

Money literally rained on the purple-carpeted steps leading to the altar of this urban church, and I was in awe. Dollar bills, five-dollar bills, ten-dollar bills, twenties, even hundreds, fluttered out of hands and onto the steps, along with hand-written checks.

The music boomed and this weekly ritual continued for quite a while. It was fascinating to observe how obedient the men, women, and children were as they headed up to give their offerings, their tithes, as the Christian Bible dictates to give 10 percent of one's earnings to the church.

I was attending this service alone and happened to sit next to a woman who pulled out a tiny, beaded change purse. She unzipped it, pulled out crumpled bills, and held the money firmly between fingers whose red nail polish was worn down so much that only uneven splotches remained at the centers of her fingernails. The purse, her fingers, her clothing, the crumpled small bills—all signaled that she was not affluent, and that she was perhaps a member of the working poor.

Unlike the congregations at some churches that I have attended, where I recognized doctors, lawyers, CEOs, and socially prominent and affluent people in my large metropolitan area, the people at this particular service did not appear wealthy or professional. They were everyday people trying to make it through life, and this religious inspiration every Sunday kept them going. In exchange, they tithed what they could, including the woman beside me. This was many years ago, and the image of her fingers gripping that little purse and her clump of cash has remained in my memory, along with the extraordinary vision of cash and checks raining down on the purple-carpeted altar.

Typically, in church services that I have attended, a basket is passed from the ends of each pew and handed to each person until it reaches the other end of the pew, where another usher retrieves it and takes it to the next row of worshipers.

Sometimes, white-gloved ushers, who are usually male, pass gold bowls for these offerings. Some churches have everybody come up in an orchestrated procession to the front, row by row, to drop offerings into large baskets. The music blasts and it's a show of pageantry and celebration that feels joyous.

This is all well and good. A church is a business and must pay its mortgage, light bill, heat bill, insurance, employees, and all the other financial obligations required for running any building and organization.

However, this structure often becomes lopsided, as the church leadership lives like kings and queens while the congregants live like paupers. Examples include the preacher driving the most expensive luxury vehicles, owning private airplanes, living in mansions, taking extravagant vacations, and living an extremely opulent lifestyle. I've heard people say that congregants prefer that their leaders live a lavish lifestyle to represent them as if they are a king or a queen.

Let me be clear, I love church so much that it always makes me cry. I love the intoxicating energy of the music, the sermons, the feeling of being amidst dozens or hundreds of people who are all praying, crying, wailing, and bursting with praise. I also love the church leaders who are providing this spiritual sustenance for the masses. They are dynamic and charismatic people who do great things in the community, especially to uplift people most in need of food, shelter, jobs, health care, and legal assistance.

Some of my favorite churches on the planet include Detroit's Little Rock Baptist Church, where Reverend Jim Holley preached for 40 years. I have felt so much love there, and he is an amazing leader from the pulpit and in our city, where he has spear-headed many community development projects that have helped countless people.

Likewise, I love International Gospel Center in Ecorse, a downriver community of Detroit, where Pastor Marvin Miles electrifies the audience with powerful sermons that are broadcast around the world, and where the congregation is welcoming and loving. Pastor Miles is such a trailblazer that he produced two powerful Hollywood films: *Silent No More* (2012) and *Anything is Possible* (2013) with Los Angeles-based director Demetrius Navarro of D Street Films. I had the honor of playing a major role as an actress in *Anything is Possible*, which is now streaming on Amazon Prime and Peacock.

Likewise, I love mega pastors whose sermons I watch on YouTube. They include Joel Osteen, Joyce Meyer, and Reverend T.D. Jakes.

When I'm attending a religious service and tithing time arrives, I happily make my financial contribution, because the experience of attending service is so enriching to my mind, body, and soul.

I absolutely love religious leaders who provide the spiritual nourishment that we humans crave and deliver it in ways that sustain us through our days, especially during challenging times.

All the while, I recognize that religion is a business.

And for some, that is a turn-off. Some religious institutions require that members submit their tax returns so that the religious institution can know exactly how much money the person makes, and therefore demand 10 percent or more. Some mega churches have businesses within their business, such as a credit union and travel agency. This may be perceived as a convenience or a control tactic.

Every person has the freedom to decide if and how they want to financially commit to a religious institution. For some, in addition to complying to religious doctrine, one's financial contribution is an investment in so many benefits: having a community of friends and congregants who share common beliefs; securing a social calendar that includes post-service meals, holiday parties and programs, picnics, and even travel clubs, book clubs, and other events; enjoying the security of a "church home" (or another name for that in another religion) which makes one feel embraced and valued; networking amongst congregants that can enhance social circles and even marital match-making, as well as building business relationships for professional advancement; and the backing and support of the religious leader, should one need prayers for a sick relative, legal advocacy, and a platform should a member decide to run for elected office, or invite their favorite candidates to speak during the service.

Many religious leaders wield tremendous power in swaying their congregants to vote for particular local, state, and national candidates for elected office, ranging from city councils to state legislatures and the governor's seat, all the way up to the U.S. Congress and the U.S. Presidency.

This is powerful!

Being part of this experience is a choice. For many, it's beneficial. For others, it's a turn-off, because the aspects of money and power can, for some, taint the altruistic mission of a religious institution.

I've heard friends cynically call tithing time during a church service a "shake-down" as the preacher rouses the crowd and passes the offering baskets. Some services have multiple rounds where the pastor asks for money, not only for regular offerings, but for the building fund, the first lady's birthday party, and other events. Other religious institutions have a screening process during which the applicant's financial profile is evaluated to determine if they are a good fit for membership.

This raises questions about the institution's motives and can lead to religious hurts, making someone feel that they are not welcome by virtue of being a believer seeking spiritual guidance, and instead are seen as a potential financial asset for the institution.

Likewise, in more affluent religious communities, sometimes people feel that they do not have adequate educational degrees, or designer clothing, or luxury cars, or prominent job titles, to fit in with the well-heeled and potentially pretentious and "boogie" congregants. This could spur someone to not attend those services, even if they love the leader's style of delivering uplifting religious messages.

These dynamics can cause religious hurts in the form of suspicion, cynicism, and rejection.

What are your thoughts and feelings about the business of religion?

REFLECTION QUESTIONS

Has the business of religion ever hurt you? If so, how?

_____

_____

Have you found a place where the balance of tithing and financial support for a religious institution has been equally balanced with the benefits that you receive from contributing money?

_____

_____

Do you think it's fair that people have to pay for private religious education? Why or why not?

_____

_____

Who are your favorite religious leaders? Why?

_____

_____

The Business of Religion
By Zamber Knight

During the late 1980s and into the 1990s, I was discovering "me" as I grew from teenager to young professional woman. This journey in self-identity happened at a time in our culture when "who" I am came with a lot of risk for prejudice to live authentically.

Through self-reflection of experiences and emotions, I determined: I am an American; a Jew in religion, race, and culture; and a bisexual woman. People could choose to disregard me for many aspects of myself. I chose to be me, taking all of the risk. Now 57, I am not only surviving, but have gained acceptance in all areas of my life.

Family

In 1995 at age 28 over brunch at The Original Pancake House, the table talk with my parents and sister centered around current events in our lives as we chatted feverishly. Then the focus shifted to future aspirations. The family insisted that I would find the right Jewish guy, build a home, and have children. I am sure they thought that they were being supportive, telling me not to be concerned that I was single, and that it would happen in due time.

This was not the vision I had for my future. I had no intention of sharing what I had slowly discovered about myself over the past 10 years, here in public, over pancakes, but I found myself impulsively responding, "Maybe I will not marry a man. Maybe kids are not my future; I may be with a woman."

I watched my Dad drop his fork on his plate, drop his head below his shoulders, and sit in silence for the rest of the meal. My Dad and sister had the hardest time accepting me. In time,

Dad gave me the gift of unconditional love during a "goodbye" visit; I was moving out of town for work. I did not know this would be the last conversation we would have; he died two days later.

Religion & Community

As I grew into my identity, I started to withdraw from organized religious activities in which I had been immersed since I was a toddler and groomed for organizational leadership roles, of which I held many.

Activities, conversations, and worship services seemed heterosexually-based "matchmaking" and family focused. I could no longer relate and lost interest in participating.

Over the years, I have gone to all kinds of religious services and celebrations with an open mind to learn and experience new views; so many religious sects have opened the aperture to include diversity in their congregational approach.

I healed the pain of not belonging with the belief and ability to talk to God in my mind when and where I want, by being still and looking within myself. My base foundational values align with Jewish teachings, but I do not ascribe to any established religion. It's a business like any other, selling the products of hope and support, which I already have within myself.

Every human hurts. How we embrace our insight through healing the pain becomes our life. The world has evolved, too. I am no longer tolerated as an American, Jewish, bisexual woman; I am sought after.

Zamber Knight is artistic and bold, dedicated to bringing joy into the world with art, horticulture, and relationships.

Tips

for healing hurts by religious leaders
and the business of religion:

- Recognize that religion is a business whose products are support and comfort, and many other benefits that include a feeling of belonging and having a social community.

- Journal about your experiences in a way that purges out the feelings and memories, so that you physically release them from your heart and mind onto the pages, as a step toward healing.

- Seek religious or spiritual leaders who nourish your mind, body, and soul.

- If you desire membership in a religious community, ask for personal referrals and research online to find places where you feel that your financial contribution is merited because you are receiving back the love, peace, community, and religious leadership that enhance your life.

- Know that you have the power to decide how and where you will engage in a religious community, under which leaders, and by contributing financially in ways that you feel good about.

- Understand that you have the power to opt out of organized religion altogether, and find your own path to love and peace.

Seek religious or spiritual leaders who nourish your mind, body, and soul.

Aja Walker

Michael Irby

Tay Ryan

Eric Williams

Rosie Robles

Jill Prioreschi & Janet

Ruthie Murray

Michael Hensley

Pamela Ross McLain, PhD

Deborah Randall-Kravitz

Rev. James Martin, SJ

Janell Monk

Susannah Stokes

Viv Ashton

Chapter 5

Marriage and Death
Eternally Yours

Healing Religious Hurts around Marriage and Death, Widows, Orphans, and Quails
By Joanie

During my book signings for *Nun Better*, I meet amazing people who ask questions and share stories that touch my heart. Here are a few that I want to share with you.

My partner died, what do I do?

Friend: "My male partner died suddenly, and his family doesn't want my name listed as his partner in his obituary."

Me: "That's so crazy!"

Friend: "What do you think?" He pauses long and sighs, "I'm going to do it anyway."

Me: "I think you can decide when, where and how. He was your partner and you are adults. Did his family know you?"

Friend: "I hope his family, in time, will accept me and will understand our love."

Me: "This is the time for you to stand up for the love you shared with him. God hold you, dear friend. Do you believe in heaven? Eternal love?"

Friend: "I will for him, for us. Yes I have a strong Christian faith. I miss him so much," as snot billows, tears stream and eyes are glassed over; deep, deep sorrow my friend is in.

What churches and places of worship celebrate LGBTQ+ weddings?

Friend: "I wish more churches celebrated LGBTQ weddings! Which ones do? Love is love."

Me: "Great question. Me too, I wish more churches celebrated LGBTQ+ marriages and weddings! It sounds like you or someone you know wants to get married in a church? Or in a faith community that is LGBTQ+ accepting and will celebrate and honor queer love."

Friend: "Yes, definitely. Can you help me?"

Me: "Yes. Let's start with Googling LGBTQ+-friendly churches! Even better, why don't you call your local churches and places of worship and ask them extraordinary questions about LGBTQ+ same-sex marriage? First consider LGBTQ+-friendly western Christian churches that are standing in favor of same-sex marriage unions: Unitarian, Episcopal, Methodist, ELC Evangelical Lutheran, UCC United Church of Christ, and Presbyterian. It's good to also know which ones don't. Southern Baptist and Latter-day Saints/Mormons come to my mind. Churches seem to be either very rigid-minded and closed in thought, while others are welcoming conversations and debating the issue. It's funny, I don't see it as an "issue," but I see it as two people in love, so follow your heart and explore your options while educating yourself. Have fun!"

My new LGBTQ+ Jewish friend

Friend: "The Jewish faith supports LGBTQ marriages. How about trans partners?"

Me: "I believe yes. Why don't you set up a meeting with a Rabbi to answer your specific questions and to have a companion on your spiritual journey? I recently met a LGBTQ+ Rabbi. They had been hurt when their synagogue found out. I am extremely proud of this person for telling their truth as a Rabbi."

Friend: "I would love to read about spiritual religious leaders who have such a compulsive faith to do what God, Jesus or their Higher Power says to do or be: totally honest."

Me: "They touched my heart that amazing day!"

Married Until Death Do Us Part

Here's the ultimate connection of love: commitment to your lover(s) at the beginning, middle, and end of life. It's magical and mystical.

Dear Reader, get the full stories from Joanie about marriage and death in Nun Better. Read about her wedding with Carol from pages 232 to 233 and about the miraculous moments preceding Carol's death on pages 254 to 256. They include Joanie hearing an angelic voice saying, "I bring glad tidings of joy" along with flashing lights that came from the heavens.

Carol and I fell deeply in love in 1983. It took us several years to figure out what to do and more importantly what God was calling us to do and be. We were both vowed nuns at the time and there wasn't legal marriage for LGBTQ+. We weren't using any descriptive LGBTQ+ words to even describe our relationship. Simply, we were two women in love and committed ourselves, forever, to each other. We moved in together in 1986. Within a month, with our first paychecks, we chose our Black Hills gold rings as our outward symbol of our never-ending love. Without fanfare, without a large crowd celebration, we hugged, kissed and devoted our whole selves in the jewelry store, parking lot and our rental home. We lived private lives together, cherished, respected and grew closer as time went on. Our life was bliss: sensual, sexual, and spiritual. The three S's!

In 2012, we obtained our official Oregon Domestic Partnership, and in 2020, we officially and sacramentally married in our living room with an Episcopal Priest. Because of COVID, present at our wedding were our two witnesses, Tim Guzik and Sarah Tierheimer, priest celebrant Fr. Bernie Lindley and his wife Paige and us the "newlyweds." Yep, do the math, from our first meeting in 1983 through 2022, we were unified as one heart, one mind, one soul; 39 AMAZING years before we were **officially** and **sacramentally** married.

Let me repeat, "Married until death do us part." That was me and Carol. Monogamous and golden! Yahoo! Yippee and more yahoos!

Not all relationships are that way. We each have our own vocation and journey to follow and live. Live every day to the max! Hopefully joyously free and healed from hurts. *What's your story?*

So, let's resume with more questions that have struck my heart since the 2023 writing of *Nun Better: An AMAZING Love Story.*

LGBTQ+ Funerals and Death

Wow, this is a huge topic. Thank you for asking questions and thinking of the entire spectrum from first love to first death.

Friend: "Have you ever been to an LGBTQ+ funeral or memorial service in a church or with a church officiant?"

Me: "Yes, we have."

Friend: "Do they have LGBTQ+ funeral services? I never hear about them."

Me: "Yes, celebrations of life vary as much as LGBTQ+ marriages do!"

A Church Funeral for my Gay Friend

I've only had the privilege to attend one gay funeral service *in a church*. It was in the 1990s and it was at a rural Catholic Church. The air was thick and heavy for me and Carol because the families of the deceased and his husband's family were not allowed to give the Eulogy during the church service. The deceased's husband was not allowed to receive communion either, that was a total bummer! Our hearts and minds felt betrayed and helpless. Thinking how cruel the church was! Where was compassion? Sadly, not there. It was excruciating and depressing to see their families witness church discrimination.

Maybe someone right now is reading this and can relate. Peace be with you! Healing!

Carol and I, a known lesbian couple, but not officially married, did receive communion that funeral day. After I received Jesus in the body disc host, I walked past the deceased family members all snuggled shoulder to shoulder and squished in the first rows, and I pretended we were all sharing a bite of the holy sacramental bread. I noticed from my widower friend, his pale face, the tears welling in his swollen red eyes, so, so, so, so much pain, loss and hurt being expressed; this is a constant theme for us older gays and lesbians. Healing is ongoing!

Hidden and invisible, we grew up with a way of life as we safely lived as LGBTQ+ people during the 1980s and 1990s. Suffering inside, without a way to let it out. This was just another one of those days. The numbness of grief saved him temporarily. But in consolation, he knew his LGBTQ+ FAMILY was there with him. Healing is ongoing!

An intimate group of friends and family traversed the wet grass to his graveyard burial site under big trees and a sprinkle of rain. Holding onto each other, gay and straight alike, one simple prayer was read, flowers placed on his casket and we, straight and LGBTQ+, ended in great big hugs. We will miss, we will move on; John was in a happy, heavenly place singing his heart OUT! Healing is ongoing!

Back on the church grounds, the parking lot filled to the brim, the music blared, our smiles returned, and we said, "Let's go celebrate! That's what flamboyant John would want." Healing is ongoing!

Oh how fun and happy the reception was, with an abundance of home-cooked, aromatic and delicious Mexican food, along with tequila shots and a variety of other drinks for toasting. Laughter, live guitar music, and family and friends' hilarious testimonials seemed to go on for hours! The black microphone with its long cord tossed and circled around the huge community hall of lover-ly friends and family kept everyone in robust laughter and grieving giggles. Anyone who wanted to, spoke happily, freely, and with excitement. It was totally awesome! This was the way! Jesus was there in humanity and divinity without the staunch rigidity of priestly hierarchy. By the way, the priest officiant never showed up. Next time, Father. You missed an incredible gay bash! Healing is ongoing!

Today, 30 years later, I have reflected on that incredible holy day. Was the widower's family oblivious to the homophobic act of the church? It hurt me deeply, because I represented the church, and I've been privy to live on the inside of it. On that day, the holy church did wrong. Maybe the family covered up their disgust and pain, knowing the real fun celebration of life would occur at the reception, at the other church—the hall! I pray that healing and scars have been released by his widower and family. Time does heal. Mine included.

LGBTQ+ Funeral Services

Most LGBTQ+ people don't have a religious memorial or funeral service for two reasons. First, many LGBTQ+ people are not OUT, and secondly, they don't belong as members of a faith community. Somehow, we, society, associate marriage and death services with church and places of worship. That's not always the case for LGBTQ+ folks.

My life experience shows about 90% of LGBTQ+ deaths end with no, nada, zero closure for family and friends. How sad! Sometimes the only public closure is a tiny required legal newspaper death announcement and a drop off of their belongings at the Goodwill.

Thank goodness for emails, message alerts, and social media postings. Hope you have a hotline of sorts.

Carol and I vowed to be available, take charge, organize, attend, or comfort our LGBTQ+ family when death stung. One end of life celebration was in a funeral parlor, one in a backyard, one at a banquet hall facility, and one on the riverbank. Similar to weddings, celebrations of life and death take on a life of their own. It's all about LOVE!

Spiritually, we are reminded that at death, love does not end; it changes. Radically for most of us who face it head on.

Would you join with me to become more compassionate in celebrating LGBTQ+ marriage and death without stigmas or prejudice? We need each other, allies and family!

Until death do us part is an all-encompassing phrase better known as the dash between the year of marriage and the year of death. It's the dash of living one's truth to the best of their ability. A dash that is filled with incredible moments: successes, failures, disappointments, and dreams come true.

Carol's life celebration was a *partttttttyyyyy!*

She had been Catholic for 79 years, yet she did not want a Catholic Church mass or rosary as her memorial service. She chose to have a place where everyone felt welcomed and could share a spiritual communion, to eat mouth-watering pizza and fresh green salad, munch on homemade cookies, and drink root beer! She wanted people to tell happy stories, laugh, have big smiles, and wear bright colors. Her wishes came true. Throw in non-stop, happy-feet-moving, dance hip bumps, and Carol's favorite songs played from Andrew's portable speaker. Daffodils sprouted on every table, thanks to Val and plenty of joyful happy tears. Carol enjoyed her celebration, being present to each of us, about 100 people, in a spirit heavenly way! I loved it, too! Friends told me afterwards, "This is the best memorial service I've ever been to. Truly a joyful celebration!"

For me, it was a double party commemorating our marriage and death!

I was blown away when Father Bernie remembered and blessed me at Carol's one-year anniversary of death at St. Tim's Episcopal mass.

"Strength for the journey, Joanie," Deacon Linda told me at Eucharist. That meant a lot to me! They are phenomenal pastoral leaders, knowing each of us as special persons. I'm amazed how they know and remember everyone's name and crucial things about their life. Sort of like, in scripture, "I've called you by name!" Smile, sigh!

Many faiths are decades into discussions to confirm or deny their position on LGBTQ+ issues. The flip side of that is, people die and people want to get married all of the time. How pastoral are you, church leaders?

My dream is that religions would publicize and spread the word like a popular national TV Super Bowl commercial, a local newspaper ad, a fun dancing lights billboard, or a jingle-jangle song informing and recruiting LGBTQ+ people for marriage and funeral celebrations. Imagine what a business or religious mission that could be? AMAZING!

Everyone, straight and LGBTQ+, needs to know who to turn to when death strikes. Will it be you, your community, or your Higher Power? My hope is in your promise! Yahoo! Shazam!

Tips about LGBTQ+ Marriage and Death

Yes, I group two big life events together. You may think this is strange, but to me, marriage and death invoke similar questions and decisions. This inspires us to examine our perceptions and opinions about LGBTQ+ marriage, death, and funerals. It's different in a variety of ways because of how we, LGBTQ+ people, live. We have our own uniqueness, struggles, and celebrations. Healing is ongoing!

Widows, Orphans, and Quail

Oh golly, I've been watching for weeks a beautiful California quail with a plump body and tassel of elegance atop its head. Mr. Quail stands so pristine, statue-like, holy, and elegant. It reminds me of the John Paul Getty Museum gardens and courtyard, the Louvre in Paris, and Roman and Greek sites where noble figurines guard and grace the grounds.

Then, out of nowhere, for no reason at all, I saw the quail, quick-footed, skinny with a sucked-in breast, running faster than a speeding roadrunner. He crossed the freshly mowed emerald-green lawn, I awaited the *beep, beep* sound, but heard only the high-pitched quail call, for he was looking for his lifetime mate. *Click, click, click.* Just as Carol and I were lifetime mates!

Cocking his head from side to side, not hearing any signal from his mate, his statue-stillness resumed. Minutes later, I spot quail, camouflage colored, invisible to friend or foe, basking on the telephone line directly above my head, 20 feet up.

I think, *What a wonderful world you have up high, but where is your sweetheart? Are you a lone quail? Without your better half to fly, play, and run with?*

Am I, and is Mr. Quail, the widow and orphan that I read about in the holy Bible? During Jesus's time, two thousand years ago, many stories of widows and orphans were recorded as cultural events and used as parables for masterful teachings.

The Bible mentions widows and orphans 15 times. That's plenty of time and examples of how we, you and I can be compassionate. Do widows and orphans need extra special attention? Are they frail? Do they need tender healing? YES, YES, and YES. Widows and orphans are often invisible, forgotten, and discarded. The Bible says to take care of them.

Quail, tell me, are you a widower or an orphan? One in the same, deserted in loss and love. I haven't seen your partner, and you have not seen mine. For they are missing or dead, leaving us all alone? It's a strange empty feeling of being off kilter, not myself. You look like you are afraid to venture further, Mr. Quail. You and I both are experiencing fear, pain, agony, trauma, spaciness, and bizarreness. Being a widow or an orphan is the art of living in the scary unknowns. Scary! Day and night!

I feel like I have also died. Will I ever FEEL love again? You and I are going through our daily motions, but our routines have been altered for this new way of life. Are you healing from this grip of grief, Quail?

What do you miss most about your mate? What was she like? Tell me your love story. Maybe that will be the puzzle piece to enable me and you to heal and move on?

Oh my God, Quail, you and I are the same creature . . . we are both widower and orphan. We are alone without our soulmates. Me, after a blissful 40 years with my beloved Carol.

For years, Mr. Quail, Carol and I would watch the two of you and your little ones, frolic in the green grass, and hide in the wild black berry and flowering pink fuchsia. It was fun to see all of your family flit from cypress tree to hydrangea.

Now, I see you stop, look in many directions for your mate, but she does not appear. I do the same.

I, too, make loud quail-like song calls, day or night, hoping to hear her voice twitter and answer me in her precious beautiful song that only I could recognize. Your harmonic call returns without response as well. It's been two years since Carol died and YES, I still grieve a little. You too, pretty quail?

I cry at the strangest times, when it's loud with activity and in the silence of the night sky. I heard you also cry really loud one day. Do you feel better after a few sobs? I sure do!

It's okay to be sad and happy at the exact same moment. My loss of her love broke my heart! How's your heart? If it's like mine, it feels tiny, then it feels overflowing with something.

I can't even imagine the terrible, violent loss people or animals experience in tragedies far beyond a peaceful death. How did your spouse die, Quail?

Carol's death extended for a long period of time, years turned into months, then days, then hours, then minutes. All along, my letting go was healing. Unbelievably difficult at times but such joy, too. It's best described as I cry tears of sadness and smile beams of joy.

Yes, I take flight, Quail, and explore new things. I've learned to stop pacing while looking for her, because I've found her in my heart forever! No further explanation needed! You will soon fly to more wires and trees, unafraid and happy.

She goes where I go; her angelic powers continue to surprise me every day as positive things happen like magic and the downer-depressed days are further left behind. A new day, with a bright, color-filled sunrise like never before, happens every single day! AMAZING! You know, Quail, the early bird gets the worm. I see you also greet each new day with prancing and dancing. You are bouncing with every step and your tassel is no longer crooked. It is reaching for the sunshine.

I went for a long beach walk today. My new heart songs burst and blast forth from my smiling lips as I walked faster, my heart beating stronger as my pink-laced tennis shoes stride on the high-tide, dark beach sands. Teaspoon-sized, white angel rocks guide my steps.

I am thanking God for new friends who live around the block and some many miles away! I wave my hiking stick as if I'm the marching band director. Up and down over my head and all around. The long, pointed stick circles and makes figures of eights to the stereo-sound music happening in my mind as I belt out the lyrics of "This Little Light of Mine." Louder and happier I sing as the crashing Pacific waves harmonize.

It feels good to have new fresh breaths, for I have left the old. Like you, single quail, leaving the seeds and berries (the daily memories) for others to gulp. I feel Carol within me, but it is not all-consuming anymore; it took time and peace, surrender and prayer. Every creature moans and groans in their unique way and in their special time. I hope you will soon be marching, waving a stick, and singing your new song in a new place. It's okay if you need to leave my yard. I get it!

Life is different. Today was joyful. How about your day? Have you surrendered, let go, and moved on without your soul mate? You look happier as you share the seeds with the pretty blue scrub jays. You have new friends, too!

Did you know that sometimes I can actually feel her skin touch my skin? She holds my hand; it feels warm to my touch. I'm amazed that her spirit is in my every move and every musical note, and I don't even consciously think about her. It just happens.

Miracles from above are gifts of the Holy spirit.

I bet you feel your honey scratching your back feathers and looking you in your gorgeous eye.

Have you noticed how, Quail, we don't eat as much anymore? It's not as much fun to eat alone. I see you walk and fly more and eat fewer seeds. I'm still healing, with one thing at a time, since EVERYTHING is brand new! Healing comes in spurts. Put your patience cap on, Quail; your time will come. Just like it does for me. Let's continue to be kind to ourselves.

Quail, what's your story going to be? What's your tip on how you conquered grief pain? Can you describe how you healed from your loss? Did you have a church, a support group or a safety net to catch or hold you? I did! It was wonderful!

I think you and I have shared similar yet unique experiences. How odd, yet how beautiful. Pain and agony do turn around to that incredible joy that scripture describes. Jesus will take care of you as much as He does me.

How, you wonder? Believe that your quail life has a great purpose! Have total faith, trust and HOPE! Divinity and Higher Powers exist. We are both profoundly loved. Believe in life everlasting, comprehend, and understand that there is a bigger picture to everything and everyone. Even you, Quail. No exceptions.

Quail, I found myself a new name, a new label, a title. I am no longer a grieving widow or an orphaned little one. I am single and extraordinary! Just like you! We were both blessed with lifetime soul mates, so let's hold fast to our blessings, be grateful and most of all, look forward to each and every new day, with new adventures.

Positive self-talk, invigorating happy words make a difference in my mental and emotional psyche. Try it, Quail. It comes in your language, too.

In the last year and a half, I have made and met so many new friends! I do new things and with my old friends I am embarking on new and improved, deeper relationships. My friends say that I'm sweet! Of course, probably more gentle? You and I, Quail, have been forever influenced by our mates.

I have no worries and I hope you don't either. Everyday weather surprises us, angels twirl around us, and I think less about myself and more for others. Have fun with your neighborhood bird friends. Reach out, let your voice be heard, and be the best you!

I so strongly believe in God's plan for me and for you, Quail! Our past pains, fears, rejections, hurts, and losses can and will be healed if we/you allow it. Yes, you and I have been in pain; we've been through tough times or are going through it now, and there is a lot of light streaking and overpowering the dark. Do you know that I am loved and irreplaceable? You are, too! Did I tell you that I found rest and peace because Jesus carried my burdens? I am so grateful for the gift that Jesus gave me to watch over Carol and for her to watch over me, to create such an AMAZING, loving relationship. It was centered on selflessness and joy.

Now it's our turn, Quail, to accept healing, and to let others know they can have it, too.

Quail, thanks for talking and being with me this morning. It's the absolute best to have a friend like you. Thank you *so* much for being you—plump and elegant, a gorgeous blue-green, tassel-topped quail. I promise to hear your song call and please listen for mine as well. Happy healing life to both of us!

Healing Religious Rifts in Marriage
By Elizabeth

Marriage starts in a purple haze of romance and the wedding often happens with a religious officiant as a blessed occasion. It is one of the most beautiful life experiences, and many call their wedding day the happiest day of their life.

But if divorce occurs, the union ends in the stark, cold contrast of a courtroom and breaks down as a business deal dividing up money, property, and rights to seeing your children.

The dream can quickly turn into someone's worst nightmare!

When I divorced and this harsh realization struck my heart, I wondered,

What is the role of religion in marriage?

In most religious doctrines, it is the ultimate goal. Marriage is expected, encouraged, and even forced in some religions. It's viewed as the framework of stability for society. A man, a woman, and children together comprise the building blocks of what religion considers the ideal world.

But fewer people are marrying today, more are choosing non-traditional love-styles such as polyamory, others are adamantly committed to staying single. Many young people have no desire to conform to society's heterosexual norms, and some are opting not to bring children into a world plagued by so many problems, including global warming.

The religious aspect of marriage has inspired many questions for me, and I hope that exploring them can enhance your perspective on this topic. Here are some questions. Please share your opinions on the lines after each one.

What if partners have clashing religious beliefs and practices?

Many people fall in love across traditional barriers of race, ethnicity, national origin, and religion. For example, if a Christian person and a Jewish person marry, which religion will they follow? Sometimes one person converts to the other person's religion. Sometimes couples celebrate both, creating traditions that are a fusion of both beliefs and cultures.

But while it may seem simple for their love to create a whole new and unique way of connecting with God, their family members may not be so quick to participate in this religious union. Sometimes parents from one Christian denomination have deep-rooted prejudices about another Christian denomination. This can cause religious hurts, for example, if a Catholic daughter wants to marry a Protestant man, and the Catholic parents oppose this so viciously that they refuse to attend the wedding. This type of rift can occur if a Jewish person wants to marry a Muslim person, or a Christian wants to marry an atheist, and so on.

The families will argue against the union by saying it will dilute their son's or their daughter's beliefs and practices. Critics will also say that it will confuse the children if they have to hopscotch between two religions.

What happens when your spiritual journey takes a new path while your partner takes another road or stays stuck in old ways?

I've often heard married people complain that their partner had a radical shift in their spiritual and/or religious beliefs and practices, and that it caused a major problem in their union. This can happen when one person has a spiritual awakening and steps into a new lifestyle that includes:

- a daily spiritual practice that takes time and energy away from their partner.

- travel to retreats that one partner does not want to join.

- new ways of thinking about life and love that make one person stop drinking alcohol or partying or eating junk food, thus treating the body as a temple and refusing to engage in activities that once were a happy, fun focal point for the couple.

- a sudden immersion in a righteous religious program whose doctrine and practices make the other partner feel condemned (such as a Christian man who happily married an atheist woman, but after some years espouses conservative viewpoints that he learned while attending all-male Christian rallies and as a result spouts hurtful things to her about going to hell for not being a believer).

- an intolerance for misogynistic music, too much negative news, violent movies, gossip, and other low-vibe content for the eyes and ears, that once were the norm for the couple.

- no longer wanting to socialize with certain people and couples, or attend events that had been a mainstay of the courtship and marriage, but now ring hollow or even intolerable to the spiritually-awakened partner.

- wanting to opt out of an established place of worship where the couple has always attended—and perhaps even married there—and instead desiring to explore new religious and/or spiritual communities.

- and speaking a whole new dialogue and doing things around chakras, energy clearing, high-vibrational frequencies, plant-based eating, and other things that dramatically contrast with the status quo of the marital lifestyle.

There are so many other scenarios in which religion can cause a rift in a marriage. These often occur without warning, as people evolve over the years and lifetimes, and certain experiences such as trauma, grief, loss, disillusionment, and spiritual awakening can jolt a person into a new way of thinking, praying, and connecting with God/Spirit/Higher Self.

Can this be avoided? Communication that starts very early in courtship is key. Our ideal mates share our vision for how to receive love and peace from God/Spirit/Higher Self. The goal is to stay open to the evolution of our partner's spiritual journey, and hopefully take their hand and travel with them. When love and the committed union are the anchor, you're both free to sail into new experiences and beliefs.

However, if the differences are too extreme, it's up to the individuals to decide if the union should continue. That is a deeply personal decision. Spirituality and religion should never be forced on another person, and the best case scenario is for partners to evolve together on their spiritual path to deepen their love for each other and for God/Spirit/Higher Self as one.

REFLECTION QUESTIONS

Have you experienced a spiritual or religious rift in your marriage or relationship if you or your partner took a different path? How did you resolve this?

_____

_____

How can you heal a religious rift in marriage?

What if you're both Christian, but one is Catholic and the other is Baptist? Do you baptize the baby in a Catholic Church?

Do you raise the child as a Baptist? Can you do both, by exposing the child to services in two church communities? You can interchange the denominations and religions in this scenario.

The solution is communication and keeping the best interest of the family's harmony intact. That means compromising and brainstorming creative solutions that create a win-win-win outcome for you, your partner, and your child or children.

If you have a religious rift in your union, resolution requires an evaluation of whether it can make or break the marriage. That is a profoundly personal decision. For many, the call to follow God/Spirit/Higher Self in a particular way is a much stronger calling than the need to partner with another human. Of course, when children are involved, this is complicated.

What is the ultimate expression of love between people? Is marriage required?

_____

_____

What is love? Does love last forever?

_____

_____

Is love defined by living together, marrying, committing to one another, having kids, and/or dying in your lover's arms?

_____

_____

Catholic Annulment Pain and Healing
By Ruthie Murray

I didn't have any religious hurts growing up. I didn't attend any church or synagogue. I didn't follow any church rituals or rules. I was proudly raised with a strong Jewish heritage. My Jewish grandparents immigrated from Russia in 1905, met at Ellis Island and settled in New York. My parents were non-practicing Jews who instilled the teaching of the Ten Commandments and "The Golden Rule" in their children.

I attended many churches with friends. I loved the community feel of each denomination, but due to my Jewish background, I never invited Christ into my life.

In August 1981, I married a life-long Catholic. I had a large wedding held in the Catholic Church. Our wedding date was moved up to accommodate the schedule of my maid of honor, Joanie. She was leaving the same month to join the convent to become a nun.

In December 1986, during the Christmas season, my spouse asked for a divorce. I was shattered. The divorce was granted under a Bifurcation in 1987, while the settlement agreement was not resolved for three more years.

During that time, I received a jarring call from the Catholic Diocese asking me for my payment to begin the annulment process. I responded by saying:

"I'm not Catholic. I don't want an annulment. You must have the wrong person."

How could this happen? I felt betrayed, scared, and invisible. I had to be continually strong and now had the added burden of responding to an annulment that I morally didn't believe in. It was a devastating blow to my character, my values, and my beliefs. I took my wedding vow with a pure heart.

154

I was now a single mother of a beautiful two-year-old, teaching elementary school full time while simultaneously working on a Master's degree, as well as dealing with the unresolved issues concerning my civil divorce.

The grief, the shock, and the loss of the marriage were overwhelming, yet the breaking of a Sacrament was more than I could bear. As a non-Catholic, I surprisingly felt the annulment on many levels was a deeper wound than the painful civil divorce because I took a vow before God, my husband, family, and friends in the church.

It was a challenging and emotionally exhausting experience as I agonized over composing my written response as the Respondent. I didn't have an advocate in the Catholic Church to guide me in the process.

I chose my best friend and maid of honor Joanie, who had become a Catholic nun, to provide a written response as my witness. Surely with her heartfelt input, the Diocese would not grant the annulment. So I thought.

During the tribunal panel interview, I felt a pit in my stomach as I tried to defend myself. I felt small, humiliated, and harshly judged for something I didn't initiate. I felt as though I had a large Scarlet Letter draped across my chest. I felt like a second-class citizen in the eyes of those on the panel.

No one walks down the aisle thinking their marriage will be dissolved and then nullified with an annulment. The annulment experience felt like it was the other party's agenda to be accomplished, a checklist of man-made laws, not God's intention.

In 1988, when I received the notification letter in the mail which read: ANNULMENT GRANTED, I was surprisingly overcome with a peace I had never known before. The burden was lifted. I could feel God pouring His love over me. Although it was not my desired outcome, I knew God had something better for me. He was showing me His compassion for me in the midst of my suffering.

I accepted Jesus during that difficult season when a co-worker handed me a Bible scripture on a 3" x 5" card one day on the school playground. It read:

Philippians 4:6—"Be anxious for nothing, but in everything by prayer and supplication with thanksgiving let your requests be made known to God."

My Jewish mother, Esther, proudly clapped as she sat in the front row watching me get baptized in a non-denominational church.

As we go through dark times, the pain can seem unbearable, but there is always hope. The future can be better than the past. The storms of life can make us stronger, so we can help others and be a light for them. I have more joy, gratitude, and love each day. I've gained more than I have lost.

Ruthie Murray is a retired educator who is blessed and thriving.

Tips

for marriage, death, and funerals

- Create a personal spiritual connection.
- Believe.
- Prioritize your life your way and try to live it.
- Make God/Spirit/Higher Power the center of your existence.
- Focus on relationships, work, and service.
- Do not be afraid.
- Know that risk and rewards go together.
- Love deeply and have fun.
- Trust your body, mind, and soul.
- Know that love always wins.
- Hurt goes away when you surrender.
- Be you and love yourself.
- Communicate, understand, and clarify.
- Don't compete.
- Forgive yourself and forgive others.
- Live life to the max.
- Wear bright colors and have big smiles.
- Love who you want to!

- When a loved one dies, celebrate their life.

- If you want, be creative with funerals and memorial services in non-traditional settings such as a restaurant, a garden, a beach, a clearing in a forest—a place that reflects your loved one's character.

- Include the loved one's friends, family, colleagues.

- Honor the loved one's wishes for the type of wedding, funeral, or memorial service that they want.

- If you can, ask your loved ones to write out their preferences for their memorial service or funeral.

- Take the time to talk openly and honestly about all three love adventures. You never know when it's your time to tie the knot or untie the knot.

REFLECTION QUESTIONS

Is a legacy important to you? Do you want to write a book about your life?

_____

_____

When you die or have a commitment ceremony, do you want a service? A place of worship? Outdoors? Nothing? Why? Think of your friends and family, do they need to be included, welcomed, receive closure, to have the opportunity to let go of you in a communal gathering setting?

_____

_____

What and who would you like to read, write or speak about you? Would you like something printed for your family and friends to take home or share with others? How about pictures depicting lifetime memories? Want to post or stream them? Pre-planning can be a benefit to pass on more joys and ease the pain for those left behind.

_____

_____

Is a legal marriage important? Great question! Will it affect your days after your death?

_____

_____

You may need to consider financial benefits, name changes, ease of paperwork, wills, trusts, assets, a prepaid cremation or burial plot, remembering to name your executor(s), and who you want to gift sentimental property to. Do you want a DNR (do not resuscitate)? Hospice involvement? Do you have a health care directive? Who will need to be notified? Do they, extended family and friends have your contact information, phone numbers and web addresses?

_____

_____

_____

_____

Let's talk about support. Who will be there to hug, hold or support your child(ren), your spouse or partner, your parents, and your dear friends when you live as a couple and when you die? Months later, even years later, it's strength and love mixed together. Who will be your true emotional supporter(s)?

_____

_____

Chapter 6

Hypocrisy
Please, Practice What You Preach!

Hypocrites: How to Cope and Heal

By Joanie

Hypocrisy: the practice of claiming to have moral standards or beliefs to which one's own behavior does not conform; pretense.[5]

I've been hurt by a hypocritical Catholic Church and other church preachers. I've been a hypocrite, too.

Bummer!

But there is plenty of hope and light!

I've also been healed, cured, and fed compassion numerous times along my life-long journey. It's been an AMAZING roller coaster ride of twists, turns, and exhilarating lows and highs. Even some upside-down moments! I wouldn't have it any other way, riding with my hair blowing, my eyes squinting and watering, and even my *yahoo* screams as my arms and hands flared into the air. All because it brought out the best and better ME.

I am wonderfully made and made in the image of God.

You are, too! Yes, you can be cured as well!

Let's start with the positive life lessons I've learned.

The opposite of hypocrisy is walking the walk and talking the talk. One step, one leap turned into scouring over walls, ducking around and under rocks and climbing mountains, all in the name of soul truth with my God. It took courage, honesty, faith and perseverance to admit my failings and to accept and forgive the huge failings of the church and church people.

Who are hypocrites?

Sit, think about, and pray as you name the churches, denominations and specific people, especially those ministerial leaders who preach beautiful homilies but live a life of "sin" or contradiction. *Absolutely disgusting.*

Let's be real, hypocrites come in all sizes, shapes, ages, and religious affiliations; they are the trusted leaders who molest children, rape, squander money, cheat the poor, steal money, claim land for greed, and betray trust.

They embezzle funds, deflate people's self-worth, gossip and spread rumors while sitting stoically at the committee forum! This, while often hiding it from the public or hiding themselves by asking for or miraculously being transferred before they got caught!

They throw fire and damnation at LGBTQ+ people, at immigrants, at people whose skin is a different color than theirs, at those of "other" ethnicities and nationalities, all while displaying their plaques of excellence in education, theology, or counseling on their ivory-painted office walls.

I've heard preaching, written and sung, proclaiming bold and proud antisemitic messages. Hypocrites do that! I cringe with disbelief, anger, and sadness.

What places of worship or organizations "cover-up" their wrongs by pretending it's no big deal? Hypocrites do that!

Religious leaders of private institutions, schools, or non-profit entities develop policies and protocols that judge and mistreat people! Hypocrites behave with power and ego.

Discriminatory actions get buried under the carpet because there is no accountability. Hypocrites can be manipulative and make it difficult to trust others. Hypocrites can be silent killers as they stick their heads in the sand and avoid taking a stand for others!

Have you been hurt, victimized, scarred, or lied to, all in the name of a holy Church or other religious institution? What's your story?

I'm sorry if you've been hurt in any way—emotionally, physically, spiritually, or sexually. I feel your pain! The great news is, YOU CAN HEAL! If I can heal, you can, too. As I've said, I have been hurt at different times in my life by church, religion, or its people.

The biggest tip I have to share for anyone experiencing emotional pain from religious hypocrites is to recognize hypocrisy, name the hurt, write it or talk about it, forgive all involved—including yourself—and somehow get over it, forgive again, and move on. Some hurts may prompt you to choose legal action, therapy, counseling, and making amends with yourself and other individuals. Seek help or a confidant.

Scared to be me!

The Catholic Church has for centuries squashed people who are LGBTQ+. We were not seen as valuable members of a faith community. Yes, we were "accepted" as long as our sexual identity was invisible or we were celibate and not living in a committed, loving, same-sex relationship. I don't think Jesus would reject people based on who they love, and I see churches being contradictory and hypocritical.

My greatest and deepest hurt came when I was scared to be ME in my house of God where the redeemer lives. It boiled down to three main things: age-old teachings, closed-minded-ness of my local parishioners, and the demonstration of ego power, including chauvinistic priests and women leaders who felt threatened or jealous. Hypocrisy radiated from their fake-ness, and in them pretending to be higher than God. He and she would strut the church aisles and altar, dressed in their clerical robes and sashes, albs and stoles, chests pumped out and all alone without a smile or a nod to us peons in the pews. It seemed like a one-person performance.

It was a norm, an attitude of not including me, not being willing to love me unconditionally so that I could even feel safe to tell you that my true self was LGBTQ+! We worked side-by-side while serving meals and planning parish events, where I heard negative, crude, rude comments and jokes about gay people, such as, "Why don't they zip up their pants in the front like real men? The rainbow flag is a stupid way to promote divisiveness. They don't like us! How unnatural for two women—how do they even do it?"

I wanted to tell these critics who blabbed their opinions, that they were mean, sarcastic, anti-gay bigots. Yet, in the church building, you would smile and not even realize the nasty filth that your words hurt me with. You were a hypocrite. It was a cut-and-dry issue with you; it stabbed me in the heart for myself and for my LGBTQ+ friends. Never did I hear anyone stand up for me. Some people spoke one way, then turned and spoke another way. It was an upside-down, twisted turn of hypocrisy that made me scared to be the real me.

If you don't have anything good to say, don't say it.

Often in church, the unspoken words were just as hurtful to me. It was avoidance, sticking one's head in the sand, mak-ing me feel invisible. I was just a butt in the seat, a no-name, a number on my tithing envelope box that appeared on the table in the vestibule at the annual pledge time. It was the glare of my church-mates during the *Our Father* prayer when Carol and I would hold hands as lovers or at the sign of peace when I wanted so desperately to give her a lip-to-lip kiss, like the heterosexual people—married or not, husband and wife, man and woman—did in front of us did every week. Instead, we hugged.

Am I considered a hypocrite because I cannot be the real me?

I felt like a hypocrite, hiding my true self and hiding the love that God had blessed us with. I knew God was bigger than church and yet being stifled by church practices and customs hurt my insides so badly. Did the church realize they were being hypocritical by believing and teaching that love was confined to a man and a woman? *How narrow, ridiculous, and limiting!*

Oh, the tears would flow as I sat on the hard pew, bent over, my palms open, with the communion of Jesus's body traveling from the top of my head through every cell and down to my little toe. I knew without a doubt that God loved me, but I knew that the church as an institution disowned me. What a contradiction! It was not a synchronized walk and talk; it was God versus Church in my mind.

It hurt so deeply! Yet I was not bold enough to speak up. I convinced myself, *it's only an hour a week.* I can tolerate this. I can sit and be with Jesus, and not worry about the people around me called community; there was no COMMON or UNITY.

Carol's faith, stronger than steel and diamonds put together, assured herself and me that all was well today during this ritual Saturday night. Carol and I were comforted in prayer by knowing that God blesses us and always takes care of us.

Forgiving Myself

Every week, members of many Christian faiths say aloud every week: "Forgive me for the things I've done and forgive me for the things left undone."

I asked Jesus to forgive me for the times I was a fake. I attended weekly Catholic mass, received communion, and was an adult living a beautiful loving intimate sexual relationship with Carol, a same-sex union. According to the Catholic Church teachings, I was a sinner, a hypocrite in their eyes. I thought I could do all three: love Carol, love Jesus, and love the Catholic Church.

After five years as a nun, Jesus called me to leave the convent, release my vows or promises, and to serve others by being more worldly while loving Carol and Jesus with all my heart and soul. Here's the part where my hypocrisy was hidden. I did not speak up publicly within my church or within my community about my monogamous commitment with my same-sex life partner. I lived two lives. I prayed, *"Do I need to proclaim my LGBTQ+ status while heterosexual people don't?"*

However, internal healing came after discerning that this was not the time to speak OUT. In the 1980s and even today, it is not always wise or safe to expose one's sexual identity. Follow your heart to know when, where, and with whom you come out! You know best!

Through major gut-wrenching discernment to hear God's will, my answer shouted from my and Jesus's eyes: "I was really not being a hypocrite!" I, 100-plus percent, devoted my life to Carol and she to me, not to the church. Jesus made it extremely clear that Carol and I were formed together for a bigger purpose, to spread joy and peace in both a human and divine way. We were God's messengers, angels on earth, and that by our actions and examples, all would be well for our world and for us. We would constantly invite people to our home for breakfast, lunch or dinner, for games and for visiting. We valued quality time with people, laughing, talking, telling stories and dreaming of adventures to be held by the grace of God.

Our hope that something great would eventually come our way said, "Yes, so just hold on!"

Our victory happened in God's time . . . the Episcopal church wanted us! They accepted us as LGBTQ+, celebrated us, and believed in same-sex and trans marriages. We had found an institution, a priest, and a community that naturally walked the walk and talked the talk, alongside us. They served others as a priority, not as a fundraising event.

It felt freeing and AMAZING! We had moved on after waiting long enough! It was pure JOY, a healthy cure, when we were married in the open arms of the Episcopal Church! There was nothing fake or pretending about this proclamation.

The Episcopal Church is not hypocritical! Yahoo!

Does the Catholic Church see itself as a hypocrite regarding same-sex marriage?

I think love is meant to be shared.

Did the Catholic Church realize that they lost two beautiful, prayerful servant leaders named Carol and Joanie? Maybe others, too.

How many same-sex relationships have been forced out of their religion or faith community? Who do you know that has broken the chains to find paradise in a welcoming home community?

So, what is healing and being cured really all about?

I think it's about feeling and being welcomed! Unconditionally!

If I drove or flew to your house and appeared on your doorstep today, in a totally unexpected visit, what would you do? How would you respond? Would you greet me with smiles, joy, and happiness? Or would you be a hypocrite and pretend you are happy to see me? Tolerating me with a fake smile? It's your choice.

I'll know your answer in a millisecond by watching your face! I'm a very spontaneous, joyful person and love to surprise people! When I lived in the state of Washington, my family was 1200 miles away. With my younger sister Terri's help, we concocted a way for us to surprise my parents with my unexpected spring visit. I had goosebumps for days leading up to pulling this off. Ter picked me up at Lindbergh Field, the San Diego International Airport, and we immediately drove to my parents' home on New Jersey Street. Jumping out of her Jetta Volkswagen, named "Ter's jet," she grabbed the cupcake pan she was returning to Mom as our reason for stopping by.

The beautiful afternoon sunshine and warmth tickled my face. We bounced up the two maroon-painted, cement stairs of their Spanish-style home to the screen door. We smiled at each other, then Ter pulled open the screen door, and said, "Hi Mom and Dad, just here to return your cupcake pans." I followed behind her, nonchalantly, sauntering in the door and stood there in silence, as she hightailed through the living room, pretending to go to the kitchen.

Mom watched Ter bolt through the living room, and with a blank expression turned to see who was with her.

"Hi Mom!" I cheered, so loud and strong that Dad heard me while he was sitting in his recliner.

"Oh, Joanie," Mom exclaimed. "Oh, Joanie, it's you! You are here! What a surprise! Hi honey! What are you doing here?"

We hugged and twirled; she squeezed the sides of my cheeks and gazed into my tear-filled eyes and said, "You are here!"

Wow! Wow! Wow!

"Yes, Mom! I wanted to surprise you for Easter! I just wanted to be with you!"

She was stunned, I was in glory land, and she wondered if she was seeing a ghost. She stared at me, eyeball to eyeball, and she probably wondered, *Is this for real or am I dreaming?* Her profound love for me beamed from her face like a burst of sun rays at sunrise.

Dad jumped out of his recliner, with smiles bigger than the universe. "Joanie! Joanie, is it you?!"

"Yes, it's me, Dad. Hi! Surprise!"

We hugged tight and close! Ter, standing in the dining room, never made it to the kitchen, was crying, laughing, and loving this surprise moment!

Mom, in her large-framed glasses, reached for my hand. It was lovely! Our hands fit together like a glove! The welcome was a magnificent delight, an overflowing of love! No fakeness or pretending.

The welcome by my retired parents was beyond my wildest dreams! It was a dance celebration welcoming me with their whole beings and I could hear the Disney electric light parade joy filled melody playing in my thoughts. I felt so weak, yet so, so, so jubilant! Hap . . . py!

It was my honor to be reunited in their presence. I happily welcomed them as they had welcomed me. By the way, it was my first time seeing my parents since I had told them over the phone that "I am gay." Yahoo, yippee, a bonus!

Imagine if we could greet people in our faith communities with this much joy and love! This feeling was a stark contrast to the hypocrisy and fakeness that I had experienced in religious settings.

That celebratory moment with family set the standard for the love and warmth that I share with people whom I meet during my travels promoting *Nun Better* and *Joyously Free.* I share smiles, hugs, comfort, and blessings with people—especially those who share their religious hurts with me. Please be that change you wish to see in the world, by opening your arms and heart to others to provide the love and comfort that you may have once yearned for. Together we can all help each other heal to find peace and love.

In my living room prayer corner stands a six-foot tall oak bookcase with shelves loaded with Mother Nature's wonders: sand dollars, rocks, stones, gems, sea shells, pieces of wood, figurines, and pretty colored glass. Two framed artworks showcase peace and love. One is a wooden 5" x 5" block with a picture of a gray-blue ocean, cloudy white sky, and ocean waves gently splashing into the rock cliffs with the caption "Trust in the Lord with all your Heart" from Proverbs 3:5.

Beneath it at eye level is a golden frame holding a piece of paper from Carol's journaling days with her favorite Trinity person, the Holy Spirit. In her bold hand-printed ink she declares, **"and Jesus went home. You can imagine the expression on the faces of the people in that house when he opened the door. And how about your house, when you . . . walk in?"**

Contemplate that one! See where the spirit takes you.

Guitar music healed us

When Carol and I played guitars as liturgists at church for 25 years, I had these similar welcoming feelings at every mass. I loved that the songs were love prayers and spoke of God, Jesus, and the Holy Spirit. That was my way of coping with the hurt and the hypocrisy! Music is a place beyond hypocrisy!

The lyrics brushed aside the strict catechism, rules, and regulations that were the hypocritical causes of hurt, the behind-the-scenes causes of the unwelcome feeling. At mass, I tuned in to the God moment, not the structure of an institution that I disagreed with and saw as hypocritical on many issues. I believe that it is hypocritical that only men can become priests, only males make decisions for the World Church, and birth control contraceptives such as pills, condoms, and vasectomies are not approved for Catholic women or men. My view of sexual health is more encompassing, holistic, and up to the person or the people involved.

Change in the Catholic Church has been extra slow and is very frustrating. As women of the cloth—I for five years and Carol for 32 years—we experienced this firsthand. Lots of discussion that went nowhere. I hope that decisions will be made quicker to lessen the hypocrisy. I hope it makes historical new decisions to admit its contradictions. May healing come in gentle, kind and sincere ways, making faith institutions open to hearing the voices that silently scream for help. May we be open to receiving God's abundant forgiveness and spark of life as we ride the fun roller coaster of life.

Let's be careful in choosing words, to speak compliments, not condemnation. Let's get better, not bitter. Pay attention to how we greet and welcome others at the door, in an email, or in a text. Let's lovingly, kindly, and compassionately care more deeply, so that hearts will be turned into sparkling rainbows.

Churches have had centuries of downpour rains that have excluded people, enabled hypocrites, and separated the flock of sheep.

Carol smiled, wore bright colors, profoundly loved me in a personal and special way. God knew we needed each other, and we were part of the spreading of the kingdom. She often repeated her wise and holy words, "Joanie, change has to come from within." Her quote erased our pain and welcomed our joys.

Let us separate from hypocritical, fake, and pretending attitudes and behaviors. We are all on one roller coaster, breathing the same air and having the sunshine and moonbeams tickle our faces, as we are on the greatest ride ever, speeding towards everlasting life!

Be healed. Be cured!

Religious Hypocrisy is an Outrage
By Elizabeth

Some of the worst religious hypocrisy is sexual abuse of children by leaders who are supposed to be the most trustworthy, holy people in the world. People whom families trust. People whom their flocks admire and rely upon for spiritual sustenance.

A horrific example of this involved the Catholic Church in the United States, which for many years hid these crimes. After being exposed in the 1980s, the Catholic Church has paid four billion dollars to victims, with perhaps billions more payouts to come as more victims continue to come forward.

Somewhere between 17,000 and 19,000 people have come forward with stories of how priests raped and sexually abused them as children, traumatizing them for life. This is a terrible violation of trust and one of the most evil modern-day examples of religious hypocrisy in the United States.[67]

Shame is a Weapon

Many religions are very secretive and use the weapon of shame to keep victims silent. This is especially effective in religions where women are required to be submissive and sub-servient to men. The women must obey the husbands, fathers, brothers, and uncles. And when the women are confined to the home, prohibited from working and having their own money, totally reliant on men for food and shelter for themselves and their children, they are financially powerless to escape. They are also indoctrinated with this unfair culture from birth.

These women are also brainwashed to believe that no other men would want them because they are so deeply shamed around sex and so-called "purity." That they have lost all value along with their virginity, and therefore are "used goods" and not worthy of another man's love and financial support in marriage.

Some religions exert so much power and control over women, that they allow women to be killed if they don't follow the rules, especially regarding relations with men and specifically around sex.

If you Google "honor killings," you'll immediately see pictures of faces, mostly female, and names of girls and women who were killed because they disobeyed the rules that girls are expected to follow. Oftentimes, the girl or woman's own father or male family members killed her and were acquitted of any crimes!

You can read stories of "honor killings" from a list of stories in *The New York Post* at this link: https://nypost.com/tag/honor-killings/. The stories are deeply disturbing.

Killing people in the name of religion and/or the cultural norms that are inspired by religion has been, unfortunately, a historic nightmare for centuries. In fact, the Catholic Church led the Spanish Inquisition that started in the 12th century, killing estimates that range from 300,000 people to millions of people, according to some historians.[8] The Inquisition aimed to punish Jewish and Muslim people, as well as people accused of heresy, which is a belief or opinion that contradicts doctrine from orthodox religions, especially Christianity. The Inquisition used torture to make people confess to heresy.

Similarly, the 19 terrorists who carried out the September 11, 2001, attack in New York City expressed a belief that their religion justified their crimes and that they would be rewarded in heaven for hijacking airplanes, crashing into the Twin Towers in New York City, the Pentagon, and a field in Pennsylvania, killing 2,996 people.

Similarly, some churches are guilty of financial fraud. In 1999, the Baptist Foundation of Arizona, which was a charity affiliated with a church, was caught in a fraud scheme in which a respected pastor and his son, among other leaders, bamboozled congregants in financial schemes that totaled $460 million.[9]

All of the above are crimes, so these stories stand alone as tragic.

Hypocrisy Erodes our Trust in Religion

Once we witness religious hypocrisy, or worse, become a personal victim of it, how do we stop that anger and disappointment from clouding or stopping our ability to find peace and love with God outside the man-made rules of religion?

When we equate our connection to Spirit with whatever a deceptive and/or secretly criminal human has told us, and that human now has no credibility due to their scurrilous and even illegal behavior, how can we clearly and confidently free our minds and hearts from that confusion and step forward into our best spiritual life? One that's free and clear of human foibles and provides a clear, joyous connection to the divine energies that are within and around us, ready to comfort and guide us 24/7?

In order to clean the house, we need to see the dirt. So let's get a clear understanding of what's happened to you and/or what examples of religious hypocrisy have tainted or blocked your ability to connect with Spirit. Writing is a powerful tool for self-exploration that leads to healing and releasing any kind of disappointment and trauma.

These leaders are supposed to practice what they preach about living a pure, godly life. They're telling dozens, hundreds, thousands, and even millions of people how to think, act, live, love, work, and play. They tell us to follow the rules of the religious doctrine that they teach, but what they're doing behind closed doors may be quite the opposite.

Having adulterous affairs. Paying for sex. Using drugs. Embezzling money. Using money from struggling churchgoers to live an opulent lifestyle. Beating their wives and/or kids. Espousing hate toward people who are different religions, ethnicities, or nationalities, or people who are LGBTQ+.

This is an outrage! When these stories are exposed, they tarnish the credibility of all religious leaders, because they cast a tinge of suspicion over all the others who may be totally ethical and integrous.

Some of the most highly publicized examples of this relate to homophobic religious leaders. He who shouts loudest may be the most guilty.

We've seen many examples of when the preacher who rants loudly every Sunday in the pulpit about "the homosexual agenda" gets caught in a gay sex scandal . . . because despite the picture-perfect female wife and kids . . . and adamant declarations of being "heterosexual," he's exposed for having sex with men in his office and in hotel rooms . . . or worse, for molesting boys.

The many highly publicized cases of this phenomenon include male religious leaders who are engaging in sex with men behind closed doors. Several high-profile scandals have demonstrated this profound hypocrisy.

For example, America's once-top evangelical pastor, Ted Haggard, who founded a mega-church and who publicly condemned same-sex marriage, sparked a scandal after admitting that he had paid a male prostitute for gay sex. And a young man from the church revealed an ongoing, consensual relationship that was sexual. This story was told by HBO in 2009 in *The Trials of Ted Haggard*.[10]

Ousted from his church, he blamed his desire for having sex with men on being molested by a man when he was a boy. Then Haggard opened another church, inviting LGBTQ+ people to join. All the while, he said he was heterosexual. Throughout the scandal, his wife stood at his side.[11]

His story is among many others about religious leaders who condemn gay people publicly but engage in same-sex relations behind closed doors. This is extremely hypocritical and emphasizes the old saying that people who live in glass houses shouldn't throw stones.

Our mission is to find love and peace with God by establishing personal relationships with Spirit that do not rely upon humans and their foibles that are sometimes criminal, to taint our spiritual experiences. And when we do decide to partake of organized religion, we carefully vet the leaders and the organization to ensure that our intuition is giving the green light that this is a safe, trustworthy person and place of worship. Should anyone demonstrate evidence that suggests otherwise, then we have the power to go elsewhere.

What examples of religious hypocrisy in the news and/or in your community have tainted or blocked your ability to connect with Spirit?

REFLECTION QUESTIONS

How does religious hypocrisy make you feel?

_____

_____

Now that you have a clear understanding of religious hurts that you want to heal and release, it's time to clearly define what peace and love with Spirit and/or God looks like to you. Describe the type of relationship you'd like to have with Spirit and/or God.

_____

_____

If you are atheist or agnostic, describe this experience from your Higher Self, which is the essence of your truth, your intuition, and the greatest potential of your heart and mind.

_____

_____

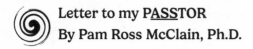

Letter to my P<u>ASS</u>TOR
By Pam Ross McClain, Ph.D.

Dear P**ASS**TOR,

My heart aches as I write this letter to relinquish my church membership. Over the years, I have become estranged from our church under your pastoral leadership. I have witnessed and experienced unChristian behaviors and toxic attitudes that deeply contradict the teachings of love that should guide us as children of God.

You wage war from the pulpit. You use your pulpit as a bullying platform and regularly throw jabs at your critics. Your chauvinistic, misogynistic, and homophobic teachings have caused pain and division among us. The empty pews should alert you that you've alienated many who sought solace and acceptance within our church family.

You often weaponize God's teachings. You distort the word of God by preaching self-righteousness and judgementalism. Added to that, your preaching undermines empathy, inclusivity, and human decency, which are fundamental principles in leading a community of faith. Your words and actions have contributed to the marginalization and invisibilization of vulnerable groups within our congregation.

I am a cisgender woman and while I am not the object of your homophobic rhetoric which perpetuates discrimination, I can no longer subject myself to a leadership that brazenly exhibits malformed attitudes and behaviors.

My faith is stronger than ever, but my place within this church community has become untenable. I pray for a future where our church can truly embody the principles of love, acceptance, and equality for all. There is no place for hate in church.

With a heavy heart but a hopeful spirit,
Peace out!
P.S.
I wrote a haiku just for you:

Seek First Kingdom of God
A Haiku by Pam Ross McClain, Ph.D.

Satan's handiwork
Left a stench in God's temple
I left to seek God

Dr. Pam Ross McClain is a career educator and community builder who wants to advance a new research tradition—vulgar scholarship—which will resonate truth and speak to the sensibilities of everyday people. She can be reached at prossmcclain@ umich.edu.

Healing Through Love and Acceptance
By Jill Prioreschi

My German/Irish mother was born in 1941, raised Roman Catholic in Cincinnati, Ohio, and attended a Catholic high school. My Italian father was born in 1937, raised Roman Catholic in Cleveland, Ohio, and did not attend a high school, but went to trade school instead.

My parents were sanctioned in holy matrimony in Cleveland in 1959 and later moved our family out west to California in 1967. A short while later, my very Catholic grandparents on my mother's side followed us out to California. This laid the foundation for my baptism and first communion in the Catholic Church before I knew any better. Then came Confraternity of Christian Doctrine (CCD or otherwise known as Catechism) classes that then lead to my confirmation in the Catholic Church.

Church, when I was little, was fun at times; there was a family that played guitars and bongo drums which made the nine o'clock mass a fun event with lots of singing. I especially liked the song lyrics, "Amen! Hallelujah! Amen! Hallelujah! Amen! Amen! Amen!"

When I had a hard time sitting still in church, my mother would tell me to hold out my hand, so I would stretch out my palm as far as I could open it, and my mom would lightly tickle the palm of my hand, running circles over it. This calmed me to the core and enabled me to sit through the very long stories.

I barely remember my father attending church; he did, but it seemed like he wasn't there all that much. On the other hand, my grandmother was a fixture in church and always had her special seat in the front row. We didn't always sit with her, but we always saw her there.

Somewhere in between my first communion and confirmation, my parents divorced. So, at age 10, after the divorce, was the first time I questioned the Catholic Church's rules. My mother could no longer receive the holy Eucharist (communion) for divorcing my father and was no longer accepted in the church because of the sin of her divorce. She could still attend, but she could no longer participate in the rituals.

As a child, I bore witness to my father striking my mother, and to the bruises she tried to cover up with makeup as she went to work. My mother was a very strong-willed person and even though my father tried to emotionally and physically break her down, she always kept us children safe and out of harm's way from him. He was an alcoholic, and she became the punching bag.

My patriarchal father believed and stated out loud that "women were meant to be docile and obedient, and barefoot and pregnant." He would recite things out loud over and over in a kind of joking yet preacher-like manner. I didn't find any of it funny back then, and only the men in our family seemed to find him amusing. He was a character for sure, and I have truly never met any other father quite like him.

Yes, I felt cursed from a very young age. One night while I was sleeping over at my grandparents' house, my mother came barging in, saying she was "leaving your father for good." This was one of the happiest days of my life, and I was absolutely thrilled for the divorce and to escape the monster that made our lives so miserable.

Later, after the divorce, when it came time to go back to church, my mother explained that she could no longer partake in the communion because of the divorce being a sin. She then tried to make me walk down the long aisle and take the communion without her. Well, this made absolutely no sense to my 10-year-old brain.

So, I began to despise the Catholic Church and its dumb rules. I started kicking and screaming: "I don't want to go to church! It makes no sense!"

Questioning myself in my head, I wondered why would they (the church) force her to be with him when she is being beaten? Why would they force her to be with someone who was so mean to her? It was all too much for this little kid and nobody really explained anything in enough detail back then. We were just told to do things, and we did what we were told. Inside, I was not happy about any of it, and built a deep resentment because it did not make sense to me.

Despite my feelings regarding the church as a child, in my early teens I attended CCD classes and continued on to make my confirmation, taking on my mother's middle name as my confirmation name.

My mother had remarried but was not allowed to remarry in the Catholic Church, so her second marriage was sanctioned in a Methodist Church. She married a wonderful man who showed me that men were not all bad. He turned out to be a great male figure in my life who really showed up for me as a father.

My mother also had a son with my stepdad, and to her, this meant that God had blessed her decisions and her new marriage by the birth of what my older brother and I refer to as "the love child."

One of the last times my mother received communion was at her mother's funeral in 1994. She was so riddled with guilt from not receiving it at her father's funeral 15 years prior that her brother supposedly had a conversation with the priest about it. Her brother assured my mother that it was okay for her to receive it. However, to this day, she's not so sure her clever brother actually talked to the priest about it.

After my confirmation, the only time I willingly stepped foot into a Catholic Church was at my grandparents' funerals, and my grandmother's funeral was the last time I remember receiving communion in a Catholic Church. I received it from my grandmother's favorite longtime priest who actually reeked of alcohol while he handed me the bread disc representing the body of Christ. This left me with a bad taste in my mouth for my beloved grandmother, and it was another bad experience within the walls of a Catholic Church.

In my later teens, in 1982, I had my first romantic encounter with a woman. I had always known I was a bit different from other girls my age but could never quite put my finger on what made me so. This woman turned on a light bulb inside of me and made everything seem so true and clear within me.

I was so very happy to finally find the truth in myself, but was also extremely petrified. I knew my mother would never understand me and would blame this woman for converting me. Although my mother was no longer very active in church, Catholicism played a huge role in my fear because I knew it was still ingrained within her deep-rooted Catholic ways.

We struggled for years after she found out. She believed that because "my first" was a woman, that is all I would know. So, I distanced myself and went into the "closet" and did not share things with my dear mom whom I had loved with all my heart because of all that we had endured together. Yep, I went into the deep dark closet, and in 1984 I decided to join the U.S. Army.

I hid from myself, and even dated men to "try the other side" for my mother's sake and her Catholic ways. This was the most painful part, and this gave me more reason to despise the Catholic Church and its deep-rooted judgment on my life.

As a result of all of this judgment, guilt, and rules, I lost faith in church and religion. I decided instead to pursue my own made-up church in nature and the universe because nature was magnificent! That way I knew my God was with me everywhere

I went and He was with me without judgment. Yes, I still prayed; I have always prayed. I believe in a Higher Power, and I feel that God is within all of us, regardless of religion.

After many years of hiding my true self, in 1991 I had a girlfriend who put pressure on me and basically forced me out of the closet at work, with my family, and with my friends. This got crazy for me, but it forced everyone to finally look at my life and accept me for who I am. This included my mother who had many years of looking the other way or sticking her head in the sand.

As I boldly stepped completely out of the closet, my mother and I went through a full year of not talking to one another. This was very painful for me, and for her. The girlfriend was not right for me, but she pulled the scab off for all of us and forced us to deal with the very large elephant in the room. The girlfriend was a steppingstone to a bigger picture, and I thank her for pushing me out, but I really give thanks to TV shows like *Donahue* and *Oprah* for shedding light on interviews with gays and lesbians and their families back in the 90s.

Once we started talking again, my mother intently watched those shows and read books that I gave her on the subject. My mother and I put in a lot of hard work together, and with time, I sure feel I was one of the lucky ones, because my mother always loved me, gave an effort for me, and never gave up. She recalls a particular *Donahue* episode that really spoke to her; in it, the father of a lesbian stated, "She is my daughter; I will always love my daughter, no matter what." And that is how we got through everything at the time.

Being a lesbian was another thing that the Catholic Church obviously frowned upon, but at that point, I really didn't care any longer about Catholicism. I did attend an Episcopalian lesbian wedding once, and I thought that that was cool and very accepting, but I still did not pursue the church setting.

So, staying true to the church of nature and the universe, I married my wife in 2013 in a circle of friends outside on Goleta Beach in Santa Barbara County with my mother and stepfather on FaceTime. We were married by our dear friend who became a minister or justice of the peace, and who married us without church walls, church rules, or church rituals.

My wife believes in more eastern spiritual philosophies like Taoism, and yet also considers herself a nature worshiper like me. Atheism has never really appealed to either of us, as we both believe in reincarnation. Purgatory is another thing that never made sense to either of us.

Fast forward to 2024 . . . I have been happily married to my wife for 28 years (legally married for 11 years). We moved to Brookings, Oregon, in 2017.

My stepfather and my mother moved in with us in 2018 and lived with us in our basement until my stepfather passed away in 2019. After my stepdad's passing, my mother decided to go back to the Catholic Church! Well, okay, let's see how that goes for you, Mom. She then found out that she can receive communion again if she went to confession, and that it is okay now. Go figure!

My mother still has a lot of guilt about receiving it because she has been told it is wrong for over 44 years! So, she was 78 years old then, she walked with a cane, and she returned to the Catholic Church. She regularly went and no one really talked to her, no one embraced her or welcomed her. She even tried going to coffee afterward, and she sat there alone, while others sat with their friends at other tables. Still, no one reached out to her.

She would go, and the church would ask for money for the general fund, and then for the building fund. My mother is hard of hearing, and she has trouble understanding the priest because he is from another country and has a very thick accent. All of these things were not making my mother's church experience very enjoyable. And so, she would sit there and pray independently for three long years.

In May of 2023, I was so grateful to have met Joanie Lindenmeyer while playing pickleball at our local high school gym. I had heard, through a friend, that she had written a book called *Nun Better*. I was able to purchase the book from her that day at the gym. I was purchasing it for Mother's Day and asked Joanie to autograph it for my mom. I was completely unsure how my mother would receive the content of the book, so I took a leap of faith and did not read it before I gave it to her. Well, my mother loved the book and exclaimed that she is "pretty open when it comes to reading real life stories." She also said that she "related to Carol" in the story.

After reading and loving the book too, my mother and I had some follow-up questions for Joanie, specifically regarding communion. Joanie graciously gave of her time and called us to answer any questions we had. My mother then told Joanie about her experience with the local Catholic Church and how it was "not fulfilling" to her and that it felt "cold and non-inclusive to newcomers" and that she just didn't feel "moved anymore." Joanie had recently joined St. Timothy's Episcopal Church and suggested my mother also try it out. She then mentioned that Father Bernie gives a marvelous sermon, and that it is very similar to the Catholic Church. So, we tried it. I went for moral support for Mom.

Enter Father Bernie! A guy who makes you smile! Mom and I showed up at 10 AM for Sunday mass. Joanie was out of town that day, but Father Bernie saw that we were new faces in the crowd. He zeroed in on us straight away.

"Welcome," he said, and proceeded to get to know us by asking us, "What brings you here today?"

He took us under his wing before, during, and after the sermon. It was a unique experience for sure. He said we could receive communion if we wanted, that the church service was very open in most ways and that "all people are welcome here."

My mother explained that she was from the Catholic Church, and I said, "Yep, and they don't like my kind," referring to the Catholics, and then Father Bernie said again, "All are welcome here." He then opened up his arms and his heart and proceeded to give me a huge hug that brought tears to my eyes and that I felt to my core. We then smiled and laughed.

The people in the church were very welcoming and inclusive, and the sermon was relatable and enjoyable. It brought up community issues, and we all said prayers for people in need. It felt a little like when I enjoyed church as a child. Then came time for communion. My mother got in line, and I stayed in the pew. A lady came up to me and said, "You could just go up and get blessed if you don't want to receive communion."

So, I thought, *okay I'll just be blessed.* So, I caught up to my mother and we proceeded to the altar. I kneeled and Mom stood. Father Bernie came to me first and offered communion, and I said out loud, "You could just bless me." Father Bernie then said, "Now Jill, I was so hoping to be the first one to give you the holy Eucharist in a very long time." So I stuck out my tongue and proceeded to take communion.

Then my mom took it. Next came the wine. I took a sip of that, too, and so did Mom. We crossed ourselves and walked back to our pew, sat down, looked at one another, cried, and hugged.

This felt like full-circle healing inside, and it flooded me with my childhood memories with Mom in church. I could hear in my head the sound of guitars and bongo drums playing, "Amen! Hallelujah! Amen! Hallelujah! Amen! Amen! Amen!" and I could feel the fun that it used to be.

After mass, Father Bernie gave us a tour of the whole church, including the garden. It's a small church that does very big things for a lot of people. I felt nothing but pure love and joy after everything that special day and I thank you, Mom, Father Bernie, Joanie, and thank you God for this healing of our hearts through Jesus and communion.

My mother is now 81 and currently loving church again at St. Timothy's, and she even watches it online when her back and leg pain flares up. She loves people and feels excited about having a community connection again, and that makes me very happy for her.

For me, I am back to the church of nature and will go to St. Timothy's on occasion. It is just nice to know that there is a place that I can go to worship, if I want to, a place that puts love first and accepts people like me and my mother without any judgment.

Jill Prioreschi loves to play, laugh, dance and swim in nature and in sport.

Tips

- Identify examples of religious hypocrisy. Journal about how this makes you feel.

- Release anger about religious hypocrisy through healthy outlets such as exercise, walking in nature, getting therapy, and talking with trusted people.

- Should you speak up when you witness religious hypocrisy? When?

- If you witness religious hypocrisy that is breaking the law, contact authorities in a way that puts safety first for you, your family, and the victim(s).

- Be strong in character.

Chapter 7

Forgiveness
How to Forgive Religious Hurts

A Deathbed Request for Forgiveness
By Joanie

The afternoon had turned to evening in a quick snap of the fingers. Carol was laying on her single mattress covered with her electric blanket, in an extra long hospital bed in our home's master bedroom. The room we had remodeled and converted into her sanctuary before death would take her away and turn her into a heavenly angel.

She was already an angel in my mind and heart. The kindest, most loving person I had ever met and the only woman I had ever loved with my whole body and soul, for 40 years.

Here, all of a sudden, she lay sobbing as I heard her from the kitchen where I was cleaning up, stacking the dishwasher and wishing she was able to stand and do this simple daily chore together with me. But I knew, no longer was this our way. We had a new way of living and loving and the days were numbered, but we forgot how to count. It was now about God moments, not minutes, hours, or days.

Every moment was special, every look in her eyes was PRECIOUS! She lay more motionless every day since she and I had chosen to agree with the hospice program to have her come home from a care facility for the last time.

Oh the sobs, the wails got louder, then, "Joanie, Joanie come be with me . . . I need you."

So I stopped everything and hastily walked to her bedside. I rolled her wheeled table out of the way. Her eyes looked so, so, so sad. I knew it wasn't physical pain bothering her, but something more. I bent over, wrapped her in my arms, putting my face on her cheek, tasting her salty tears that had streamed down to soak her flaming Valentine's red nightgown that covered her chest and torso.

"What's wrong, Carol?"

"Joanie, I'm so sorry. I'm so sorry. I'm so sorry. Please forgive me."

"What sweetie? Of course I forgive you!"

Not having a clue what she was thinking and why my emotionally strong lover was so upset. We hadn't had any secrets!

"You've worked so hard, doing extra things for us to have money! To pay our bills, to buy the extra things I've needed since my stroke. You've done so much for me, for us! Do you remember that man we loaned $2,000 to?"

She paused and her sobs began again. This was so unlike Carol. She was not a crier. She had always left that up to me, saying, "You have enough tears for both of us."

"Yes, I remember."

"He never paid us back! I feel so bad! Please forgive me for having us loan the money to him! It was my fault!"

Oh, the tears flooded! The dam had spilled every drop of water from her pool! From both of us. She was so remorseful. She was in agony from the inside out.

I never knew this was something that she held on to! Out of all the things in the world, here she was, dying, and she wanted to make amends with me and her God about being gracious to someone who took us to the cleaners. OMG!

I laid my body from waist up, on top of her as much as I could without hurting her. Carol was so fragile and had lost 80 pounds in the last 60 days. I kissed her over and over, on her lips, her cheeks, her arms, her hands, and her eyes. Those gorgeous green eyes were now red and swollen. Snot was coming out of both our noses as we sniffled and snorted. She only could use her one hand to blow her nose and she was not going to let go of my hand to do that. So I, like I'd done for the last eight years, held the soft, fragrance-free white Kleenex to her nostrils and she blew; filling one, two, three, and many more Kleenexes. She tossed them into the blue, plastic bag-lined wastebasket, missing several and scoring a few.

"I forgive you, love!" I said. "I absolutely, totally forgive you, Carol! We both made that decision to give him the money. We gave him the loan, and we never thought he'd skip town. I feel so sorry that you've hung on to this. I'm so glad you told me, Carol. So now, we both forgive each other! Right?!"

I wiped her last bit of wet tears off her neck and face with the back of my hands, she said, "Right! Yes, thank you, Joanie! I love you so much!" Her voice quietly turned to calm and peace. She stopped crying and her brilliant smile flashed.

"I love you more, sweetie!" I said.

We gently long-kissed and gazed into the depths of each other's souls; each other's eyes offered our special view of heaven on earth! We laid there in silence and warmth, our breathing and heartbeats returning to being one rhythmic melody. Our healing on the spot!

"Let me get a warm washcloth for you, Carol. I'll be right back."

"Okay, Joanie, whatever you say!"

This was her repeated pat answer response lately, another part of her letting go and letting God be God. This was her way of letting me know that no longer did we make decisions together. She conveyed the message that, *Joanie, you will be on your own to make decisions and I will always be there for you to talk them over with me!*

I grabbed a pretty purple—her favorite color—soft washcloth from the hall closet, warmed it in the bathroom faucet, returned to her side and she confidently said, "I can do this!"

She swished it over her face, under her eyes, and over her eyebrows. The eyebrows she would tame by licking her fingers and running them over the hairs. She was so beautifully vain. Then with one hand, she positioned the washcloth, reversed its side and wiped my face, too. Oh golly! Wow, I started to cry again, enamored by her selfless love.

Time was running short and this was her chance to care for and be tender with me. We both knew the specialness that had just miraculously happened, yet had been there all along for decades.

This meltdown of asking, sharing, and granting forgiveness is the art of contrition, reconciliation, and peace! It's God's enormousness of profound love!

So, what's my tip about forgiveness?

Say sorry, forgive, say thank you, and love more!

Your turn.

Give Yourself the Gift of Forgiveness through Meditation
By Elizabeth

Forgiveness is the act of healing yourself by releasing painful feelings that were caused by something that you or someone else did. Merriam-Webster's dictionary defines the verb "to forgive" this way: "to cease to feel resentment against" an offender. Did you notice that forgiveness is an inside job? It's a shift in feelings.

Nelson Mandela once wisely said: "Resentment is like drinking poison and then hoping it will kill your enemies."

If you fail to forgive yourself or someone else, it only hurts you more, long after the offense was committed. Forgiveness is a major tenet of spirituality. In fact, *The Lord's Prayer* says, "Forgive those who trespass against us." But how? I did not understand how to truly forgive until I was 49 years old, standing at my ex-husband's bedside in the ICU while a breathing machine kept him alive.

"I forgive you," I said aloud. I was motivated by love for our son. The power of forgiveness lifted a heavy weight from my shoulders and enabled me to help my ex, and to bless our son with a fully functioning father. Plus my ex's near-death experience made him a much nicer person and we finally achieved "the harmonious resolution" that I had scripted and prayer for so many years.

I have since applied my *PowerJournal* technique of combining meditation and journaling to forgive myself and other people for things that gnawed at me with guilt and anger. For me, forgiving means releasing. Releasing bad feelings toward myself opens space for love and peace to pour in, which makes me feel and function better. Forgiveness is a gift that we give ourselves.

It has nothing to do with the other person. They don't even know that we may have spent years seething or hurting or ruminating about what they said or did, even if they had committed a terrible act. Oftentimes people such as narcissists who are so self-consumed with greed and oblivion to how their selfish ways hurt people, are unaware and totally unconcerned with how their words and actions affect other people. Even if it's criminal. So dwelling on them and wishing they would apologize or repent is pointless.

This healing is all about **you.** Period.

It's our responsibility to forgive. I'm not saying *excuse.* I'm saying release the emotional burden of dwelling on the hurts that someone caused. Forgiveness can also be applied to yourself. For example, in the past, I have forgiven myself for allowing myself to waste precious time and energy ruminating over someone else's hurtful words or actions. Journaling, meditation, and therapy are excellent ways to help expel these feelings from our minds. There is no shame in speaking with a therapist or counselor whom you trust, to help you unravel the thoughts and emotions so that you can release them and free your mind and heart of the burden of angst caused by religious hurts.

No, this is not easy. But it is possible.

So I want to guide you through an exercise called PowerJournal for Forgiveness, by combining meditation and journaling. First, let's talk about the healing of meditation.

look at the words "meditation" and "medication."

Notice how only one letter is different:

Medi-**c**-ation.

Medi-**t**-ation.

For me, these words are one and the same, and they can be for you, too. It's an honor to introduce you to the idea, or emphasize it if you already know, that meditation can heal you emotionally, physically, and even spiritually.

If something has been blocking you from healing your religious hurts, then we can clear your path with the help of my "PowerJournal for Healing with Archangel Raphael" technique.

Disclaimer: **I am not a physician.** *If you have a serious mental health condition or medical condition, please continue with your doctor's prescribed medical regimen.*

This healing experience can help unblock anything that's obstructing, delaying, or derailing your healing journey. Likewise, meditation can help you find inner peace, tap into your creative genius, sleep better, lower your blood pressure, boost your mood, connect with Spirit, and amplify your intuition.

You are about to experience my "PowerJournal for Healing with Archangel Raphael" technique that I conceived during my year-long spiritual retreat in 2013, when I empowered myself with forgiveness while healing and releasing many emotional, physical, and ancestral wounds by combining journaling and meditation, while calling upon non-denominational, all-loving Archangel Raphael.

Angels are not human and do not have genders. The most powerful angels—known as archangels, who may have gender-specific names, such as Archangel Michael—are not male or female.

Very importantly, these angels who include Archangel Raphael are all about spiritual power that is bigger than the doctrine of a single religion. They are always with you and available for you to call upon their power to protect, heal, and manifest.

You also have at least one guardian angel who has been with you since birth; you can get silent and still and ask them in your mind to reveal their name and signs of their presence in your life.

This might sound far-out if you only believe and trust what you can see, hear, touch, taste, or smell with your five physical senses. We've been programmed to live in 3-D since our souls left the higher, invisible dimensions and came into the physical world at birth. We've learned to ignore our intuition and not acknowledge that humans have supernatural powers, or that angels and spiritual beings are real.

Why? Because for centuries, the powers that be haven't wanted the masses of humanity to know that we have access to a sixth sense—the supernatural power of the Universe—to heal, receive psychic knowing and downloads, find power, and conceive innovative ways to do bold, brave things in the world. This power is also known as intuition.

In general, those institutions that lead masses of people, such as the world's major religions, want people to follow like sheep behind the "leaders" who know and use this knowledge to their advantage for power, wealth, and control—under the guise of the religious guidance and comfort that religion is supposed to provide.

You can skip to the next section if it sounds too bizarre to trust invisible forces to help change your life. But if you want to learn how to harness this power and use it to heal and thrive, then please keep reading.

The Universe is charged with infinite energy and information that we can tap into and use. This energy is invisible. It's "the force" that Obi-Wan Kenobi made mainstream in *Star Wars* movies.

Let's explore this in terms of your cell phone. You trust that it wirelessly connects you with people, information, videos, music, and so much more, from sources around the world.

These sounds and images are beaming through the air—invisibly!—all around you on energetic frequencies that match with your phone and other devices. These frequencies are being transmitted from towers that carry voices and images to your specific phone number.

All thanks to the unseen magic of electrical energy currents known as wi-fi. Wi-fi that you trust and know is there—electrifying the air!—as something we take for granted in this digital age.

You also know that all you need to tap into this magical information source is a wi-fi network and password to receive those frequencies that enable you to talk with anyone and receive any information from anywhere, 24/7!

Here's where the spiritual energy in and around our physical bodies is just like the wi-fi that powers our wireless devices. Frequencies from the Universe are pulsing through the air—and through you. Our souls, which live in and around our physical bodies, are individual starbursts of this Universe/God energy that is the pulse giving life to our human bodies.

In fact, the spark that's keeping your heart beating and your brainwaves moving is an electric current that can be measured by monitors. If you doubt what's keeping your heart beating, remember that a person suffering cardiac arrest is brought back to life with **an electric jolt** from a defibrillator.

This electricity is the starburst of God's energy inside you and it is your soul. Your soul is your true identity. Not your name, your appearance, your family's history, your education, or your job.

This soul-power current of energy in your body is connected to the energetic frequencies of the Universe all around us. We are transmission towers that can send and receive information. Have you ever thought of a friend, and they immediately texted or called you? That's not a coincidence. That's confirmation of the energetic connection that we have with each other, and the more we hone it, the stronger it becomes.

You can access this cosmic, divine source of energy and information when you connect to its frequency, just like when you turn a radio dial to receive the clearest reception of a channel.

So how do you tune in? With meditation. It's the best way to activate this power and use it for your benefit, starting with healing your religious hurts.

So, back to our healing with Archangel Raphael, who will perform powerful alchemy to transform negative emotions into peace and love. To start, take out a notebook, a journal, a laptop, or the notes app on your phone, and write on the blank line the following, along with the name of the person who caused your religious hurts. You can also fill in the appropriate information for each blank line.

PowerJournal to Forgive _____.

Date, time, location

My intention is to ask Archangel Raphael for a healing to forgive _____ for _____ so that I can replace hurt, shame, and fear with peace and love.

List reasons why you want to forgive that person. I recently listed everything for which I needed to forgive someone, then I released it in a state of peaceful prayer and with confidence that God would relieve me of this emotional burden. You can use this process to forgive yourself and any person for any offense. For example:

My Intention is to forgive my religious institution, its leader and/or its congregants for my unhappiness because they guilted me and forced me to live by their beliefs.

Another example could be, *I forgive Pastor Jones for shaming me for being gay.*

Feel grateful and confident that this healing will rid you of bad feelings toward Pastor Jones that fester as negative, toxic energy within your own mind, body, and spirit. Write: *"Thank you God that I forgave the people who caused my religious hurts"* or *"Thank you God that I forgave Pastor Jones."*

It is extremely powerful to give thanks for something before it has happened. That demonstrates your faith that you believe that God/Spirit/Higher Self will divinely orchestrate circumstances to answer your prayer, either how you request it or in an even better way.

To do this, start by taking several deep breaths. Now let's meditate to connect with Spirit for a healing with Archangel Raphael. We are going to meet them in the Upper World, a divine dimension that we reach through meditation by ascending a golden beam of light that serves as our imaginary escalator or elevator into the heavens.

If you'd rather listen to Elizabeth guiding you through this healing meditation, please use this QR code:

Meditation

Get quiet and still in a place where you will not be disturbed. Sit with your spine straight. You can also lie down, but not if you think you might fall asleep.

Close your eyes. Become aware of any tension in your body and imagine your muscles softening like warm butter. Take deep breaths to relax.

Then begin by envisioning a huge sunbeam, the kind you see shooting down from the sky through the clouds that look so majestic, especially around sunset when they glow with golden light. In your mind, call out to your spirit guide who will escort you into the spiritual dimensions.

Your spirit guide may show up as an angel, a passed-on loved one or ancestor, an ascended master such as Jesus or Yogananda, or your spirit animal, which is an animal that comes to you in spirit form to teach you characteristics that can help you.

For example, one of my spirit animals is a cheetah. It's the fastest land mammal on the planet, able to run 78 MPH, yet turn quickly while running at a high rate of speed, because its spine is more flexible than the spines of other animals. The message to me from Spirit by assigning the cheetah to escort me into the divine realm during meditation is that I move really fast through life, and am able to quickly shift directions to move from one project, such as editing and publishing a book, to another, such as coaching aspiring authors to write books, recording my podcast, traveling, and attending events. By embracing the cheetah spirit, I am empowered to accept rather than resist my life mission to be involved in many activities that require quick shifting to ensure success.

Here's an amazing benefit for you. Once you begin to learn about all the backup and insights that Spirit can bring to you when you awaken to its magic, your outlook will be enriched and expanded in ways that make life feel fascinating and that leave you in awe of the simplest moments. That is joy!

So, call out to your spirit guide to escort you into the divine dimensions for this healing, and remember that golden beam shooting down from the sky. Imagine that you, with your spirit guide at your side, are ascending this golden beam like a feather in the wind. See and feel yourself gently rising, ever so lightly, going up, up, up. You may feel a flutter in your stomach and a lightness of being. Just keep floating upward, knowing you are safe and surrounded by an army of angels.

Ponder your intention to forgive a specific person as you ascend into a higher dimension where you're free to converse with God, Spirit, angels, ancestors, divine beings, your Higher Self, and/or the wisdom of the Universe. Imagine yourself floating up this beam, safe and surrounded by pure love and peace.

As you ascend, you'll reach the lavender veil that separates the physical dimensions from the spiritual realms. This veil is similar to the layer of clouds that an airplane has to pass through as it ascends toward the infinity of sky and space. Above the veil, continue to float up. Soon you'll reach your "power spot" in the spiritual realm. This is your unique space where you're free to adjust to this experience, then journey through divine dimensions to connect with spiritual beings and learn what you need to know.

You may experience this Upper World as an enchanted forest, a mountainside, an Atlantis-type underwater wonderland, a rocky terrain, or something else. Simply observe what you hear, see, and feel. Your spirit guide will remain with you. You are safe, surrounded by a team of angels.

Next, allow your spirit-self to call to Archangel Raphael, whom you may see, feel, or simply know that they are there. God's healing angel performs healings amidst the emerald-green light of the heart chakra, which symbolizes pure love. So you may notice flashes of emerald green, or you may see a giant angel, or the outline of wings.

Express your intention to forgive your institution or the example of Pastor Jones. Archangel Raphael may take you to a particular place or lay you on a bed as if a medical procedure will be performed. Other beings may appear. My healings with Archangel Raphael sometimes include Indigenous medicine men, as well as wolves and bears. Also, during these healings that have stopped sickening migraine pain and back pain with no medication, I am suspended in the air as Archangel Raphael performs the healing.

Since the Divine communicates through metaphors, you may envision that Archangel Raphael is removing an object representing the offense for which you're seeking forgiveness. For example, if you want to forgive someone for something that has manifested as shame, Archangel Raphael may pull a slimy net from your body, symbolizing how the negative emotion had permeated your entire being. Every healing meditation with Archangel Raphael is different, depending on the nature of the ailment. Sometimes, no physical object is removed.

Archangel Raphael's healing power is all about trans-mutation. In physics class, we learned the Law of Conservation of Energy: Energy can be neither created nor destroyed. It just changes form. Well Archangel Raphael takes the energy that's hurting you and transmutes it into healing energy. This happens as the angel removes your affliction and puts it in a lavender flame that activates metaphysical alchemy. The lavender flame appears to me as a shallow gold cauldron of vibrant purple fire, similar to the one that holds the Olympic flame. It may appear differently for you.

Your ailment crackles, transforms, and shoots up from the flame in golden sparkles or an emerald-green mist, which Archangel Raphael directs back into your body as healing energy. This golden sparkling healing energy looks like the arc of gold sparks on the cover of this book. Joanie calls them "angel healing kisses."

"It is done," the angel declares, indicating that your healing is complete. Thank Archangel Raphael and listen for instructions, which could include praying, journaling, having direct commu-nication with someone, engaging in acts of gentle self-care, or something else.

Next, your spirit guide will return you to your power spot and escort you down the beam, ever so gently, like a feather in the breeze. And just like the airplane passes through the layer of clouds to land on earth, you pass through the lavender veil that separates the divine dimensions and the physical world. Float gently down, down, back to your body. Savor this deeply relaxed, peaceful state of being, and know that you can return here anytime, to seek forgiveness or to ask Spirit to provide guidance on any topic.

Now, wiggle your fingers and toes to re-acclimate to your body. After you adjust, write as many details as you remember. Use Intuitive Writing to answer more questions; this means writing in this meditative state with a clear connection to Spirit, so that you can channel messages clearly and unhindered by the fears and doubts of the thinking mind, which is calmed and quieted by meditation. I do this daily and it feels wonderful.

Remember that forgiveness doesn't mean forgetting. It's important to remember what caused the need for forgiveness; those incidents helped form who we are. We survived them. And we have the divine right to thrive! Healing and forgiving religious hurts with Archangel Raphael is one way to do that.

How to Forgive People Who Caused Religious Hurts
By Rosie Robles

Forgiveness is really hard. It's a concept that you have in your mind, but when you need to pull it forward and talk about it and do it, that's another thing.

Because sometimes we don't want to let go of what hurt us that we need to forgive, because it gives us a reason to continue to be angry and *I'll show them* type of a feeling.

I have two stories to share around forgiveness.

The first story began after I was appointed by my Archbishop to pastor to two parishes. There was no priest in those parishes, so he asked me and another sister, Lynda, if we would take on the responsibility of two parishes. Lynda and I were already working in these parishes and the parishioners loved us as the sisters who were leading trainings and doing different things with them.

But as soon as we became the Pastoral Head and our title was Parochial Minister, a lot of their feelings shifted, because we weren't priests and in the Catholic Church, a priest was traditionally the person who pastored and this was usually a man. I was one of the first few women in our church to be appointed in a pastoral role.

This was not celebrated by the people in these rural parishes. They were angry that they were assigned two women and many of them felt they were being punished because they didn't get a male priest.

Unfortunately, this situation strained the wonderful, 15-year relationship of harmonious teamwork that I had enjoyed with Lynda. We had worked well together, until we became Parochial Ministers to two parishes. Both of us have two completely different styles of ministry and they complimented each other. Unfortunately, when we were forced to blend them, it was not successful.

206

After a year, Lynda left the parish, which left me with the remainder of the six-year term that we had contracted for. Those six years were so difficult! I was appointed to be the spiritual head to make sure that the parishioners' spiritual life was fed and that I could do all I could to keep the doctrine of the church viable in their lives.

But I was at a deficit because I wasn't a priest and therefore I couldn't administer the Sacraments of the church. It was like somebody said, "I want you to build this house, but I don't want you to use a hammer or nails or anything, but I want you to build it and keep it standing. So we want you to be the Pastoral Spiritual Leader of these two parishes, but you can't do anything with the Sacraments. You can't offer the Eucharist. You can't baptize. You can't officiate weddings. You can't do any of those things, but keep the church open."

Consequently, a lot of anger and meanness were leveled at me. When I would get up to preach, about 10% of the people would walk out of the church in protest.

Even worse, I received death threats over the phone. Others said:

"Don't take this personally, sister, but we wish you weren't here."

"You're only good enough to do the linens!"

"Who do you think you are, acting like a priest?"

I would respond by saying, "I'm doing this to keep the doors open. If I weren't here, the parish would close. There is no priest available."

This continued for five and a half years. Every day I tried my hardest to be what I was supposed to be, knowing that I would never be enough. Having to deal with that 10% of parishioners who were in my face all the time, I had a slight heart attack because of the stress.

My Archbishop who appointed me, retired. A new bishop came in, who was not in favor of what I was doing.

My community pulled me out. And during that time of recuperation, I discerned that I wasn't going to die for this. I was hurt and I was angry because of the way I was treated and because the church put me in that position. I prayed about it, then opted not to reassign for another term after my six years concluded. I just couldn't do it.

The church wasn't ready for me in a ministry like that and the hurt and the pain, the anger, and feeling that I was abandoned by the church that appointed me was almost too much for me. I got sick, so I took that time off and I made the internal discernment to not return for another six years. I told the people there when I finally came back that I was not going to re-up.

The 10% who didn't like me were elated.

The 90% of parishioners who liked me had never told me that they did, until I said I was leaving. Then all of a sudden, they were saying, "You don't know what you're doing. You're doing a good job!"

I knew by the way they spoke that what I was doing was valuable and it was important. I knew in my heart that God was asking me to have a ministry, but how it was going to happen, I didn't know. What I did know was that it wasn't going to happen within the church. They weren't ready for Rosie.

I took three years off, then decided I would ask for a dispensation of my vows. I left Community after 35 years, which was the hardest thing I ever did because everything I knew and everything that defined me was in the Community. I love the Community, but for me to stay was going to restrict me from being who I really was in ministry.

I had to forgive the people in those two parishes who were so harmful to me. This led me to a scripture passage in Matthew's gospel where Jesus says to his disciples, "Whatever you bind on Earth is bound in heaven and whatever you loose on Earth is loosed in heaven."

I'm talking about what that passage said to me, because there's a difference between studying scripture and praying scripture. When you pray it, it becomes personal. Whatever the words were meant at the time, you have to ask, *What do they mean to you now?*

And so, when I came across that passage, it said to me that I have bound those parishes to be nothing more than what they always were to me. I had to let them go and loose the hurt that I had from them so that I could heal. When we hold on to anger or pain, we don't move and we don't grow and the person who hurt us doesn't change in our eyes, because we have bound them to be who they were when they hurt you.

Forgiveness is letting go with open hands and letting God take it from there. I couldn't change them. I couldn't make them love me.

When I left, I had no money. I had no job. My pension went to the Community and so it wasn't mine because the vow of poverty means you don't own. I thought, Well I had a pension from what I did, but the Community said, "No, it goes into the pot. You don't get to take it with you when you leave."

So there I was. No job. No money. No credit. I had been Sister Rosie for 35 years. They did eventually pay into Social Security for me, but during my first year teaching, I made less than $6,000 because it was just a stipend. So my Social Security was hardly anything.

So after I left the Church, I showed up in the world as if I had been born in my fifties. Someone at my bank playfully asked, "Where did you come from, lady?"

I had to build up my credit, so I was taking out credit cards to do that. I had a car that the Community gave me that was a lemon and it died. They gave me a few thousand dollars to get a new car.

People in my valley that I had been with since 1981 and ministered to as Sister Rosie—the people who loved me and validated my ministry every month—they would send me money. I wouldn't ask for it. I didn't expect it, but I would get checks in the mail that enabled me to pay my rent and pay my utilities, because I was now on my own.

For a lot of years, I marketed myself to the churches in the area because I was trained as an advocate for annulment. When I left the Church, I was in the process of helping with 40 annulments. So the priest hired me back to finish them, so I parlayed myself into a position. Then a new priest came in and was threatened by me and he fired me, so I had nothing. That was another hurt that I had to let go of.

Then hospice found me.

"We know who you are," they said, because as Sister Rosie and as a minister, I had done a lot of funerals. "We need a chaplain. Come in for an interview."

I did.

The woman who interviewed me said, "I'm not even putting this out for anybody. You got the job."

This gave me financial security because I was bringing in a paycheck and I had benefits, thank God!

I also got married to my beloved husband, Ron. In retrospect, my husband saved me. While working in hospice, I learned a lot about myself and about God in that process while dealing with death and your mortality. It taught me:

"Rosie, don't hang on to the things that hurt you or to the people who hurt you. Let it go. God cannot force a gift into a clenched fist."

I once heard the phenomenal actress Meryl Streep say something that I'll paraphrase: *I'm at this time in my life where I want to let go of people and events that bring me down. I don't need them. I want to surround myself with positive things that encourage me and foster my personal growth. I have just decided to let go of people and events that no longer foster my peace.*

That spoke to me.

"That's it," I said. "I'm 78 years old. I'm on the downside of life. I don't want to go around with this sitting in my chest."

It includes a lot of hurts that I've incurred in my position as a woman in ministry. But since I left and affiliated with the Federation of Christian Ministry, they endorsed me as chaplain, thanks to my background and my education.

That endorsement enables me to witness marriages, officiate funerals, and perform Christian baptisms. I remain spiritual director to some and the church cannot interfere. Everything I do has a spiritual overtone. I've officiated hundreds of weddings and more than 400 funerals. I can share my faith and I can help people who are not affiliated with the mainline church to find God.

I don't have somebody standing over me saying, "Thou shalt not! You can't do that! You're a woman!"

Yes, I can and yes, I do and yes, I will!

❦

My second example for the need to forgive religious hurts involved two priests who abused me. Their behavior was especially hurtful because it contradicted holy behavior, plus I was young and I had no recourse. Who would listen to me? These guys were prominent and far superior to me in position. And yet for some reason, they felt entitled to make me their personal property. They were extremely inappropriate with me.

Their behavior violated my vow of chastity. I knew that it wasn't something that I enjoyed or wanted, so I didn't feel that I had done anything to tarnish that vow. I was intelligent enough to understand the concept of abuse and that it was outside of my control and the only way I could deal with it was to leave the situation.

One night, I drove away from the retreat house in the dark in my little VW Rabbit. I left. I didn't even say goodbye. I just left.

I moved on to another ministry. But the abuse stayed in my heart for years and years and years. When the Me, Too movement happened, I realized that I was a Me, Too—I also was a woman who had been abused.

Before that, my lawyer, John, who had become a very special person in my life, was providing legal services for women who had been physically and sexually abused by priests. For many of them, the abuse happened when they were young girls.

John asked me if I would serve as the spiritual director for these women. So I worked with them spiritually to help them heal and in doing that, a lot of my own feelings were coming up. I shared what had happened to me and they could relate to me as a counselor, because I knew what they were feeling.

At the same time, John was advocating for them financially and getting some kind of retribution. So in that process, John and I helped a lot of women. He became very disenchanted with the Church because their lawyers were trying to get out of it, accusing the victims of being responsible for the abuse. This was ridiculous because the abuse happened to innocent children.

I was able to help the women, but opened the emotional wound that I had from the abuse. So I wrote a letter. I wanted to contact the two priests to get some resolution. I found out that both of them were deceased, but I noticed on the roster of pedophiles that one of them was on the list, but the other one wasn't.

I contacted a priest friend of mine who had become a Bishop. We had done retreats together and I respected him. I was going to mail the letter to him, but I wanted to talk. So I found his phone number and I called and left a message, saying, "You may not remember me, but I'm Sister Rosie who worked with you at The Retreat House."

He called within 20 minutes. He was retired and said, "Yes, I do remember you, Rosie, how good to talk to you!"

I told him about the abuse by those two priests.

And he said, "On behalf of the church, I apologize to you."

That was all I needed!

I didn't want money.

Although I could have used it. It could have paid for the counseling that I had financed to deal with this pain.

My lawyer informed me that there was a fund with at least $10,000 to compensate victims of abuse by priests.

"I'm not asking for money," I said. "I want to be relieved of this."

After that, I received a letter from the then-Bishop of the diocese, and he said he was sorry. He said he didn't know the priest in question, but he promised to put my name on the altar on a card and pray for me.

I laughed and said, "All this pain and I›m relegated to a card on the altar, but that›s better than nothing."

Most importantly, when the priest said, "Rosie, on behalf of the church, I apologize to you," that meant a lot to me! Those powerful words were like the absolution. I took it in and I thanked God and I let it go.

The priests who abused me are wherever they are in glory or in heaven. They know what they did, because I talk to them. I say, "You know you hurt me and I let you go!"

I had another hurtful experience with my next-door neighbor who was my landlord. He came over and pushed me up against the refrigerator and started kissing me.

I angrily pushed him away. He was embarrassed. Years later, when he was dying, I went into the hospital and he was in his bed and I went up to his ear and I forgave him. My work in hospice had taught me that hearing is the last thing that leaves us.

"You hurt me," I told him, "but I forgive you and I want you to go to God peacefully." That's my credo. We have to forgive or we will be pulled down. The more that we hold on to things, the more we have it on us, and eventually we're sinking into the ground with all the hurt.

When you let it go, it's like being able to take a deep breath that you've been holding for so long. It's not to say that those feelings won't creep back into your consciousness. They do. It's a conscious decision every day to let it go. It doesn't happen one time. What happened was so traumatic, it altered your perception of God and of yourself. When people say, "We don't want you here," and "We wish you were dead," and priests inflict abuse, that is very scarring. After awhile, you start questioning your self-worth.

All of this can be healed with forgiveness, which means letting go of something that is well beyond your control to change. It means letting go from the heart, not just with words, but by really asking God to change your heart.

Let go and let God. I stopped trying to be God a long time ago. I don't do as good a job. You have the power to forgive people who caused you pain, and it will help heal your religious hurts.

Rosalie G. Robles is author of Memories of My Life: Reflections of a Former Nun Led by the Spirit.

Tips

If you're in a difficult position and need to forgive religious hurts, here are Rosie's tips.

1. Go into a room and scream. Get it out! Find someone that you can confide in as counselor, as a spiritual director, or a good friend that you can share the situation with. When you don't let it out, it remains in you and it festers. It takes on a life of its own and it can make you sick.

    Once you get it outside of yourself to another person and they reflect back what they're hearing, you can better deal with it. Then you can start to sift through and say, *I don't need this. I don't want that.*

    You don't want to go through your life carrying this heaviness sitting in your chest and bringing you down.

2. Find your prayer spot and pray a lot.

3. Go run, go swim, go walk, do physical activities to burn off the stress.

Chapter 8

Go Within to Find Your Answers
Let It Be!

Prayer Creates Joy from Within
By Joanie

*C*arol, as a Catholic "woman of the cloth," an official Sister of St. Joseph of Carondelet for 32 years, taught prayer by her example! Her life! She uplifted women at parish retreats including Cursillos, a type of Catholic retreat, and she created her own retreat called Luminaire, which provided self-discovery through her certification as a graphoanalyst/handwriting expert. Carol had a blast sharing faith, spiritually leading men and youth at locations in many cities and parishes. She created many prayer services, while she fostered, changed, and opened people's hearts to spread joy and bring Jesus to them.

Here are her handwritten keynote talk notes about prayer, scribbled on a lime-green, polka-dotted, 4" x 6" piece of wrinkled paper. I hope it helps you as much as it has helped me. I've been reading it for 35 years:

☙

Purpose of prayer? Is to surrender your life to God; begins with WONDER . . . not happy, not to get an answer, but just truth. Ends with SURRENDER.

Pray about the things in your life, be calm and peaceful, turn to scripture.

Prayer is the ERUPTION of God within you!

Focus your mind on a point.

Prayer is the whole person, body, and spirit. Keep your body alert, put it in a position of reverence, sit up straight, take a few deep breaths, relax your body, let your arms hang, and close your eyes.

Carol and I loved to sing our prayers. Especially the song, "Make Me a Channel of Your Peace," written by Sebastian Temple and sung by Susan Boyle.

REFLECTION QUESTION

How, when and where do you enjoy or desire to pray?

_____

_____

God is Within Us
By Elizabeth

"Be still and know that I am God."
Psalm 46:10

You may interpret "I am God" as an entity outside of yourself. And you may envision God as a male figure looking down with a scrutinizing, scornful, even punishing temperament. Please allow me to share how I encounter God in my meditations, as I am often led by my own father's spirit. My father died in 1990, and remains very much alive in spirit.

"Come," my father said, taking my hand during a meditation. In the spirit realm, my father is a very tall, powerful being cloaked in long robes. He glows with pure love, peace, and wisdom.

"I'm taking you to God," he said as a floaty sensation fluttered through me and I ascended into the fifth dimension where I was no longer conscious of my body.

First, I saw a golden throne. Rather than witnessing a bearded man in a white robe, or any human form, I was overwhelmed with blissful peace and knowing that I was with God. And God is pure energy that appeared as an infinite, golden glow that flowed in vast streams and swirls, engulfing and permeating everything, everywhere.

Beside this indescribably huge, warm glow of love, was Jesus, who first appeared to me in 2011, and is now a constant presence in my life and in my meditations.

In this one, the pure golden energy that is God emanating from the throne suddenly rolled toward me. This golden flow tapered to a point that entered the center of my abdomen, and the God energy poured into me, fusing with every cell in my body, setting me aglow from the inside out. Then this God energy exploded inside me, spraying gold sparkles brilliantly and beautifully in every direction. Like I was at the center of an exploding star.

As this occurred, I absolutely knew that I am one with Source.

God was showing me that *I am* the God energy.

And you are the God energy.

God is within us.

My life's divine assignment is to teach how to allow God's light and love to set you aglow from the inside out. This will help you attain inner peace, and feel fulfilled and prosperous by discovering and living your life's purpose.

What's the goal in doing that? To serve humanity and Mother Earth so that love and peace prevail everywhere. God is pure love. God is the Source of all creation.

Our souls are individual starbursts of this God energy that is the pulse-giving life to our human bodies. Your soul is your true identity. Not your name, your appearance, your family's history, your education, or your job.

When you cultivate a spiritual lifestyle, you can activate that starburst of God energy within. You can expand it, strengthen it, and utilize it to maximize your potential on every level: health, love, joy, relationships, career, wealth, and what you contribute to the world.

Unfortunately, the human condition is fearful, and that breeds hatred; we're taught that we're different, superior, inferior, and separate. We ignore our intuition and our soul's calling, and instead shape our lives on the external expectations, rules, and restrictions of our families, religions, and society.

This makes it easy for forces of evil to hijack our lives and stop us from fulfilling our divine purpose. Negative forces—including people, situations, religious hurts, and our own fears and bad habits—distract us from our God-given missions to do good things for ourselves and for humanity. We have the power to eradicate war, hatred, famine, disease, discord, inequality, and injustice. We have the power to heal Mother Earth and make peace prevail.

But first we have to find it within ourselves.

As you go within to heal your religious hurts and step into your spiritual power, you will be awed by seemingly miraculous synchronicities, psychic flashes, inner peace, vitality, and better health. The light of God glowing within you will burn away your old self, and you will feel reborn with the power to serve as a change agent to help yourself, humanity, and the world.

A version of this passage was first published in *God's Answer Is Know: Lessons From a Spiritual Life.*

Accepting the Gifts & Communicating with the Divine
By Aja Walker

For many years, I have struggled with my place in religion, because it was forced upon me by several family members. At age 11 or 12, I was told that I had to be baptized and I did not have a say in it. I just did not feel right.

I have gone to so many different churches over the years, and none of them resonated with me. When I became an adult and had my first child, I decided that I would become Muslim for my husband at the time. I had something to prove to so many people, which, in turn, made me lose myself before I ever found myself.

After my divorce, I divorced the hijab, the Qur'an, and the Muslim faith. I could finally breathe!

For years after that, I was mentally tormenting myself, trying to figure out where I fit in the world of religion. The pressure was astronomical!

It wasn't until I was in my thirties and living for myself and my two children, that I realized that religion is not for me at all.

Spirituality is my love. I feel most comfortable when I align myself with the universe and the almighty intuition. I thank the universe daily for allowing me to receive what I need and even what I want. The God that I believe in is the Higher Self.

We are all reflections of one another. I get this confirmation over and over from the people I meet and relate to. All the hardships I have ever been through—and boy, there are a lot—are not in vain. I can talk to most anyone and be able to relate to them and comfort them on a deeper level. I am forever grateful for that.

In the last six months, I have delved into tarot cards, and I have been getting readings from gifted individuals to get confirmation that I am on the correct path. The tarot cards are helping with boosting confidence in myself and with gaining more patience. They help me to see things in a way that I never would have thought of in relation to my life and the people around me.

During this time, my beloved grandmother came through from beyond for the first time in 20-plus years. If that wasn't confirmation enough, I don't know what is!

She let me know that she had been by my side for the entire time, but I just had not been ready to receive it. I was not working on myself to be able to "hear" her. Don't get me wrong, I have received several signs from her over the years, but I just doubted myself before.

This has healed the 17-year-old me (when my grandmother died) so deeply. I light a white candle weekly for her, per her request, and I light a cigarette for her as well. That woman was and is so important to me.

For anyone who doesn't know where to start, just sit and ask the universe some questions, then simply breathe and listen. You may not hear actual words, or you may, but you will get your answers.

Believe in yourself and your spirit guides. If you feel something in your gut, then go with it, always! It may sound silly, and you may not understand, but it will definitely work out in your favor.

Aja Walker is a talented chef who loves helping people.

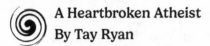

A Heartbroken Atheist
By Tay Ryan

I . . . am a heartbroken atheist.

My favorite early memories of church were full of warmth as I sat small amongst smiling strangers while the well-dressed man at the pulpit spoke of Jesus and his infinite patience and love for all the sinners of the world.

My young heart soaked in "Love thy neighbor" and "Let he who hath not sinned throw the first stone." My cup overflowed with hope and joy because a being of infinite love was watching over me.

And then it happened. Hate in a sermon. Subtle, slippery, said-but-not-said. At first it was hard to put a finger on. A tone of judgment, a word that "others" another human being, the very concept of the devil and hell. Each utterance steeped in complex language, tradition, and the aura of deep, indisputable fact.

In that moment, the tall gothic spires of my local Catholic Church became imposing. The high ornate ceilings became oppressive, its stone imprisoning me within. It chilled me and I reached out, asking questions as I tried to claw my way back into the light.

For years after that, I clung, accepting that I had to have faith and that I simply didn't yet understand the true glory of God's plan.

My last question was, "Can a gay man get into heaven?"

The negative answer was the final straw; my heart was broken. If God couldn't accept a gay man, then how could he ever accept me? I wasn't gay. In fact, I didn't know what I was, but I surely wasn't a straight male.

I felt betrayed, unloved, cold. How could God be all-loving if he invented the devil, and hell, and intended to send me there? I felt, well, quite frankly, damned.

In my mind, it was a great favor that my heart broke that day. It sent me first to other religions, then to every book on philosophy and psychology that my young mind could find.

I substituted "Love thy neighbor" with the Golden Rule: "Do unto others as you would have done unto you." I exchanged God's love with my own, and the love of my family. I sought to learn and make the world a loving place on my own.

And in education, my heart broke again and again as I learned how the best of humanity could be used against us.

How the words we lovingly craft can steer souls. The very things we build through color, shape, size, and style can impose or welcome or reject or even control.

Our fear of death—or often worse—the cold terror we feel when confronted with losing a loved one makes the idea of heaven so convenient and so desirable that it almost screams to use me to control others. If I were to manipulate man, it's easy to see that this would be a powerful place to start.

To my mind, reading is what has both broken and saved me. Through time, I've learned lessons like the Golden Rule is for noobs, the platinum rule is much better: "Treat others how they would be treated."

Put simply, just because I would like someone to treat me to a nice rare steak doesn't mean that's appropriate for or desired by or even safe for someone else.

Through language and education, I evolved my morality. And as most humans do, I yearned for good people to share in my life and philosophy and experiences.

Over time, through bars and hobby groups, jobs and online forums, I tabulated odds of finding certain types of people. While one job draws in a particular personality type, another might draw in people of completely different morals, goals, and beliefs.

Eventually this drew me back to religion. Not because I again saw God because again, I am a heartbroken atheist, a joyful atheist in a reality of infinite complexity. A dance of energy and matter that fills me to the brim with wonder, terror and hope.

But because some of those who do find their way through religion become so inwardly beautiful, so loving and full of grace, that my attraction becomes inevitable. My want to join in and share in their lives and deeds is infectious, my need to share love fulfilled.

The paths we walk are varied, forged by stars and dust and the soles of our shoes. We don't have to walk as one to find ourselves in the same garden sharing a cup for a moment or two.

"Never Get Rid of The Chair, My Love!"
By Michael Ray Hensley

I have experienced sadness and emotional hurt.

"How?" you might ask.

By sharing a gift granted to me from our Creator and by helping hundreds of people, I have had religious and strong church people who insist that my gift is coming from EVIL, pretending to be good. They see my spiritual gifts as something that goes against the teachings of their Christian and biblical church interpretations. This makes me very sad, because churches proclaim that they are open to everyone, but not to me and my gifts.

My emotional pain from many overzealous religious people who only live in a realm of their strict practices, does me harm. Throughout my life, one hateful remark from someone would create two- to three days of worry and self-doubt. When I heard, and still hear today, negative accusations, it deeply drains me and tears run down my cheeks. Inside I feel crushed!

I carry on anyways, through LOVE! The power of LOVE is infinite! This was written with the assistance of Carol and Angels. Okay Carol, we are listening.

Thank God, most people I have been able to help are thankful.

They understand that my gift is from light, Angels, God, Jesus, and all the good energies above us, around us, and within us.

I am NOT comparing myself to Jesus or Joan of Arc, but sometimes I understand what they (Jesus and Joan) must have felt. They helped so many people, yet many people turned so cruelly against them. I wonder how people could be so judgmental. It makes me so SAD!

It deeply hurts me. Thank you to those who know that I go to the LIGHT, not the Dark!

My visions and messages always start with an INCREDIBLE feeling of LOVE, and sparkling lights, orbs, that come quickly towards me. It starts a tingling between my elbows and wrists, with goosebumps and a crawling sensation on my arms.

While praying, I heard my Aunt Thelma's voice (who has passed away) and my Grandma Nano's voice with a clear message and vision of my cousin Wanda. So I telephoned Wanda and asked, "Are you at the hospital where your brother Steve is a patient, as we speak?"

Wanda said, "Yes, I'm in the waiting room."

I responded to her and said, "I have a message for you from Heaven. The message is, 'Please thank the Man of God first, church second, pure of heart, that is leaning over my son, Steve. As Steve is coming home within an hour.' "

When Wanda got to Steve's hospital room, her younger brother Kirk was there.

"Kirk, was the preacher just here?" she asked. "And was the preacher leaning over Steve?"

Kirk said, "Yes," and Steve passed within an hour.

During my conversation with Wanda, I heard Angels singing and saw fluffy white clouds parting.

The chaplain preacher who had just visited Steve told Wanda, "We have experienced a miracle from a man that doesn't go to church."

I am thankful that what came through me was relayed to Wanda.

I was raised by an atheist father and a Roman Catholic mother, yet my mother did not attend the Catholic Church very often. As a youth, I was free to go to church with my mom or not to go to any church. I tried going a few times, but didn't like them because they just did church stuff, and no one talked positively about gifts that I had. I knew I was different.

When my brother Mark was dying of stage four cancer, I stopped by a church to get a rosary. The priest acted like he didn't trust me. He wanted me to leave and so I left. This answered my prayers asking if I should go back to church. The real answer for me was, "I don't need church, just a strong belief in my heart."

My grandmother Midge, my great-grandmother, and aunts on my mother's side, all had psychic phenomena experiences—Creator "gifts"—but had to hide them most of their lives because of the strict beliefs taught by their churches. Living in the 1940s, people with spiritual gifts were stifled and seen as a threat to the church.

My family members were rebuffed, ridiculed, and thought to be "crazy" when they shared their gifts with people or with church leaders. Many of my cousins and aunts were Catholic nuns who had taken their vows, yet were deathly AFRAID they would be excommunicated if their gifts were exposed. It was a family secret. Secrets only breed fear and hate!

My mom, Margie, a kind loving older woman, tells me to be careful with my gift. She's afraid that I might be put in a mental institution, as was her aunt who had strong gifts. Mom's aunt was put in an insane asylum by her uncle while he had a love affair with another woman. He used the fact that my great aunt had visions and heard messages in order to put her "away." He also used her as an excuse to have the affair. The uncle took mom's aunt out of the asylum after his affair ended. This ordeal still haunts my mom today at the age of 93.

My mom, sincerely and heartfelt, recently told me on the telephone, "Look what they could do to you. I love you and don't want any harm to come to you, Michael."

When I was a little boy, my mom's aunt placed her hands on my head. I remember it so vividly! She told Mom that I would be special and have my "gifts" late in life. But during my younger years, I would just know stuff. Unexplainably, I would see things in my mind before it happened and like a magnet I could feel and sense things. This was me. Yet, I was around 50 years old before my gift was amplified and I could share it with people.

I was with my life partner, Richard, when he had a heart attack, and coded twice in the same day. Richard coded first in the ambulance and the paramedics were able to bring him back. The second time, he was at the hospital when he coded. I was with him through the whole ordeal. This particular time, I stood in the doorway of the emergency room, watching as they attempted chest compressions and the use of paddles as they worked very hard to bring him back to life. They then said, "It's not working; we need to call his time of death."

Upon hearing this, I fell to the floor on my knees in shock and disbelief. I immediately offered myself in the place of my life partner. It was ALL of me who asked God, "If Richard comes back to me and I get to live, I will use the gifts YOU have granted me to help people through LOVE and Angels."

The machine immediately started beeping, Richard came back to me! They said it was a miracle! I stood up, walked over to a chair, feeling exhausted and filled with happiness.

Ever since that day, I try to remember to ask people for their permission to tell them what their deceased loved ones wish for them to know.

I do not know when or where it will happen, but I'm like a transformer-tower messenger. It reminds me of the sound at the beginning of old RKO (Radio-Keith-Orpheum) movies: *beep, beep, beep.*

Once, I was granted visions and messages for a nice man who was working next door for our neighbor. When he got home, he shared the messages and visions with his wife, to which she said they were true. The man said the wife was very touched. She asked him to let her know anything I told him, as she is not allowed to personally ask me or see me because it is against the teachings of her Christian biblical church. This makes me very sad because her church and many churches proclaim they are open to everyone—but not to me and my gifts.

I am very thankful to live in a beautiful area next to the Pacific Ocean and the majestic Redwood forest in Northern California. I believe there is a wonderful energy here that helps and amplifies my psychic gifts. I am able to give people peace and a feeling of love that is validated through my gifts.

My partner and I recently became friends with Joanie and had never been to her home on the Southern Oregon coast. After lunch with her and a friend, she invited us into her home and yard to see the beautiful memorial rose garden planted in 2022 after her life partner's death. The love of Joanie's life, Carol, has come through love to show me her strong connection with the color purple. I had no idea that it was Carol's favorite color or that the living room walls would be painted purple. Joanie's house is filled with the love between Joanie and Carol and represents the intense forever-love they have for each other.

When I sat in Carol's chair, which I was drawn to, I felt an abundance of CALMNESS and LOVE. In my mind, I saw chakra colors of red, pink, orange, yellow, green, blue, and purple. All sparkly, while I heard angelic singing and monk-like chants. I silently invited Carol to join me as I sat in the low-back swivel chair while looking out to the front yard. As soon as I heard this singing, I felt warm hands touch my arms. That day I heard, "Never get rid of this chair, my LOVE!"

I stood up while feeling so much LOVE radiating from the chair. I kept feeling Carol's touch on me. Then while standing in the large, open living room, I told Joanie that I heard a song and in my spirit, I said aloud, "Carol wants me to relay this to you.

Could I have this dance for the rest of my (our) life?"

Joanie burst into tears and said, "Wow, that is one of our precious songs that we danced to. In fact, Michael, just a few days ago, I felt Carol here and we danced in this very living room spot."

Joanie cried as I said, "Carol is telling me she'd like to dance with you." Without hesitation, Joanie asked, "Alexa, play Anne Murray's song, *Could I Have This Dance?*"

The music serenaded us and through my gift, Carol and Joanie slowly hugged, swayed, twirled, and danced. I was Carol for that magic moment with Joanie. Joanie's tears stopped and she said, "Michael, it was just like Carol and I were happily dancing. Thank you for being the connection between Heaven and Earth today. It reminds me of the movie *Ghost* with Whoopi Goldberg. This is real."

It's not me; it's the gift granted to me. It's from our Creator. It comes through me. I am a messenger of their words and sometimes actions.

I see sparkles of multiple colors and I know the message is from that beloved person, because it's an unknown voice to me. I trust it is their unique voice and unique words. And, IT IS!

I'm sure God, our Creator and Jesus (who is kindness and LOVE) are okay with my gift, but sadly, churches are not!

My gift scares religious institutions and church leaders. But I carry on and let it happen.

Maybe someday the church will let go and let be.

That's healing, that's LOVE.

I hope that those who read this entire book, *Healing Religious Hurts*, receive all that is good, feel LOVE, healing, forgiveness, and protection, and believe in miracles. Know that you are loved in Heaven and on Earth.

Even if you don't go to church!

Michael Ray Hensley is celebrating 25 years with his protector, lover, friend, and husband Richard as they enjoy their 70th birthdays on the Northern California Coast.

Tips

about prayer and going within to find love and peace.

1. Don't overthink it. Simply say, "Hi, God!" God will respond.

2. Prayer is talking and listening with your Higher Power, with the divine made flesh. It is a solution on how to deal with life.

3. The more often you freely and honestly talk and listen in prayer, the easier it becomes. Just like two friends talking.

4. Be patient with yourself and with your God. God hears you and God answers you.

5. Dedicate specific time every day to make it a habit in building your unique personal relationship and friendship with your God, Jesus, Holy Spirit, and Higher Power.

6. Sometimes you feel something extraordinary and divine; sometimes you don't. That's faith.

7. Pray in silence everywhere: with others, with readings, with scripture, with music, within a church building, at the river/lake/beach, in traffic, in a restaurant, at a concert, while walking the streets, and with a lover. Prayer is anytime and any place you allow it.

8. Be THANKFUL, pray, speak, listen, and be quiet with an open heart and open mind.

9. Meditate, do yoga, stretch, run, walk, hike, sit, and stare. Revel in your surroundings and your body. Clear out junk, negative thoughts, sin, and evil.

10. Ask for forgiveness in your failings and move on. Get rid of the past anchors that hold you back or keep you stuck.

11. Plug into The God Minute app or other phone or computer prayer teams that resonate with your beliefs.

12. Ask for interventions and spiritual guidance from angels, ancestors, and saints. Holy beings are real!

13. Be you! There is no wrong or right way to pray. Discover your truth.

14. Ask and it will be given, seek and you will be found. Believe in the unbelievable. Miracles happen!

15. Heal, forgive, be grateful, and grow in the love of God/Spirit/Higher Power.

16. Check out tunes that Elizabeth likes: "Oh Happy Day" by Aretha Franklin featuring Mavis Staples and "Here I Am to Worship" by Hillsong Worship and Reuben Morgan.

17. Joanie's playlist includes:

    The Dameans Album, *Beginning Today*

    The St. Louis Jesuits Albums from the 1970s

    and 1980s

    "This Little Light of Mine" composed by Harry Dixon Loes

"Take my Life and Let it Be" by Paul Baloche

"Seek Ye First" by Maranath Singers

"How Good You Are, God" by Millie Rieth and Miriam Malone

"All Are Welcome" by Marty Haugen

"I feel You Everywhere" by Jan Phillips

"Behold What Manner of Love" by the Maranatha Singers

"Open My Eyes" by John Michael Talbot

"El Shaddai" by Amy Grant

"Remembrance" by Hillsong Worship

"Was It A Morning Like This" by Sandi Patty

"Mary Did You Know" by PentatonixVEVO

Chapter 9

LGBTQ+ and Religion
When You Least Expect It . . . Rainbows Appear

It's Bigger Than Us!
By Joanie

*W*e, LGBTQ+ people, are in every church and faith community around the world. We invite you to reach out, get to know us as individuals, and understand our needs. If we don't feel loved, we will not disappear from the planet. But we will find other ways to enhance our closeness to a Higher Power and find a faith community that loves us for who we are.

The day was sunshine bright in the entrance foyer inside the big wooden doors of the First Presbyterian Church in Ashland, Oregon. The wall displayed a seven-foot-long painted rainbow with the inscription: ALL ARE WELCOME with GOD WELCOMES ALL! My heart leapt for joy!

This was probably the identical feeling as in the Bible story when Elizabeth, pregnant with John the Baptist, saw Mary, who was her cousin pregnant with Jesus. I was overwhelmed with the signage and artwork that matched the robust smiles, twinkling eyes, and salutations of "Good morning, welcome to our church!"

Another time, the night was sparkling, the air warm, a plethora of cars carefully carousing the streets in Balboa Park's 6th Avenue area, looking for a place to shelter and convene as the Pre-PRIDE, the opening ceremonies of San Diego's Pride Festival. Oh, in glory, minutes away from starting the weekend celebration of DEI: Diversity, Equity and Inclusion for LGBTQ+ ministers of all faiths: Jewish, Muslim, Hindu, Protestant, Presbyterian, Episcopal, Catholic, Universal, and more. All were gathered in their bright-colored albs, robes, heart glasses, multi-colored shirts, dresses, and even lit-up tennis shoes.

It was the July 2024 night of St. Paul's Episcopal Annual LGBTQ+ Lighting of the Cathedral. A two-hour gay prayer service was a dream of mine. Tonight was the night! There was the spirited vocal group, good-looking in age span and hair styles, with the women's gay choir front and center. The LGBTQ+ symphony was positioned on the huge, marbled altar. An entourage of church ministers, LGBTQ+ people and allies, who pranced and danced forward, speaking boldly and reverently to read poems, scriptures, and prayers.

We were all one around the world on this night! On the right side, Patrick, Michael, his mother Paulie, and I sat shoulder-to-shoulder, tight and cozy, holding hands as a few tears shed throughout. A moving, loving vibe circled around the church celebrating its 150 years of dedication and decades of peaceful activism.

Our light, our God, our source of life is all-powerful and all-loving. Oh it's an "ahh" moment, an unexplainable lifetime of experiences where there is but one holy deity, a transforming being, something bigger than all of us.

It's amazing to me how many times I've been asked, "Are LGBTQ+ people spiritual people?"

My simple answer is, "Some are and some are not. I am!"

Please Don't Label me as "Marginalized"

As LGBTQ+ people, we have been viewed as a taboo group/topic and more recently labeled "marginalized."

What the heck does that mean? Living on the margins? It sounds to me like I and my LGBTQ+ family are an object, an agenda item, a category on an Excel spreadsheet, a designated place on a page as a mistake, somewhere between disgust and broken, with no hope for repair. Because we are "not normal." I definitely don't like the word marginalized because it seems tiny and sets me apart as insignificant and powerless.

Margins are the sides of a piece of paper. We, LGBTQ+ people, are a colorful book of pictures, artwork, quotes, and stories! We are included on the front, in the middle, and on the back pages, not on the sidelines, not on the margins.

All we want is to be on an equal playing field. Please don't label me or anyone "marginalized;" we are all important and living on the same page to do the best we can.

Some of us have been forced to live on the fringe of life, but we don't choose it. Sometimes, we do need extra help and attention, only to help you see our value.

We desire and love it when we are appreciated and celebrated. We pray and hope to be understood, listened to and cared for like everyone else. When individuals, organizations, businesses, governments, and faith communities take the time to really get to know us as individuals, the discovery of more similarities becomes more clear. That's a win-win!

As my mother used to say, "It takes all kinds to make the world go round!"

LGBTQ+ friendly places of worship

So, do you know which places of worship support LGBTQ+ people? Which places of worship support same-sex or trans marriages? Which faith communities adamantly disapprove? Find out!

It's time to learn, ponder, and know the differences and similarities. Many churches have specific congregations or sects that either support or do not support LGBTQ+ laity, ministers, and same-sex relationships.

Searching is great! Chasing a spiritual connection and direction is about what feels happy to you. Go visit people, churches, and holy places. Personally, I think it's beneficial, wise, and fun to Google and explore national and local websites, shop around, attend, walk in, and get the feel of it.

It could be a pickleball court, a gym, a book club, a fashion show or theater group that gives you joy as well as a church, synagogue, or temple. Learn and love as you go. Within your town, village, city, state, or country, people, customs, and services can vary in drastic distinctions.

Be an explorer, meet new people, read new books, watch and listen to spiritual documentaries, podcasts, meditations, and music. See what brings you joy and peace after you ponder and wonder in your quietness.

I was overwhelmed at the All Saints Episcopal Church in Bentonville, Arkansas, last year, when two gorgeous ladies stepped forward to face the 75 people attending a communion service. They spoke of their long-time membership and the faith community unity they feel with all of us, the parishioners. Then, in a shock to their partner and to all of us, one knee was bent, a black ring box was presented, and a marriage proposal occurred. They asked: "Will you marry me?"

Oh the applause, clapping, standing ovation and the lesbians kissing delighted all of us.

"Yes, I will marry you!" the other person responded.

Go deep within to find your spiritual happy place! Stay open and honest; maybe a bolt of lightning will strike you like it did St. Paul. Remember, "It's always bigger than you think." Expect great things to happen. How fun is that?!

Historically, some churches since the 1960s have ordained LGBTQ+ people and affirmed LGBTQ+ faith communities. I invite you to look at your past and current faith community with beautiful, mirrored glasses that show the many angles and colors of light. Project onto a screen, magnify, and watch yourself in a movie of your spiritual journey. Be open to what you learn, be well-informed, YOU are the captain of your own ship . . . your discipleship.

Basically, for years The Christian Churches of Unitarian Beliefs, United Church of Christ UCC, Episcopal and Evangelical Lutheran have been known for being OUTspoken and all-inclusive, as LGBTQ+ friendly and as supporters of LGBTQ+ marriage. Alleluia! Yippee! High tens!

Does your God or faith community discriminate?

Some religions or faith communities do not accept LGBTQ+ people, nor do they agree or approve of relational, intimate, or sexual acts between same-sex people. I don't get that; love is meant to be shared!

I guess it boils down or boils up to what kind of a supreme being do you believe in? Is your Higher Power more judgemental or more merciful? Do you think a score card of your success and failures tells the entire picture? I don't! Forgiveness is paramount and **LOVE ALWAYS WINS**!

The anti-LGBTQ+/same-sex marriage churches include but are not limited to: Southern Baptist, Roman Catholicism, Orthodox Jewish, Church of Jesus Christ Latter-day Saints, and Pentecostalism. Remember though, theological debates are ongoing! What may be true today may change tomorrow.

241

Churches move very, very slowly in making decisions. So first, find your heart's truth and live it.

The Presbyterian church voted in 2023 to formally sanction same-sex marriage. The 2019 PEW research surveys show about 61% of mainline Protestants favor allowing "gays and lesbians to marry." In contrast, 31% are against it. The cup is more than half full and that is a promising hope for all of us, straight and LGBTQ+ people.

Allies are warriors

Seek straight allies who provide support and tell you, "I got your back." It's reinforcement by a team of earth angels and encourages forward-moving, open and honest communication related to sexual orientation (who one is attracted to) and gender identity (how one views their gender identity)! Thank you God for the Lutheran Reconciling Works training program called SOGIE, Sexual Orientation and Gender Identity Expression. It is available for all denominations to learn and grow from.

It's always bigger than you think!

Allies have provided me with guidance ranging from my fear of coming out or not, while knowing whom to avoid, and whom I can trust within my faith community. (Think smart and be safe.) Allies are awesome warriors as they speak up for LGBTQ+ people in casual conversations that ricochet back in positive ways with happy endings. All of a sudden, I hear a congregational pulpit sermon and a general invite to be more included. Allies are one of our secret weapons!

If it's important to you that churches support and celebrate LGBTQ+ people, then talk about it! Spread the news, be bold and bring it up in conversation with family, work, school, church, sports teams, etc. Fund and support the churches that support

LGBTQ+ people, get involved, and invite others to feel the love! Grow in wisdom, grace, and spirituality. It's bigger than us!

What does your spiritual path look like?

There is nothing wrong with choosing other ways to be spiritual. I think about health class when eight dimensions of well-being were taught: Emotional, Physical, Occupational, Social, Intellectual, Environmental, Financial, and Spiritual. Listen; follow your heart. It's okay to change to a different faith community! I was a Roman Catholic all my life, until I was "called" to change. Now I'm a practicing Episcopalian. I'm so HAPPY, so joy-filled, with no more walking on eggshells! It's so nice, comforting, and healing! Walk your walk! You can do it! Yay!

I am so honored to belong to an Episcopal church! The passing of the USA baton from the first African American Bishop Michael Curry to Bishop Sean Rowe will occur at the end of October 2024 and Bishop Diana Akiyama leads us from Oregon. In August of 2023, Bishop Diana laid her hands on my head and shoulder in a receiving ceremony mass. She consecrated the bread and wine into the body and blood of Jesus at that celebration ceremony. It was very cool! She is living out her calling to priestly servanthood! By the way, she looks great in her bright purple shirt with a white collar, called a collarino.

CathEpiscopal

I wonder if the Catholic Church will feel the love that the Episcopal Church feels in regard to same-sex sacramental weddings? It's awesome for me to be Episcopalian! It's freeing and it's a forever joy with no strings attached! The Episcopal Book of Common Prayer is packed with everything you need to know and centers on prayer, service and trust in the Lord surrounded in abundant LOVE. I don't read it a lot, but I know of its power and strength. Good idea, I'll read it more!

Funny though, I still honestly pray with the Catholic scripture readings every morning, listen to the Catholic God Minute app, play my guitar, and sing along to a variety of Christian music. I respect many prayerful proactive, all inclusive, religious leaders.

Maybe I'm really a combo—CathEpiscopal!

In both faiths, I keep getting closer to my Higher Power, enlightenment and isn't human service what it's all about?! A duo combo of humanity and divinity! A healing process of saying goodbye to one and embracing the new one. I have no regrets, no guilt and total peace . . . the result of forgiving and healing. Yahoo!

What's your story? Please share.

Hurt: it keeps poking up its ugly head!

The biggest hurt was when Carol and I were denied marrying in our Catholic faith because we were two women in love!

So simple a situation, yet a mole hill turned into a huge mountain. Thank goodness mountains can be climbed and summitted. Miracles do happen!

Me at age 63 and Carol at 78, it was time! After 39 years of living together as an intimate and sexual couple without an official marriage title/license and being "practicing Catholics," it was time for true peace and joy.

Carol and I both had taken vows of poverty, chastity, and obedience as Catholic Sisters of St. Joseph. We lived faithful to our vows until God put us together and our human love overtook our religious commitments.

Read about us in my best-selling 2023 book entitled, *Nun Better: An Amazing Love Story.*

We attended weekly mass, and sent petitioning letters to the pope, asking to be sacramentally married in the Catholic Church. We were refused, denied, and told "NO."

This hurt was big, but thankfully not deep enough to destroy our love. It was a hurt that we pushed aside for years, with it raised its ugly head at the oddest of times. Our joyful, grateful attitude about life, our prayers, and letting go with letting God handle it, combined to slowly dissipate the hurt. We didn't want to live in negativity; we knew who we were. Jesus was bigger than any church and our love was bigger than everything! We were living a true beautiful spiritual and human life, though in opposition, not sanctioned, by the Catholic Church. "Their loss, our love and the right timing will happen eventually," we said.

The main tip is in letting go, forgiving, and moving on. Try it! It's never too early and never too late.

Joy and Healing

It was St. Timothy's Episcopal priest Father Bernie Lindley who joyfully married us on August 5, 2020. A brand-new sacrament, a grace of spiritual reality, a special rebirth day called a new Jerusalem, an Easter resurrection. The seven gifts of the Holy Spirit were moving and grooving: Wisdom, Understanding, Counsel, Fortitude, Knowledge, Piety, and best of all The Awe of God.

God, someone was talking with you and you heard them . . . Thank you, Jesus, for stepping up for love! Thank you so much!

Do Churches Feel Hurt?

I wonder if the Catholic Church ever feels hurt? I wonder if Pope Francis and bishops agonize or feel remorse about their personal positions regarding same-sex or trans marriages? I bet the odds are in favor that within their family- and friend-circles, there is a beautiful queer living a committed, loving partnership. The typical bell curve suggests that. For centuries and currently, churches have been divided and split over LGBTQ+ issues. Wow!

It's fun to think about what laity or professed religious clergy would attend, support, officiate, and celebrate a LGBTQ+ commitment, sanctification, or sacramental wedding. Keep your deep heart voice stirring and you will hear God.

Eventually, not in Carol's lifetime, but maybe in my lifetime, Catholic Church teachings will be radically challenged and changed. Such as what Pope Francis is currently doing. He is tenderly and servantly bringing to the forefront the rekindling of "WELCOMING ALL," including women, laity, and LGBTQ+ people. Leave no one behind.

Pope Francis is personally having quality time with LGBTQ+ people. He is listening to, praying for, discerning, removing stigmas and hatred, and creating dialogue in the specific forum of the huge October 2023 synod process. What a great example! Get it? Sitting with LGBTQ+ and listening!

When I wrote *Nun Better* and co-authored *Joyously Free* with Elizabeth, the thrill of doing so wrapped me in a quilted comforter! I pinch myself that I have been chosen, similarly to *The Chosen* Netflix series—about a non-famous woman by societal and worldly standards—to achieve such a feat. I never imagined in my wildest dreams that I would be the magnet to share and shape love, freedom, and healing messages to ALL peoples, in five continents, eight countries, and 40 of the 50 states in America. Have I shared with you that I've converted each of my two books into a "yearbook"—a high school-style of signatures and remarks from the people who are in it, who helped with it, or contributed their writing? It's AMAZING and my next spirit journey will be, God willing, an audience with Pope Francis and asking him to sign them. It's like the LGBTQ+ and allies bible loaded with beatitudes! How fun!

Many past world and religious leaders have and continue to teach others to get rid of, destroy, overcome, and say goodbye to hypocrisy, discrimination, and judgment. Martin Luther King, Jr. and Mahatma Gandhi for example. Who else do you think of? I commend their courage, walking the walk and talking the talk!

Hope for LGBTQ+ Catholics awaits; it's the same waiting as the season of ADVENT . . . URE. Wait and see, come follow me, and be my disciple. It will be an ongoing adventure.

It's an honor to have Father James Martin, Society of Jesus, USA, as one of the key people invited to communicate with Pope Francis about LGBTQ+ issues. He is a wise man cheering for Catholic LGBTQ+ people. You can reach him at America Media, first published in 1909 as the *America* magazine and he has a wonderful written piece in this book! Thank you from the top of my heart, Father James Martin, for being in our book.

Help from Our Ancestors and Angels

I commend and thank the thousands of unnamed yet instrumental faith community leaders who have set the pace from decades ago for LGBTQ+ inclusion. We do stand on the shoulders of giants, our ancestors.

It reminds me of the miracle of all miracles when Carol was on the eve of her death. I sat sobbing in the chair next to her comatose body and in an instant my tears stopped, peace engulfed me, and in the very dark bedroom appeared one, then two, then three, then four, and then multitudes of shining bright lights on the walls and ceiling. It was AMAZING! It was miraculous divine intervention, an inter-religious experience.

All of her risen family, friends, saints, and angels were twinkling and shining, ready to WELCOME her to the place of total freedom and joy, a place or palace called heaven!

An enlightened state where **Wellcome** (I misspelled that on purpose) is synonymous with, "I love you forever; heaven is on earth!"

Imagine . . . a life of no division of LGBTQ+ and straight.

Let's add a favorite song of ours to the prayer booklets in places of worship around the world: "Born This Way" by Lady Gaga! I would love that!

Imagine this . . . would you every year help celebrate October 11th? The National COMING OUT holiday that celebrates all LGBTQ+ COMING OUT of the closet? Mark your calendars now!

This national holiday began in 1988 and has become a world holiday for Ireland, Switzerland, the Netherlands, and the United Kingdom. To me, it's a great day of solstices: summer and winter, a Christmas and Hanukkah season, and Easter and the Buddha golden rule kind of day.

An OUT LGBTQ+ Nun or Priest . . . *Hmmmm?*

Wouldn't it be awesome if on this special day of October 11th, all faith denominations, including the universal Catholic Church leaders who include the pope, cardinals, bishops, priests, deacons, sisters, nuns, and laity, COME OUT? Why not?! It's possible!

Hats off to other LGBTQ+ out denominational clergy!

Imagine the joy of university professors, religious seminarian and formation programs, parishioners, high school staff and coaches, elementary school teachers, all families, students, teachers, and staff **COMING OUT!** A worldwide positive influence of honesty and welcomeness. A celebration that God does not make junk!

Imagine the impact of the joy, the vast numbers of people **COMING OUT** every year on this special national and religiously spiritually holiday! I guess it boils down or boils up to what kind of supreme being do you believe in and what kind of Higher Power made you?

Exponentially growing, this would be the Spiritual Olympics of all nations, united in truth and freedom. Bigger than us, bigger than you think, once again!

What does **COMING OUT** have to do with **WELLCOME?** EVERYTHING!

Think how high the numbers would be if **all** faith communities, churches, and religions embraced it. Most importantly, imagine how many straight and LGBTQ+ people would be healed and given a fresh start, an earthly resurrection. So utterly exciting for me to envision. Can you see it? Would you join in?

It would be a remarkable day! Close your eyes and imagine a new day to sing a NEW Song called, "All Are Welcome!" This would happen in every church, temple, synagogue, and place of worship around the world, from the mountains to the prairies to the overpopulated cities to the islands of few inhabitants, with literally open doors and open hearts!

Spiritual services would celebrate, welcome, and include without any judgment, the holding of hands that fit like gloves, as the symbolic and real way of caring. Together everyone achieves more. TEAM "God and Company!"

Imagine the Christian religious institutions and leaders together setting the pace by their true-self actions and teaching others to embrace being LGBTQ+ or straight, being human in the likeness of a man named Jesus. It would be proclaimed to all lands and galaxies to stand tall, walk the walk, and talk the talk because "nothing is impossible with God!"

LOVE ALWAYS WINS!

That peace is here on earth and in heaven. That God's will be done! For this is the kingdom, the power and the glory of God! Alleluia!

Just Imagine! If a virgin can give birth to God, why not an LGBTQ+ gender reveal? Both are everlasting miracles!

Follow Your Own Rainbow Path to God's Love & Peace
By Elizabeth

Sinful.

Deviant.

Destined to forever burn in hell.

Sadly, many religious leaders preach this hateful misinformation from what they believe is the gospel from books that were written hundreds of years ago. Families enforce this messaging to help do its damage, and society reinforces it: starting with name-calling and bullying by children and continuing all the way to discrimination against LGBTQ+ adults in the workplace and acts of even deadly violence toward queer people. Incredibly, being queer in some countries is a criminal act punishable by death.

For example, in 2021, an Iranian man was killed by his own family for being gay.[12]

A news report in *The New York Post* says that the 20-year-old man's family found something in the mail about how he was disqualified from joining the army because he was gay. The man was killed in a brutal manner by his own family, the article says, after his relatives discovered that he was gay. The man lived in a country where being gay is a crime and sex with a person of the same gender is punishable by death.

It's Time to End Religious Hate Against LGBTQ+ People

Religious shaming and condemnation that's reinforced by families and society scars many LGBTQ+ people and forms some of their earliest memories relating to their identities. This is crushing and destructive to a child's psyche, self-esteem, and future success.

Sadly, when LGBTQ+ people grow up in families that ascribe to anti-gay beliefs rooted in religious hate, this rhetoric can be extremely harmful. So much so, that LGBTQ+ and straight people alike may become agnostic, meaning they don't know if God exists, or atheist, which means they don't believe in God or a Higher Power.

It's time to end this and heal religious hurts against people who are LGBTQ+. How? By awakening to your power to connect with God/Spirit/Higher Self to find and feel the love and peace that you had once hoped to receive from religion. Another way is to find a faith community where you feel accepted and loved, just as you are. A place that celebrates the truth that God is love and love is God. A place that feels as free and happy as a Pride parade or festival. Where you're surrounded by your tribe, and you collectively engage in worship, you exponentially multiply the power of Spirit to heal, uplift, and guide you into new levels of health and happiness.

It's scientifically proven that people who are socially connected with close friends in a supportive community actually live longer. So finding and bonding with your queer spiritual group could potentially extend your life! Not to mention, you can form deep friendships and possibly even meet your forever person.

All while healing religious hurts that may have been inflicted by intolerant religious leaders and institutions, or by family members who are parroting the homophobic teachings of religion.

That's why we're here to tell you that you are free to love God and receive God's love back unconditionally. You are beloved by the Creator, who made you just as you are.

God does not hate or punish or reject you. God loves you. So many religions are remiss in teaching that God is a mean entity who's watching every move and just waiting to punish people for the slightest disobedience to man-made rules. This is especially damaging in the context of same-sex intimacy. Love is love and body parts don't matter. Love is a connection of souls, that's why we're called "soulmates" when we find our perfect partners.

Let's please emphasize that hateful messaging from religious leaders is man-made. These leaders and their institutions want to control people and wield power over them, to grow their flocks and amass strength in numbers, along with financial wealth and even political influence.

Even though our faith communities are supposed to create sanctuaries of peace, love, and acceptance, they can instead become hornets' nests that sting with painful words and poisonous experiences.

So, we need to follow God, not man-made religious rules that breed rage and rejection.

As I said in *Joyously Free: Stories & Tips to Live Your Truth as LGBTQ+ People, Parents and Allies*, written with Joanie, healing begins with first understanding what the hurts are, and what caused them. The surgeon can't perform the surgery without knowing where the cancerous tumor is located. So doing the inner work of self-exploration is imperative.

REFLECTION QUESTIONS

If you are an LGBTQ+ person or ally, what are your religious hurts?

_____

_____

What would it look and feel like for you to heal and release the thoughts, feelings, and memories of these hurts, so your heart and mind are free to fly into your future with joy, relief, and gratitude?

_____

_____

How Do You Define a Healthy Diet? Fake or Natural?

If you strive to nourish the temple that is your body with healthier foods, then you know that a plant-based, organic regimen is best. Fruits, vegetables, nuts, and beans, as well as fresh fish, meats, and poultry, come straight from Mother Nature.

On the contrary, manufactured foods such as packaged cookies, candy, soda pop, orange snack chips dusted with imitation cheese, processed meats, and fast food, are unhealthy and can lead to obesity, diabetes, high blood pressure, and even cancer. These foods are created in laboratories where food scientists calibrate the perfect blend of salt, fat, and sugar to create highly addictive flavors and textures that activate the human brain's pleasure centers as powerfully as cocaine and opioid drugs. The goal is to make the person keep eating, and keep buying, the fake food item.

On the contrary, when you follow "God's diet," you eat whole foods prepared by Mother Nature, enjoying the most powerful punch of nutrition and wellness.

You have to learn this for yourself, often after a battle with obesity or a serious health crisis related to an unhealthy diet. The food companies and fast food restaurants want to keep people eating the delicious but potentially harmful fast food.

Similarly, we have to wake up to the reality that man-made religion wants to keep us hooked on its beliefs and fears, so we'll keep coming back to fill their places of worship and keep filling their golden coffers. Sometimes the sense of community and even spiritual upliftment that one experiences in the prayer, song, fellowship, and celebrations during religious services can be as addictive as foods that taste delicious but are actually harmful to our health. Why? Because they can trigger gnawing in a queer person's gut that the religion's doctrine is intolerant and toxic.

So which do you choose?

Religions whose rules can harm one's mental health with shame, rejection, and hate?

Or the pure love of God in its natural form that is ours for the taking to nourish our minds, bodies, and souls?

A Jesuit Priest Standing Up for LGBTQ+ People in the Catholic Church
By James Martin

Often, I'm asked, "Why do you do ministry with LGBTQ people?"
And the answer is pretty simple:

Because it's what I believe God is asking me to do, and because I believe it's the group with whom Jesus would be ministering today if He were still walking around on this earth.

LGBTQ people are no doubt the most marginalized group in the Catholic Church today. But it's not just the church that marginalizes them. In some countries, it's a criminal offense even to engage in same-sex relations—meaning you could be executed.

And in many more countries—perhaps 70—it's an offense punishable by imprisonment. In those countries, sadly many Christians, including some Catholic leaders, support these laws. Even in the West, being an LGBTQ person can bring harassment, beatings, and other forms of violence. So very much an "at-risk" population.

Those are what you might call the "secular" reasons to accompany these people, which would be enough. But on top of that, there is the great tradition of Catholic social teaching, which asks us to stand in solidarity with the "marginalized." And that would be enough, too! But on top of that is the tradition of my own religious order, the Jesuits, which asks us to "walk with the excluded."

But, as I said, the deeper reason is that I think this is where Jesus would want us to be today. After all, in the Gospels we see how he continually reached out to people on the margins, people who felt left out or were left out: a Roman centurion who asked for healing for his servant (a centurion who wasn't Jewish and probably not even a monotheist); a Samaritan woman (remember the enmity between Jews and Samaritans) who had been married five times and living with a man who was not her husband; and a tax collector named Zacchaeus, whom Jesus welcomed even when the crowd who saw their encounter "grumbled."

So basically, I feel that this is where Jesus asks us to be. Jesus was with those "on the peripheries," as Pope Francis likes to say. That's where I want to be, too.

A few years ago, for the first time, I met Pope Francis in a private audience—a highlight of my life—and he asked me to continue this ministry. I can't tell you how consoled that made me feel.

So the real answer to the question, "Why do you do ministry with LGBTQ people?" is "Why wouldn't I?"

James Martin, SJ, is a Jesuit priest, editor at large of America Media, consultor to the Vatican's Dicastery for Communication, and author of many books, including most recently, Come Forth: The Promise of Jesus's Greatest Miracle.

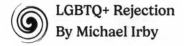

LGBTQ+ Rejection
By Michael Irby

As an ER nurse, I know what pain is. I see it on the faces and bodies of my patients, as well as in the expressions of their loved ones who are witnessing these events. I hear it in their voices and cries for help, even in the way they breathe.

Pain can be described as: acute, which is sudden; of abrupt onset, whose origin can be within; or outside the body. Pain can also be defined as chronic, meaning that it is something which the patient must live with, managing it as best they can.

The curious thing about pain is that it is never just physical, although my patients often focus on that. Pain is also emotional, psychological, and spiritual. And because of this, many of my patients will leave my care with their pain still present, lessened in some ways I hope, but not completely gone. Or if it has quieted down, this may only be temporary.

Traditional Western Medicine does not wish to give this much credence. It is too messy, too complicated, and too time-consuming to consider these other aspects of pain. In fact, some would say that they are not the problem for the ER. We draw blood, we perform imaging, we assess, all to determine where the physical pain is coming from. If the results are unremarkable, we give the pain a special name, "idiopathic." Which simply means that we don't know why it is present. We stop the bleeding, we close open wounds, we set broken bones, we give medications. If the results of our interventions remain inconclusive, the patient may be referred to specialists, scheduled for surgery, or, in rare cases, told, "We have no answers for you."

As a nurse, many people think of me as an angel. We are messengers (which is what the Greek word "*angelos*" means). We used to wear white. We are ministering people, and we are trusted. We say the things that others will not. We rush in to help, no matter the cost. We give without expectation of return.

Because my name is Michael, some call me an archangel. I have always been grateful for my name and its meaning—"Who is like God?"—the question asked by the Archangel Michael to Lucifer, the Angel of Light, during the battle described in the book of Daniel. The answer to this question, of course, is that there is no one like God. Yet, we can seek to be in His image. To be called an angel is the kindest thing a patient can say to me, because I want to serve them in this way, sharing a little of God's divinity, just as I care for them in my own humanity.

Healing is as complex as pain. I tell my patients that their recovery can be an involved process, and that it will require far more of their participation than mine. Many do not wish to hear this, and understandably so. First, they did not invite this pain into their lives. And then, to search the mind, the heart, the soul, and the spirit for the contributing causes of their pain, is far more daunting for them than my using mere blood work or x-rays in looking for the physical. It is hard to accept that while we may not be directly responsible for our pain, we are directly responsible for our healing.

The road to healing, inevitably, begins with acceptance. This is a word we hear a lot today. Acceptance is different than acknowledgement.

Acknowledgement involves the brain; acceptance requires the heart. How does acceptance initiate the healing process? It is in our assent that pain is truly present. It is in our recognition that it is not just physical. It is in our consent to what the implications are. And it is in our receiving the remedies necessary. Thankfully, our non-physical healing can include many resources: friends, family, therapy, the wisdom teachings of religion, and nature—all placed at hand for us by the God who created us.

The paradox, of course, is that these same resources for healing can, themselves, be the sources of our pain. Each of us, sadly, can tell of stories in which friends betrayed us over the seemingly most inconsequential of reasons. Of families where physical, emotional, psychological, sexual abuse were present. Of therapies which promised hope, but only stole our time, patience, and money. Therapists who did more harm than good, forgetting their role as supporters. Of churches and religions which were supposed to inspire us to draw near that which is greater, but instead, told us why we were flawed, why we were guilty of what caused our pain, or why we would never be worthy to be loved by the God who created us. Of victims of natural disasters, whose lives were never the same afterward.

But aren't these situations to be expected? Isn't this the nature of humanity? We have joy; we have sorrow. Won't our lives always include friends and enemies, peace and conflict, unity and division, stability and instability? Of course. For many of us, we seek solace in something wiser, something that encircles all of this and sees every disappointment, feels every hurt, knows every heartache we experience. For most Christians, we give this Being a name, be it God, Father, Son, Jesus, Christ, Holy Spirit, the Trinity. Also for most Christians, we learn about this Divine Being through our religion, its sacred writings, our churches, our faith communities, and the people who comprise them. Isn't religion supposed to rescue us from being defeated by the sources of pain in our lives? Ideally, yes. But what if religion becomes another source of pain?

The stories collected here are an account of that very thing: religion which assaulted us rather than comforted us, religion that was the Pharisee and not the Good Samaritan, religion which was the Thief and not the Shepherd, religion which disposed of us, because being disposed of is all that we believed we deserved. Sharing our hurts from religion, the very thing that should have been a source of healing, is not enough, however. More importantly, these are stories of hope: how each of us found healing from religious hurt, oftentimes from coming to a true understanding of the author of that religion, which had been previously misrepresented by its most vocal, zealous disciples.

To tell you of my pain is to tell you that it is chronic. It manifests in my life as anxiety and depression. And yet, I am on a healing journey. I continue to seek out the origins of my hurts, and to use the resources I have found to manage it, to change how it expresses itself in my life.

How did religion hurt me? For me, it was never one single event (what we call in nursing, a trauma) although many of my friends could share such stories. Instead, I would say that my religious pain was caused purely by never being accepted for who, what, where and why I was on my journey. Which has very little to do with how I view myself sexually. This is only one aspect of who I am, and how I fit into God's plan for me. I wonder: if you asked any random person on the street to list the first 20 words which came to mind in describing themselves, for how many would sexuality make the top 20?

As a teenager, I went on a journey of searching for a man named Jesus Christ. I had heard about him at different times during my childhood, but nothing that was ever consistent. Why did I want to know him? Quite simply, I knew he would love me. Although I did not know it then, outward unacceptance (by others) had caused inward unacceptance (within me). And love was nowhere to be found.

Initially, I read history. Sure, I knew about the Bible, but I also knew the Bible did not simply drop down from heaven. Because I love history, my interest became focused on the ancient roots of Christianity. I believe if you want the real story, you go to the source. Further, these expressions of Christianity, or denominations, included centuries, even millennia, of history, implying that there was room for all sorts of people. This was not the case, at least for me. Rather than making broad, sweeping generalizations about a few ancient branches of Christianity, I can better share my experiences at the local parish/community level.

For some of those parishes, whose origins were more geographical, or of a particular ethnic identity, I did not fit the mold. Because I was not a particular nationality, I was considered second-class. Because I was unable to understand how to worship in their original/preferred language, because I did not dress as their ancestors had, because I did not grow my hair long or wear a beard, I was made to feel unwelcome. Don't get me wrong, I am not an inflexible person; I made valiant attempts to change who I was. But it was never enough. These experiences made me feel as though I had to prove myself in order to be accepted by them, by Jesus. It was a wounding experience.

Other parishes believed that, as an unmarried male, I should be primarily focused on either seeking a wife or seeking the life of a monk. There were no other options available. Discussions of sexuality were irrelevant (not that I spoke of such, anyway).

Many parishes represented a church which legislated sexuality in minute detail. It was almost as if there was an obsession with sexual conduct, both within a marriage between a husband and wife (the only situation in which sexual activity was accepted) and outside of marriage (with celibacy being the only option). Clergy in many of these parishes were required to be male, unmarried (and thus, celibate) with no place for anyone else. There were penalties and penances for infraction of the rules, with a tremendous emphasis on sexual sin.

Independently of these examples, there was always the undercurrent, to greater or lesser degree, of thinking like this:

"God did not create them to be the way they say they are."

"God hates their sinful lifestyle."

"God will send them to hell because of their unnatural behavior."

"Their decision to live this way is what crucified Jesus."

"Jesus came to save them, but they refuse to repent of their choice."

"They don't know the real Jesus if they act that way."

"The Bible condemns what they are doing."

"Haven't they heard of the story of Sodom and Gomorrah?"

"St. Paul wrote to the Church and described that life as an abomination."

The list could go on. Words heard by many, but never directed at me, simply because a discussion of my sexuality was not something I would share at the parish level. The intimate things of my life are for intimate discussions.

As is human nature, at some point when we realize that we are unwelcome, despite our repeated attempts to make our own offering to a faith community, we just leave, in search of something else. And that's what I did, for many years. I would discover a new community, and would get so excited thinking, "Maybe this will feel like home!" Others have made journeys similar to mine and have ultimately left Christianity. I cannot blame them. For me, that was not an option. I had fallen in love with this God-man, Jesus Christ, who left heaven to come and live with us. How could I leave Him? He had not left me.

Historic Christianity also professes something at every worship service called the Nicene Creed. It is a confession of faith of the ancient church, and in it are contained words which refer to Jesus Christ having become man, by the power of the Holy

Spirit. It is a statement which has resonated within me since I first read it. We are called to become like Him, and in a similar manner by the power of the Holy Spirit, I also became a man. God the Father, in His infinite love for His continuing creation, willed that I should come into existence. Jesus Christ lovingly received and echoed His Father's will and, in union with the Holy Spirit, created me. And this is the root of my inward acceptance. Think of this: outward unacceptance had led to my inward unacceptance. In seeking Jesus Christ, I found inward acceptance, which will lead, inevitably I believe, to outward acceptance.

I have come to accept that my hurts from the Christian religion were made by imperfect people who believe differently than me. Over the years, through much reading, prayer, being quiet or in service to others, I continue to discover the sources of my pain. I am not overwhelmed or discouraged by them. In discovering them, I have something else for which to forgive others, and myself, for.

A Married Male Couple Hiding the Truth for Their Baby Godson's Baptism
By Derek

It's a shame how society treats minorities of any creed, color, or gender. We are all human! What is worse is when a non-profit organization (which really is a for-profit organization with all the riches they have) does it and hides behind their own morals to justify their "rules and regulations," when in fact their own followers break some of these rules!

Who am I talking about?

The Catholic Church, of course, and more specifically, the ones in Mexico.

As a gay man, I have been out and proud since I was 24. I have never denied or lied about my sexuality. I do not flaunt it, but I also don't lie about it if asked.

I am happily married to a man, or to be more specific, a "hot-blooded" Mexican man. Married for the last 10 years, we have been together for 19 years!

His family has accepted me as their own and I am honored! They don't see us as anything but loving individuals!

I love the Mexican culture and its heritage. So much so that I have gone out of my way to research it and embrace it and teach it to our nieces (who are my husband's brother's kids—they are American but have this Mexican heritage that they need to know).

Things like "Día De Muertos" (aka Day of the Dead Celebration) and things like knowing how the Mayan and Spanish (from Spain) cultures have contributed to a rich tapestry that is the country of Mexico. And that gives them their unique history that I hope they are proud of, because I am!

I was very excited when the next child to be born was that of my husband's sister, who lives in Mexico. This is his only sister, and as you can imagine, the family was overjoyed to hear that she was expecting! Her son, whom we all call "Rafalito" (meaning "little Rafael" or "junior") is a term we Mexican families use to honor the grandfather who died (whose name was Rafale). He never got to hold his grandchild—he was taken by a heart attack—but his grandchild will always hold his namesake and hence our family heritage goes on.

Finally, the day arrived when my sister-in-law asked me and my husband if we would accept the honor of being Rafalito's "Padrinos" (Godparents) and of course, without even thinking about it, we said YES! What an honor that will be.

Oddly, I was raised Catholic myself, but no longer follow the religion (nor any other organized religion, for that matter). Do not get me wrong, I don't judge those who are religious; I respect all beliefs! As for my husband and a lot of Mexicans in general, they claim to be religious and/or Catholic, but they really only follow the religion when it benefits them (like attending Christmas masses or a baptism). But again, I don't judge. To each his own!

So why write all these good things? Where is the bad part? That is the next part of this tale.

My husband and I have been asked to lie! And we have been asked to lie to a priest in a church! I seem to recall that lying was not allowed per the 10 Commandments so, I asked my family: "Why do I have to lie?"

Only for them to explain to me that the churches in Mexico do not believe same-sex couples should have the right to be godparents (or even parents for that matter).

REALLY!?

How dare they stand and judge me when the Catholic Church has had so many issues with priests abusing children and so many of them abusing children of the same sex!

What a dilemma.

Do I "turn the other cheek" (that's a Bible phrase, right?) and lie in order to be my nephew's godfather?

Or do I stand tall and tell the church to get over it?

Sadly, I have had to lie because they don't care! This is a situation where my hands are tied, and I have no choice. My husband and I, in the church's eyes, are simply two uncles who are NOT married and have been chosen by the mother to be godparents.

The priest will never know who we really are to this child. Which seems odd, because all we are wanting to do is protect this child should something happen to his mother (which is the role of a Padrino/godparent). I do not understand why the church can't get over themselves and understand this. Get with the times!

At the end of the day, I will stand in a church and in front of a priest and in front of all my family and lie. But if God does exist, He will know it's not a lie. And the family knows it's not a lie.

Does that mean I won? That if the deity these people all believe in knows I am doing the right thing, and He judges me, that it doesn't matter that the priest we stand in front of isn't given the chance to judge me?

What a double-edged sword! What a "two-faced" way to go about things. What a naïve and straight-out foolish and stupid thing it really is, because at the end of the day, my husband and I and our family get exactly what we want out of it . . . even if we go to hell!

The church should practice what it preaches and be open to all and let God judge us instead of some priest or some organized religion's rules.

I am human; I feel like everyone else and bleed like everyone else. I'm just attracted to hot Latin men! Sue me!

So, I will stand in a church and in front of a priest and know the whole time that this show—this spectacle—is simply for a piece of paper that says little Rafalito is "clean" in God's eyes and that should anything happen, God forbid (neat how God keeps coming onto this story that way) to my sister-in-law, Rafalito will be well taken care. He will be taught to love all and NOT JUDGE ANYONE and NOT TO LIE . . . unless it's for a good reason!

Wow . . . am I confused!

Tips

Ways to Honor Religion and Truth as a Beautiful LGBTQ+ Person

- Be YOU! Stop listening to the naysayers, homophobes, and negative self-talk.

- Find a church or community that accepts and celebrates you as a beautiful LGBTQ+ person.

- Be prayerful and thankful. Know that God does not make junk. You are made in God's image. BELIEVE IT!

- Read scripture, get to know Jesus or the spiritual beings that resonate with you and your beliefs. You are 100% in good hands and arms; hurt and tears will be wiped away.

- Help others, reach out, and do acts of kindness and service.

- Be positive and honest with yourself. This will lead to being honest and sharing your true self. No more hiding from family, friends, and others.

- Choose friends who lift you up and you lift them up. Consider the question Carol often asked, "Do you bring out the best in them by being the best you?"

- Create dialogue and conversation with religious people/ leaders and let them (you will probably teach them) get to know you as a person. Speak up, write letters.

- Seek peace in your heart and joy everyday!

- Use resources that are available: PFLAG, LGBTQ+ centers, online groups and organizations, personal mentors,
and printed materials.

Chapter 10

Trusting God's Timing
Serendipitous, Inexplicable, and
Miraculous Moments

Trust God's Timing to Heal Religious Hurts
By Joanie

It was the "pulpit hate" spoken and preached with fervor by a diocesan Catholic priest, our pastor, that hit our hearts the hardest but lasted the shortest. From the church pulpit, a priest for more than 15 years fired into the silent air, addressing the well-behaved parishioners:

"I was asked by a parishioner recently if it's okay to attend a gay marriage of a friend? No, it's not okay!"

Carol and I were stunned with such a homophobic and a stark Catholic response. The local ministerial leader went on to explain that if you attend the gay wedding, YOU would be (guilt scenario) promoting and agreeing to something that goes against Catholic teachings.

Not the answer we expected or wanted to hear, but this priest was exactly right in adamantly defending his Catholic doctrine. **From our viewpoint, it was completely wrong, inaccurate, and insane. He was missing the boat that love**

is love and love is God. I wished he had taken that angle in his homily.

Carol and I held our pinky fingers together, yet I really wanted to either walk out the side door near the altar or give her a big fat kiss on the lips for all to see. With our calm baby fingers entwined, I sensed her peace.

She leaned over and whispered, "Don't feed into his hate and let's let Jesus guide our actions."

"Yes, it's all Jesus," I quietly responded to Carol. We flashed our huge smiles and twinkling eyes to each other, continuing our baby-finger union.

We did not agree with this patriarchal, male chauvanistic, high-roller, black and white, legalistic fool. Sorry Father, for calling you names.

We did not believe in the century-old doctrines and Catholic catechism that says it's contrary to God's plan.

Sharing love and committing oneself to a same-sex union was not going against God's plans in our minds and hearts. We had joyously lived together for more than 25 years, hoping that the Catholic Church would approve and celebrate LGBTQ+ marriages. We continued to pray and wait!

Carol reminded me on our drive home that this was what Jesus had experienced and felt in the company of his Jewish leaders. They just didn't get what he was saying, and they were disgruntled and argued with him.

She reminded me that we, too, would find the way to use our voice, speak our truths, and discover the time and place to open hearts. She was absolutely correct. Tonight was not the night or place to confront, disagree publicly or be rude about it. Our time would come; healing would come. But that night, the hairs were raised on my arms for quite a while. Carol had already let go and let God handle it. We were two lovers being uniquely healed by the one all-loving God.

We cuddled in our purple bamboo sheets in bed, kissed goodnights, said I love yous, and she spoke her nightly mantra, "Put your back into me, Joanie. Let's go to sleep." We knew the angels and spirits were circling around us. Our last words spoken aloud to each other for the day were:

"Jesus hold you," I said.

"God bless you," she said.

I love you, Carol, for always teaching me new things! She always said that she loved me for being action oriented.

Our story evolved over the years. And in 2023, it was published in our best-selling, top 100, Amazon ebook for *Nun Better: An AMAZING Love Story.* Here was the way and the timing that Jesus and the Holy Spirit showed us to express God's message that love is love, and that we needed to share it to the world. The book is circling the USA and the world. Hearts are being touched by our stories of faithful love as two women in love.

REFLECTION QUESTIONS:

Are you open to trusting God's timeline?

_____

_____

How do you know when it's the right time?

_____

_____

Is a sign of God's timing always peaceful?

_____

_____

Why I Trust Divine Timing, and You Should, Too
By Elizabeth

I was devastated when my New York publisher said my first novel would be published two years later than originally scheduled. This was a blessing in disguise, because during that time, I had a baby.

Years later, my prayers for a "harmonious resolution" during a terrible divorce were answered—nearly 20 years later. During that time, I found my power, had a profound spiritual awakening, and learned what forgiveness and miracles really mean.

After that, I'd been working on my Goddess book series for years, extremely frustrated that the books remained unfinished, unpublished, and powerless to help the women around the world whom I knew needed them to find their power. Thankfully, after an especially transformative year of my life, I finished the first book and published it, following an exhilarating schedule of publishing the next five books within a year.

For most of my life, I had struggled for many years with food and fat, and the anxiety, depression, and mental hell that it caused, always praying to make peace with my mind, body, and food. Finally, after decades of struggle, that happened. I shifted into autopilot with a healthy mindset and food regimen that makes me look and feel my best. And I committed to a fitness regimen that has gotten me into the best shape of my life at age 57. I even got certified as a fitness trainer through ISSA.

For many years, I tried to learn to meditate and activate my spiritual/psychic powers. Yet the books that I read were confusing, and my attempts at meditation were awful. Until 2010, my meditation teacher, Dr. Rama, showed me how to meditate. And a short time later, Lori Lipten, founder of Sacred Balance

Academy in Bloomfield Hills, Michigan, taught me many more meditation techniques that ultimately led to her training me to get certified as an Intuitive Practitioner.

All of the above experiences exemplify how I wanted something so badly to happen immediately. But God had a different plan. He answered my prayers, often in ways that were bigger and better than I ever anticipated—but this often took *years* that included some of my worst moments ever.

This has taught me to trust God's timing. It has also shown that if we have a preordained destiny, it is written in the heavens and will unfold at its own pace. Pushing and forcing will not work.

I have many more examples of this in my personal and professional life. For example, a year-long romantic relationship that had wonderful highs punctuated by distressing lows. After the relationship ended, I walked away with tremendous insights and newfound fortitude to never experience those dynamics again.

That, like all of the above examples, show the power of learning and growing during times of trouble. While we're going through it, it's very stressful. But in hindsight, when we acknowledge the growth and empowerment that blossomed in the murky depths of despair, these experiences that feel delayed but are right on with God's timing, are a blessing.

The key here is to always ask why and take aggressive action to explore and understand what has happened, especially regarding religious hurts. Being hurt is not a blessing, but when we shift our perspective—by celebrating that we survived something terrible, that we are demonstrating strong coping skills, that we have not acted out or sought vengeance for the hurtful acts—we can see the silver lining on the clouds.

What happened is over and done with. We can't change it.

All we can do is make it a top priority to heal from it. Does time heal all wounds? Maybe. But trusting God's divine timing provides comfort and assurance that He is always working things out for us. It's our job to find meaning and clarity in how things resolve.

I have discovered that the more I reflect on instances of a positive outcome from what I viewed as a delay, but was actually divine timing, the more I have faith and trust in God's schedule, not mine.

I have listened to many sermons about how God has a "set time" for certain things to happen. For the right person and relationship to show up. For your business to take off. For you to finally lose weight and get fit. For that long-wished-for promotion to finally come to you. For you to have the money to travel see places in the world that you've always dreamed about. For you to find peace and love within yourself.

These sermons filled me with hope that whatever I was hoping would resolve as fast as possible, would do so. And they did.

So when things feel like they're moving as slow as molasses, get quiet and still and contemplate what's happening. What lessons could you possibly be learning while you wait?

This may be especially applicable for people who have been hurt by religion and are on a quest to find a belief system and faith community that resonates with their hearts and that provides the social and spiritual sustenance they are seeking. It may take visiting several groups or places of worship to find the right fit. The ones that don't fit are there to show you what you don't want, so when you do step into the best faith community, you will be overwhelmed with a joyous sense of belonging.

Trust God's timing in all that you do, and your patience will lead you to love and peace.

Just-in-Time God
By Reverend Janell Monk

I believe in a just-in-time God
      A God who continues to provide
Not as I want,
rather as I need

Time and time again the invitation is
      To trust
      To believe my needs will be met
      To remember I have all that I need
Even when I want more

The Rule[1] teaches us to
be the first to show kindness
      This is my practice

The Rule teaches us to
listen with the ear of our heart
      This is my practice

The Rule asks that
we be humble of heart
      This is my practice

The Rule encourages
us to bless others
      This is my practice

As challenging as my life is right now,
      In this season of
           Unknowing

Where so much of my life is uncertain
      I trust
      In the timing of a God who provides
Just in Time

Rev. Janell Monk

[1] The Rule of St. Benedict was written in the 6th century. A book of 73 chapters inviting one to live the charisms of prayer, work, and hospitality; benchmarks of a Benedictine life as a monastic or lay oblate.

The Reverend Janell Monk is an ELCA Lutheran pastor, Benedictine Oblate, and artist who resides in Oregon.

Tips

Tips for Self-Reflection

Look back at examples in your life where things seemed delayed, then finally resolved, and you realized that God was orchestrating circumstances on His own schedule, ultimately for your benefit.

What is your definition of divine timing?

_____

_____

How can you practice faith in divine timing every day, to have patience and await the best possible outcome for a situation?

_____

_____

- Be still and quiet with your Higher Power.

- Become a better listener by asking, "What's behind the scene?"

- Stand up for yourself in a kind and humble way.

- Don't jam things down people's throats. Let them speak for themselves and guide them with thoughtful questions.

- Put your patience cap on when confronted with stress or conflict.

- Words can hurt deeply and last a long time. Choose your timing carefully.

Chapter 11

Tips, Tools & Rituals for Healing Religious Hurts
"OMG! I've been healed!"

*N*ow it's time to identify activities that resonate with your heart and soul and that will help you cultivate peace and love with Spirit and/or God or your Higher Self. Think about what thoughts and activities make you feel peaceful and that you believe may help you release religious angst.

Here's a checklist of some ideas:

· Prayer

· Meditation

· Journaling

· Being in nature for walking, swimming, hiking, sitting in a garden, gardening, sunbathing, walking barefoot on the ground for "grounding" or "earthing," or another activity in nature that you love.

· Joining a faith community that is inclusive and that embraces and celebrates you just as you are.

· Creating an altar in your home where you display photos of loved ones and ancestors, burn candles and incense, place inspiring quotes, keep items that symbolize your beliefs, and include anything that makes you feel peaceful.

- Making a vision board of images that soothe you and accelerate your feelings of love and peace on a healing journey.

- Creating your own spiritual group where you can explore new ideas around how to connect with God/Spirit/Higher Self. You can do this by posting something on MeetUp.com and asking like-minded folks to convene at a park, a coffee shop, or another venue to talk about how you can help each other. When you start your own group, you have the ability to guide the dialogue and curate an egalitarian experience where everyone feels valued and celebrated.

- Creating a daily spiritual practice that includes prayer, meditation, journaling, high vibe eating, using crystals and essential oils, being in nature, reading inspiring books, communing with like-minded people, and other activities that inspire you.

- Eating a high-vibe diet which is plant-based and includes mostly unprocessed vegetables, fruits, lean proteins, beans, nuts, seeds, and healthy oils.

- Other_____.

A Love Letter to You

Dear Reader:

Let your light shine! You are important to us and to our world!

It's been our immense joy journeying with you in this book, *Healing Religious Hurts*. Thank you so much for reading it.

Now it's time to say goodbye, so we send you forward with hope for fresh mornings, sunshine days, and quiet nights, in a new life. This book is a gift of abundant love and peace for you. Laugh and cry from your soul, believe in miracles, and know that you are extremely precious and truly one of a kind.

Show kindness, smile more, give hugs away, spread love and joy, and give thanks and praise to God/Spirit/Higher Power/HigherSelf.

Everything and everyone is beautiful and that's especially YOU!

We love you!

Joanie and Elizabeth

About the Authors & Contact Info

Elizabeth Ann Atkins

Elizabeth's life mission is to cultivate human harmony through the written and spoken word, and through daily interactions with people.

This mission was born when she was one day old and her father baptized her in the hospital room, asking God to make her a "Princess of Peace." As a one-year-old, she helped unite a divided family, opening the door for loving unity for generations.

Elizabeth's desire to create a happier world springs from a trailblazing union of colorblind love and courage, thanks to her mother, an African American and Italian judge, and her father, a former Roman Catholic priest who was English, French, and Cherokee.

To amplify messages of peace and inclusion, Elizabeth and her sister, Catherine Greenspan, co-founded Two Sisters Writing & Publishing® in 2016, publishing their own fiction and non-fiction books that celebrate colorblind love and empowered self-identity.

They have since published more than 50 books, mostly against-the-odds success stories by diverse authors from across America. Learn more at TwoSistersWriting.com.

Elizabeth's most recent book is *The Biss Tribe: Where You Activate Your GoddessPleasure,* which is book two in a series that began with *The Biss Tribe: Where You Activate Your GoddessPower.* This six-part series aims to empower people with the tools that Elizabeth uses every day to look and feel her best, connect with Spirit, manifest blessings, and achieve a creative flow state in her creative genius zone.

Elizabeth's Goddess mission was born during terrible moments of verbal abuse many years ago. Spirit infused her with the peace and power of God energy to cultivate strength to persevere through difficulties.

She created and hosts The Goddess Power Show with Elizabeth Ann Atkins®. The podcast explores sometimes taboo topics with the goal of helping people live bigger, better, and bolder and manifest their wildest desires. You can watch interviews on the YouTube channel for The Goddess Power Show with Elizabeth Ann Atkins®. And you can listen to episodes on Apple Podcasts, Spotify, iHeart radio, and wherever you listen to podcasts. TheGoddessPowerShow.com provides links to all of the above.

Elizabeth also co-hosts an Emmy-nominated TV show about mental health.

She has written and published more than 50 books—fiction and nonfiction, published by major New York publishing houses as well as by Two Sisters Writing & Publishing®. Her bestselling books include *White Chocolate, Dark Secret,* and *Twilight* with Billy Dee Williams. She writes erotic fiction under the pen name, Sasha Maxwell, and her novels include *Husbands, Incorporated, Eleven Men,* and *Eleven Women.*

As America's book Coach, Elizabeth guides aspiring writers along the sometimes-treacherous terrain of writing, publishing, and promoting a book. Learn more about her "Six Months to Best-Selling book Success" group coaching program at TwoSistersWriting.com.

Elizabeth's education laid the foundation for her career as an author, journalist, speaker, and publisher. She earned a Bachelor of Arts degree as an English Literature major at the University of Michigan, where she began her journalism career as a reporter and editor at the campus newspaper, *The Michigan Daily.*

Then she earned a Master of Science degree from the Columbia University Graduate School of Journalism in New York City, where she focused on broadcast news and international reporting. During that time, she had a part-time job as a copy clerk at *The New York Times,* which published a portion of her master's thesis about mixed-race people.

Elizabeth is an inspiring speaker.

On diversity, she rouses ovations by performing her autobiographical poem, "White Chocolate," then invites audiences to explore their perceptions about race and identity. They walk away with a new understanding to never judge a book by its cover.

Elizabeth has spoken at Columbia University, the University of Michigan, GM's World Diversity Day, Gannett, Beaumont Health, 100 Black Men, the NAACP, national conferences, and many other venues.

As a wellness speaker, Elizabeth shares her long struggle with food and fat, and the depression and suicidal ideation that it triggered, and how she triumphed over that with faith and fitness. She talks about how she lost 100 pounds after childbirth (without drugs or surgery) and celebrated her transformation on *The Oprah Winfrey Show.*

Now a certified fitness trainer through ISSA, Elizabeth coaches others on how to achieve a mindset shift as the first step to transforming one's body and life. Learn more on the Wellness page at TheGoddessPowerShow.com.

Deeply spiritual, Elizabeth shares her experiences, perspectives, and tools for high vibe living in her best-selling memoir, *God's Answer Is Know: Lessons From a Spiritual Life.* She shares how meditation has helped her heal and awaken her most authentic self and serve as a spiritual teacher for others.

As an Intuitive Practitioner certified by Lori Lipten's Sacred Balance Academy in Bloomfield Hills, Michigan, Elizabeth teaches meditation and energy clearing.

Elizabeth has taught writing at Wayne State University, Oakland University, Wayne County Community College District, and at national conferences.

As an actress, she plays a major role in the feature-length film, *Anything Is Possible,* nominated for "Best Foreign Film" by the Nollywood and African Film Critics Association.

And she plays a 1950s journalist in the international shipwreck drama, *The Andrea Doria: Are The Passengers Saved?* The award-winning film is in Italian with English subtitles.

Elizabeth composed an original screenplay, *Redemption,* a gritty drama about a Detroit gangster and a writer.

Elizabeth has been a guest on *Oprah, Montel, NPR, Good Morning America Sunday, The CBS Evening News, Black Entertainment Television (BET), The NBC Nightly News, The Today Show,* and many national and local TV programs.

Her work has been published in *The New York Times, The San Diego Tribune, Essence, Ebony, HOUR Detroit, BLAC Detroit,* and many publications. Her *Detroit News* articles on race were nominated for the Pulitzer Prize, and she wrote a biography for the Presidential Medal of Freedom tribute for Rosa Parks.

Elizabeth runs, cycles, lifts weights, does yoga, journals, travels, reveres nature, and meditates to cultivate a joyous and peaceful mind, body and spirit.

You can contact Elizabeth at TwoSistersWriting.com.

Please subscribe to the YouTube channels for Two Sisters Writing & Publishing® and The Goddess Power Show with Elizabeth Ann Atkins®. You can also follow her on Instagram @ elizabethannatkins.

Joanie Lindenmeyer

Joanie Lindenmeyer is 66 years young, a former Sister of St. Joseph of Carondelet Catholic nun who is now an Episcopalian with St. Timothy's.

Joanie serves on the church vestry and in the local community in many ways that include speaking about faith, love, Diversity, Equity and Inclusion, and promoting LGBTQ+ inclusion.

A San Diego State University graduate, she was a member of the university volleyball team and has a California teaching credential.

She has worked at two nonprofits and a county department of health in areas of community health, addictions, teen pregnancy, sexuality, child abuse prevention, HIV/AIDS prevention, STI testing and counseling, and wellness.

She was a public high school physical education and health teacher and sports coach for 25 years. Prior to that, she taught religion and youth ministry for four years in Catholic schools/parishes.

Her dedication shines for people of all ages, making their lives brighter, happier, and healthier.

For 40 years, she was committed to her one and only lifetime lover and spouse, Carol Tierheimer. In 2022, she became widowed and is embarking on new adventures as a single lesbian woman.

In March of 2023, she wrote a best-selling memoir, *Nun Better: An AMAZING Love Story* by Joanie Lindenmeyer with Carol Tierheimer.

You can find her book trailer, events calendar, and links to the weekly podcast that she does with Elizabeth Ann Atkins on the Two Sisters Writing & Publishing® YouTube channel at TwoSistersWriting.com. There you can order *Nun Better* and

Joyously Free; the books are also available wherever books are sold online.

Joanie enjoys playing pickleball, watching sports, traveling, fishing, gardening flowers and sharing her veggie yields, playing guitar, listening to music, walking and hiking, baking treats, and hanging out with family and friends.

Joanie is extremely grateful for her dear friends and family and the opportunities to meet new friends and profoundly touch hearts wherever she goes. Her mantra is, "Every day is a new day, never been lived before and LOVE ALWAYS WINS!" HOW FUN!

She has lived in Brookings, Oregon, for 33 years. Carol's memorial rose garden awaits you to come take a seat and enjoy the tremendous peace and beauty of this colorful, fragrant sanctuary.

Filled with joy and hope, Joanie believes that Jesus is her best friend and she loves to wear bright colors and have big smiles.

You can contact Joanie on Facebook @JoanieLindenmeyer.

And she invites you to follow her on TikTok @ JoanieLindenmeyer.

Check out her author page at TwoSistersWriting.com to learn when and where Joanie will be speaking and doing book signings across America. She'd love to meet you in person!

Endnotes

[1] "Excommunicate Meaning," *Google Search*, accessed September 11, 2024, https://www.google.com/search?q=excommunicate+meaning&oq=excommunicate+meaning&gs_lcrp=EgZjaHJvbWUyDggAEEUYFBg5GIcCGIAEMgcIARAAGIAEMgcIAhAAGIAEMgcIAxAAGIAEMgcIBBAAGIAEMgcIBRAAGIAEMgcIBhAAGIAEMgcIBxAAGIAEMggICBAAGggICRAAGBYYHtIBCDQ4NjdqMGoOqAIAsAIB&sourceid=chrome&ie=UTF-8

.[2] "The Gospel of Mary," *"The Gnostic Society Library*, accessed September 11, 2024, http://www.gnosis.org/library/marygosp.htm#:~:text=Unfortunately%20the%20surviving%20manuscript%20of,Gnostic%20Codex%2C%20is%20presented%20below.

[3] "Gospel of Mary," *Wikipedia*, last modified August 30, 2024, https://en.wikipedia.org/wiki/Gospel_of_Mary#:~:text=The%20most%20complete%20text%20of,manuscript%20pages%20in%20the%20middle

.[4] Joe Dispenza, *Becoming Supernatural: How Common People Are Doing the Uncommon* (Carlsbad: Hay House, 2017).

[5] "Hypocrisy," Google, accessed September 11, 2024, https://www.google.com/search?q=hypocrisy&oq=Hypocrisy&gs_lcrp=EgZjaHJvbWUqCggAEAAYsQMYgAQyCggAEAAYsQMYgAQyCggBEAAYsQMYgAQyCggCEAAYsQMYgAQyBwgDEC4YgAQyBwgEEAAYgAQyBwgFEAAYgAQyBwgGEAAYgAQyBggHEEUYPagCALACAA&sourceid=chrome&ie=UTF-8

.[6] "How Much Has the Catholic Church Paid to Abuse Victims," Google, accessed September 11, 2024, https://www.google.com/search?q=How+Much+Has+the+Catholic+Church+Paid+to+Abuse+Victims&oq=How+Much+Has+the+Catholic+Church+Paid+to+Abuse+Victims&gs_lcrp=EgZjaHJvbWUyBggAEEUYOTIGCAEQRRg80gEHMzA1a-

jBqNKgCALACAQ&sourceid=chrome&ie=UTF-8.

[7] David Massey, "How Much Has the Catholic Church Paid to Abuse Victims?" David Massey Law, accessed September 11, 2024, https://dmasseylaw.com/how-much-Catholic-church-paid-abuse-victims/.

[8] "Search Results for 'Deaths in Spanish Inquisition,'" Google, accessed September 11, 2024, https://www.google.com/search? q=deaths+in+spanish+inquisition&oq=deaths+in+spanish+inquisition&gs_lcrp=EgZjaHJvbWUyCQgAEEUYORiABDII-CAEQABgWGB4yCggCEAAYgAQYogTSAQgzNDc3ajBqN6g-CALACAA&sourceid=chrome&ie=UTF-8.

[9] "Costly Church Fraud Cases," PSK CPA, accessed September 11, 2024, https://www.pskcpa.com/costly-church-fraud-cases/

[10] "Ted Haggard," *Wikipedia: The Free Encyclopedia*, last modified September 10, 2024, https://en.wikipedia.org/wiki/Ted_Haggard#:~:text=On%20January%2023%2C%202009%2C%20less,-consensual%20sexual%20relationship%20%5Bthat%5D%20went.

[11] "Ted Haggard, mega-church founder felled by sex scandal, returns to pulpit," The Guardian, June 6, 2010, accessed April 15, 2024, https://www.theguardian.com/world/2010/jun/06/us-gay-scandal-pastor-church

[12] "Gay Iranian Man Dead in Alleged Honor Killing, Rights Group Says," *New York Post*, May 12, 2021, https://nypost.com/2021/05/12/gay-iranian-man-dead-in-alleged-honor-killing-rights-group-says/.